BEHIND THE SCENES:
THEATER AND FILM INTERVIEWS
FROM THE *Transatlantic Review*

BEHIND THE SCENES: THEATRE AND FILM INTERVIEWS FROM THE *Transatlantic Review*

EDITED BY

JOSEPH F. McCRINDLE

WITH AN INTRODUCTION BY

JEAN-CLAUDE VAN ITALLIE

 PITMAN PUBLISHING

CONTENTS

	Introduction by Jean-Claude van Itallie	vii
1.	Joan Littlewood	1
	Interviewed by Margaret Croyden	
2.	Philippe de Broca	13
	Interviewed by Paul Gardner	
3.	Jules Feiffer	19
	Interviewed by John Lahr	
4.	John Hopkins	31
	Interviewed by Giles Gordon	
5.	Christopher Hampton	44
	Interviewed by Brendan Hennessy	
6.	Jorge Luis Borges	51
	Interviewed by Richard Burgin	
7.	Rolf Hochhuth	60
	Interviewed by Margaret Croyden	
8.	Arthur Kopit	70
	Interviewed by Brendan Hennessy	
9.	Tom Stoppard	77
	Interviewed by Giles Gordon	
10.	David Mercer	88
	Interviewed by Giles Gordon	
11.	Ellen Stewart	99
	Interviewed by ED. B.	
12.	William Inge	108
	Interviewed by Digby Diehl	
13.	Joe Orton	116
	Interviewed by Giles Gordon	
14.	Edward Bond	125
	Interviewed by Giles Gordon	

15. Arnold Wesker 137
   Interviewed by Giles Gordon
16. Frank Marcus 149
   Interviewed by Frank Marcus
17. Kenneth Tynan 155
   Interviewed by Paul Neuberg
18. Federico Fellini 167
   Interviewed by Eugene Walter
19. Harold Clurman 172
   Interviewed by Digby Diehl
20. Charles Marowitz 182
   Interviewed by Charles Marowitz
21. Richard Barr 191
   Interviewed by Barry Pree
22. Robert Bolt 199
   Interviewed by Barry Pree
23. Peter Shaffer 205
   Interviewed by Barry Pree
24. Harold Pinter and Clive Donner 211
   Interviewed by Kenneth Cavander
25. Edward Albee 223
   Interviewed by Digby Diehl
26. Ann Jellicoe and Donald McWhinnie 243
   Interviewed by Robert Rubens
27. José Quintero 256
   Interviewed by Jean-Claude van Itallie
28. Marcel Marceau 270
   Interviewed by Frank Marcus
29. Alan Schneider 279
   Interviewed by Jean-Claude van Itallie
30. John Schlesinger 293
   Interviewed by Robert Rubens
31. Tony Richardson and Lindsay Anderson 303
   Interviewed by Robert Rubens
32. William Gaskill and John Dexter 318
   Interviewed by Robert Rubens
33. Gore Vidal 327
   Interviewed by Eugene Walter

INTRODUCTION

It seems a very long time ago that I worked on the *Transatlantic Review*. It's been, in fact, about ten years (years during which these collected interviews were published in the magazine). I was new in New York then, fresh out of Harvard, and a summer of acting school in New York. Very quickly I realized that the commercial Broadway theater was not what I wanted to write for, that its economic and even physical structure made it quasi-impossible for an intelligent piece of theater to be born there (although the best pieces of the decade were imported directly to Broadway from England). But I was still ambitious in the theater. I looked for traces of genius among the directors and writers then working, and I was certain I wanted to be a playwright. The framework of "the theater" was still a valid one, even if only valid as a backboard off of which to try and spring new forms.

As it happened in about 1963, many young people like myself became very impatient with the non-opportunities offered us in New York by the commercial theater and so we started, in a completely haphazard and coincidental way, what has since been labeled "Off-Off-Broadway" or "The New Theater in America." This included jumbling together playwrights and theater groups and directors, all of whom only a few years ago were names known only to ourselves around Greenwich Village —Ellen Stewart's Café La Mama, Caffe Cino, Lanford Wilson, Michael Smith, Sam Shepard, Joseph Chaikin, the Judson Church, Maria Irene Fornes, Megan Terry, Jacques Levy, Paul Foster, the Open Theater, etc., etc. And for a while it seemed exciting. We were doing something new and we knew it, and we enjoyed being at the center of energy in the theater. Soon, too soon I think, we were discovered by the media, and articles began to appear in *The New York Times* and then *Time* and *Newsweek*. I remember taking a bus at four o'clock in the morning from Massachusetts, at Ellen Stewart's earnest behest (which none of us who have ever been "her playwrights" could ever deny), in order to have my picture taken, along with ten others, for *Vogue* magazine. I think we thought at the time that it was good to get the attention of the world because we were doing good and worthwhile things. There was then no excitement in the theater, we felt, like our own. And there was precious little excitement anywhere in America, about anything.

I come from an apathetic generation, compared with those who came ten years later. I am thirty-three now, and I regret that I was not born eight years later. In my day I was one of the few crazies on campus, and I was not so crazy. Organized Leftist political activity didn't exist and it never occurred to me to organize it. To grow a beard at Harvard and to wear sandals to dinner was a very deliberate and self-conscious act.

All of which is to say that those of us involved in the original Off-Off-Broadway movement were sincerely and organically channeling our individuality and what talent we had in an appropriate artistic form that was socially oriented, and we were not doing it for primarily economic motives because we didn't, at first, expect anyone with money would want to see what we were doing.

Then they did. And perhaps five years or so after it was born, the Off-Off-Broadway movement has become moribund; dying perhaps of too much attention, and also because the action has moved away from the theater.

There is no longer any point in shocking the bourgeois or anyone else, as I did in the *Motel* play of *America Hurrah*. The past four years have been shock after shock. It feels like the economic and social structure which is America, or at least urban America, is falling apart completely; and faster and faster. Some are appalled; some are delighted. I am not appalled, but, liking to be out in front, I find myself standing back a little, afraid to be mowed down by the avalanche.

All the social protest I see now in the theater seems puerile. All of that is really happening outside the theater, where people are demonstrating without being paid for it, where beatings and jailings and incredible court trials are far more theatrical than anything we could provide. I think the days of "improvising" group theaters are very nearly over, unless, as the Open Theater is doing, groups turn to other more stylized and more disciplined theatrical expression. It's no particular surprise that the Living Theater, or so one hears, is breaking up—at least in its present manifestation. They have reached the end of a logical road. The Living Theater Company said, "the actor in the theater is the same as that same person outside the theater," and it tried and succeeded in making the theatrical experience so "real," in its terms, that the actors and audience would all become politically activated and move outside the theater building onto the streets. They succeeded in doing this, and now they have to consider what to do with people on the street, with political movement, and they are no longer, by definition, really involved in the theater.

And, to me, most of the rest of what is going on in theater seems irrelevant. It didn't five years ago. But now a lot of the more or less well-written fun-and-nonsense of playwrights, who were trying to break through the uptight barrier in their audience and in themselves, is a lot less appealing. Again, the times have moved fast, and the theater that was alive during the past decade seems history now. An excursion to Greenwich Village to see "New Theater" is an esoteric habit, and one indulged in by a small minority of over-thirties (including me). But the vital current isn't there.

Where is the vital current? In America it's in the political movements, the rock concerts and the communes.

A few years ago in the theater we were trying, among other things, to "wake people up." Now everyone is so fully woken up to, say, the "national schizophrenia" as it is insanely expressed in Southeast Asia and Mississippi, that sitting in a theater seems vaguely irrelevant.

Still, Beckett is still with us, and Pinter, and Genêt (although Genêt hasn't written a play in ten years).

So where is the theater at now? I think, if the world doesn't blow up, or get totally polluted, that the Western theater is going to move toward the abstract (and this is wild star-gazing on my part); it will incorporate dance, and perhaps even sculpture. It will become abstract in a highly disciplined fashion, in the sense that Beckett and Pinter are abstract, in the way that painting has become "abstract." Tensions existing in mass situations will be expressed in crystallized form—a single actor of genius, such as Ryszard Cieslak of the Polish Lab Theater, will be called upon to portray the death agonies of a multitude. The psychological realities of the usual Americanized Stanislavski-type theater are no longer so interesting as more philosophical realities and spiritual ones, and the language of these last is more poetry than prose, more in a string of tightly-compressed single images (like short dreams), than in verbal virtuosity and repartee.

Theater is of its time. No plays by a dead playwright were ever discovered later in a garret. The theater is a lot bleaker now than it was ten years ago because then there was at least something to break out of. Now there is only to create something new, which is harder. "Something," as Beckett says in *Endgame,* "has run its course."

JEAN-CLAUDE VAN ITALLIE
New York
June 1970

JOAN LITTLEWOOD

This interview with Joan Littlewood took place in my flat in Dolphin Square in London where I was spending the summer. I had never met Miss Littlewood, but I had an intro- duction to her from a mutual friend. When I rang her up, she suggested that she come to my place. Promptly at six, Joan appeared (it's hard now to call her Miss Littlewood; we became instant friends). How can one describe her? Her clothes were of the forties, her figure middle-age, her hair un- stylish, her arms full of packages. But her eyes and smile were gorgeous—intensely and magnificently alive. Soon we were eating cheese and crackers, drinking sherry and coffee, talk- ing, laughing, gossiping—as if we had known each other for years. Joan Littlewood is one of those unique creatures who makes instant contact. A woman of rare warmth, she can talk for hours. And everything she has to say is pure joy.

INTERVIEWER: Miss Littlewood, you're one of the few women in the theater who's successful. How did you happen to pick directing as a career?
LITTLEWOOD: Well, I didn't pick it at all. I perhaps went into the theater for a different objective than most people. I didn't want to be an actress or director. I loved the theater in peo- ple, in the city, in life. I'm very keen on watching people. I guess I'm a voyeur. I love the patterns, and the lies and the performances you get everywhere. I just wanted to make a place where it would be fun for people to work. I wanted a place where you could just take off, take the high jump; that's why I direct.

INTERVIEWER: How did you begin your career?

LITTLEWOOD: I left home as a kid; I went on the bum and I got scholarships to study theater and painting. I went to Paris as most people do if they're in Europe; you know, you do the bohemian bit for a while. I picked up knowledge on the streets. A person like me from the backstreet slums was a rarity in those days.

INTERVIEWER: What part of England do you come from?

LITTLEWOOD: From working-class London, tough London. You know, the funny thing is I grew up on the streets and I'm back there.

INTERVIEWER: What do you mean?

LITTLEWOOD: Well, now I work a lot with kids off the street. When I started I ran around the streets. I wanted theater of messages when I was young. But I did it on the streets. Mind you, I've also done a bit of the other; I've learned to do the posh bit; because you had to, to get by in a very snobbish country, Britain. (I think all of that's breaking up a bit.) And now again I'm out on the street corner with hot air balloons and inflatables, and marvelous crystals, and masks, and games, and theater happenings. That's what I'm on at the moment.

INTERVIEWER: You're very famous for the Theatre Workshop. How did that come into existence?

LITTLEWOOD: Well, that was an old building that we could get for twelve pounds a week. And we had been playing anywhere we could to get to the people who don't go to the theater. It was like in the States. You had that big movement of "nuts" who wanted to take theater outside of Broadway, you know? Not into Off-Broadway but into the barter theaters. We'd go into a village, a mining village, and we would put up flags and balloons and we would take care of the kids. We would get the people to join in and have fun. It was like a party, and we'd almost live without money as they did.

INTERVIEWER: You were the organizer and director?

LITTLEWOOD: Yes. Funnily enough, always the oldest. I'm getting older and older and they're getting younger and younger. After wandering around like that (nobody would have us; we were not terribly respectable looking), people would say, "You're not theater," and "What are you up to?" And the political people thought we were arty, the arty people thought we were political. So we came to find this old barn of a music hall theater, designed and built in 1880 for the railmen and dockers. It was a music hall for their water shows and boxing. But, a very pretty theater, if you like conventional theater, which I don't. When I was twenty I was talking about new structures, about breaking down walls and having new theaters, and I found myself in this place. But the people who came were at home there, in the bar, in the street. It had been built, as I said, in 1880 and we lived in it and we paid very small rent. For a living we'd have to do all sorts of plays. . . . That was my theater in those days. Then it got famous, when the West End of London were so hard up that they would even take *me* in. They'd take things like *Taste of Honey* and Brendan Behan, who they wouldn't accept before.

INTERVIEWER: You discovered him, didn't you?
LITTLEWOOD: Well, I had to protect him from them, that gentle soul.

INTERVIEWER: Are you responsible for *The Hostage?*
LITTLEWOOD: Well, yes, because Brendan had a nine-year imprisonment—he was aiming to blow up Buckingham Palace. He never got as far as Buckingham Palace. He'd get to the pub and he'd have *The Irish Republican* (that was a newspaper) in his pocket, and bright green tweeds, and Brendan couldn't kill a fly anyway. So he'd always be arrested. And he'd be laughing so much even though he was sentenced to about ninety years; he'd only served nine, which was too much. He came to London, and I suppose we were the only people who were noisy enough for him. And we said, "Come on Brendan, let's have it—let's have the play." He was a great, great talker and *The Hostage* came like that, from my old man, my husband, who put a gun in his pants and said, "Now look here you dirty Irish so-and-so. You write that play." And mainly he improvised a lot with us. He had written a beau-

tiful one act version in Gaelic. Brendan was with us then
and this lovely young bird, Shelagh Delaney, whose film just
came out in New York—*Charley Bubbles,* this nineteen-year-
old girl, and many, many others, some heard of, some who
went into other things.

INTERVIEWER: Who subsidized you before you became famous?
LITTLEWOOD: Well, it was hard going. We were sometimes
glad to get a cigarette end off the floor. You know how the
experts are, so mediocre (the experts of the arts councils and
the government bodies). Even now they say, "I'm sorry, Joan,
but it's very controversial," and so there isn't a government
grant going for what I'm doing now. And what I'm doing
now doesn't matter which country it's in. I'm going to roll it
again to the Arab world, I'm going to do it in Cyprus, France,
and London because we can roll it around the planet. It's now
mobile theater, and it's made up of modern techniques.

INTERVIEWER: Is this what you call The Fun Palace?
LITTLEWOOD: The Fun Palace was always part of it. You see,
I envision a place where one works with a lot of finesse, with
a lot of grammar, self-discipline, or a very articulated piece
of art, and the next minute you're doing jazz. And you go
from one to the other, and you love the grammar of the language. And the next minute you're taking off with what the
jazz players did in their time, and that is opened to everybody,
to the genius of each child, or each older person. The things
one thinks while dancing with the feet, well this is with
everybody. Well, side by side with this campaign to live, which
is quite hard, one literally says to everybody, to about two
hundred miners and their wives and kids, "Let's play games."
They can, as you know, give you a creative notion of their
own life, or their own pain or their own laughter, maybe
only once. But it's something like the therapy of clowning
that everyone needs, not just us lucky ones who are mad
enough to spend our lives trying to get other people to enjoy
themselves. . . . Then the fabric of the theater is too dreary
and old. All of the best theater you've got in New York, Moscow, Berlin or Paris, it isn't for this century. I've always

thought this. So all my life I've been designing these crystal shapes that will slide open, or artificial suns or the fun of promenading at night, or wearing a mask, or changing your identity as they did in the old Vauxhall Gardens, and I've been trying to do all this, but I've always done bits of it. Sometimes I could only go into prisons, and say, "Well, what about the warden and the prisoners changing roles for a bit." It's that game, partly. But I've done it at all sorts of places. You know, we've jumped into the new technological age; the fantastically frightening revolution has happened and we have enough power and drops of water to live by and we don't have to work in mines or boring jobs. And so The Fun Palace was the name of one place. Now a bit that I'm doing is called Bubble City. The city as a theater . . .

INTERVIEWER: It's not an acted-out performance or anything?
LITTLEWOOD: Well, you can have Laurence Olivier at one end, provided at the other end something will grow into a ritual or a procession in which you or I might dance. You might wear a mask, or you being an artistic nut might become a scientific nut. It might change so there would be ritual in performance like the Middle Ages to which we're much nearer. There was a different god figure then. Today people need the sustenance of optimism of a new concept, of a constructive concept. . . . How marvelous the human being is, and how terrible, and they've got to face it because God, and the father and the family are dying fast. And races are dying fast, and very soon we'll be planet dwellers. Well, this is surely what the theater is, or was, in the Middle Ages; you moved perhaps for three days or nights from one booth to another where you saw creation. Then you watched bears, then you danced where you ate, or you found a lover or discarded one. Then you moved to the next tableau. People want to be mobile now. Well, imagine that, or imagine in Shakespeare's London, men talking science, or people chatting about stars with Marlowe and Raleigh, or people dancing some kind of dance which was much like a wild modern dance. . . . We are in a renaissance now, but where are you going to find it? Not with Mr. Osborne, Mr. Albee and all these characters locked up in a womb

of theater, but in opening this talent to this great wave of new, young kids.

INTERVIEWER: You want the Elizabethan Age back again, don't you?

LITTLEWOOD: It's here, I think. We can't get away from the fact that it's a renaissance; we have all this new technology in the theater.

INTERVIEWER: From the point of view of technology, yes. I don't see a renaissance in literature really.

LITTLEWOOD: Not yet, because we're all too conservative in the theater.

INTERVIEWER: What role do you think this theater would play politically, for instance?

LITTLEWOOD: Well, since the politicians have taken over the theater and L.B.J. and Harold Wilson and de Gaulle are much better clowns than Olivier, what are you to do? They've got the theater that you're talking about.

INTERVIEWER: Do you think the theater you're thinking of should have any kind of political commitment?

LITTLEWOOD: Do you know what I think? Almost every discipline, the doctors, the architects, the lawyers, know that the old systems aren't the style for today and tomorrow. And that we've simply got to make the more marvelous world or go under. I think we are in a very uncivilized time, and I think the clowns are very important. I don't mean L.B.J. clowns. I mean the think clowns, and they've been so few. And Willy Shakespeare and Molière and those glorious people of the thirties who kept you going, the real laugh clowns and the music ones. And the think people (I mean Einstein couldn't drop his boots, he was an old clown) they meet, Groucho Marx and the other ones. They're needed desperately because people are frightened of the new world.

INTERVIEWER: Do you think that the theater can have a role in bringing to light people's need to change the world?

LITTLEWOOD: I think we've all got our youth being anti. Young people love being anti. I know that hate made me write a thing called *Oh, What a Lovely War*. But I hope it turns into love because the political commitment is joy and the word, almost, for voice is joy in Greek. Theater is expression in laughter; laughter gets you by in a very desperate situation, living on this planet, which isn't much fun. I mean forget who you are, whether you're the Queen of Sheba or a bum, you're faced with the same problem, the art of living. We've forgotten that since a long time.

INTERVIEWER: You've worked on the West End in London, you've worked off the West End, you've worked in New York, you've been all over the world. Is there anybody or any movement in the West End that interests you at all?

LITTLEWOOD: Anybody at all who goes into that dusty museum, with a few racketeers, conning people into watching a boring repetition, is either doing straightforward whoring because they need the dough, or has got a very petty ego. It was dead when my life started, and it's now so bad in England that these West End managers are going to Lord Goodman's council and saying they need some money, they need support. They were finished long ago.

INTERVIEWER: Do you include in this London's Royal Shakespeare Company and the Royal Court and the National Theatre?

LITTLEWOOD: Have you seen them?

INTERVIEWER: Yes.

LITTLEWOOD: O.K. Well, they're the walking dead. I mean theater is *today*; it's so wonderful to try a new part. The excitement, I'm talking about—today and tomorrow—that is the present tense. They live in the past tense. And would you like to repeat this conversation again an hour from now? Could you, would you like to do it tomorrow and tomorrow?

Evening comes, and the day is lived and there's this wonderful time when the lights are lit, especially in our northern world, and that's when the theater is needed. My God, it's much more important than the pathetic attempt imposed on actors of this obsolete system of repetition. Those people in New York who get tickets for the latest thing, what do they see? A repetition. The good dance comes just when they're falling asleep. And we really can't be as bored as we're supposed to be because the critics have told us that this is the best musical, this is the most obtuse brilliant piece of writing, and what is it? The writing at its best . . . And they are clever, these young writers, but at best, they are in a womb, a dark womb. And theater has always been out where it's difficult, painful, marvelous, when it was alive, I think.

INTERVIEWER: What about the productions of Shakespeare today. What do you think of them?
LITTLEWOOD: I don't think they read the plays. It's much too difficult to do something simple and rewarding like read the plays but not to stuff into them a lot of renaissance setting or to do them in Brecht method or to get Jan Kott from Poland to give us the latest on Shakespeare, as if we can't read the bloody thing. They put on marvelous costumes but people are bored to death with it. They go, they go suffering; they dress up, go, and just sit there. We're getting culture, which is worse than an injection.

INTERVIEWER: Peter Hall said that nobody knows how Shakespeare is to be put on, that anybody's guess is as good as his.
LITTLEWOOD: He's dead right. What about that Japanese character who does that sculpture in New York. . . . Noguchi had them all dressed up in Japanese costumes and if they wanted to pee they had to take their heads off because the costumes were one elaborate thing. Peter Hall, he's on to a good thing there, and he's a very clever manager; but he wouldn't know theater if he fell over it in the dark. "Oh joy, we must have the classical theater." O.K., but let me have mine, you know. I don't mind if they're at one end of The Fun Palace. Let them compete with what we're doing at

the other. When you're middle-aged and get into ministries and subsidized theater that decides they don't want to take risks, you cannot discover that almost the next child you meet on the street is going to tell you something more marvelous than you can get from the geniuses all around.

INTERVIEWER: You know critics have spoken about your unusual directorial methods. Kenneth Tynan called you, I'm going to quote him now, "One of the most original non-predictable directors in the British theater," and then you said, "I'm not a professional director, I don't know what a professional director is."
LITTLEWOOD: That's all right, I'll stick by that.

INTERVIEWER: What do you mean by this, you don't know what a professional director is?
LITTLEWOOD: Well, I do really. Shall I tell you?

INTERVIEWER: Sure.
LITTLEWOOD: Right, we all sit down and read the script. Now we want this to have an original rhythm, you see. I've worked it all out for you. We'll do the floor pattern or what I feel about this character, and I don't believe in feeling. I believe in thinking. This is how it goes on, this is a director? Right. . . . But there is something else that happens. I don't care who we are. If five of us are gathered at random in this room and we have a subject and it's exciting, we'd get together on it; you read one bit, I'll read another, someone can dance, someone knows about music. The objective is just in the team looking for protein; they might not find it, but they might find something quite different. I happen to believe that the theater is more than an art, that it is also a science and a very necessary one. Films are peripheral, TV's all right; it hooks people up, but ours is to do with something else. It doesn't matter if there are no critics coming, but if it's happening in this way, this improvisational way, which is the opposite of religion, then it's operating. I know all the rackets, I know all the terms and I've seen a lot of theater, but I know that when people get together in this exciting way you'll get a

play out of it. And I've done that with Arabs mixed with Jews in North Africa. And we did a play about identity and it was very necessary and very funny.

INTERVIEWER: Did you go away from England for a while to work there?

LITTLEWOOD: Yes, I did.

INTERVIEWER: Just to digress for a second, what kind of experience was this?

LITTLEWOOD: I got fed up. Someone said to come to Tunisia, there's twenty-one acres. There I worked for what amounted to a year altogether with a mixture of nationalities to play out their fear of each other. Syrian for Algerian, Algerian for Tunisian, Arab for Jew, Jew for Arab, French for Algerian. This they played out, and this became a very exciting piece of theater, almost a therapy.

INTERVIEWER: Yes, it sounds as if it is a therapeutic exercise or an exorcism of their own psyche.

LITTLEWOOD: What about the great private anguish of the really great public poets, the ones I've known, the Dylan Thomases, the Brendan Behans, the great jokers? You know it's always the men with the saddest private lives who make the great theater subjects, and I think that applies more or less to all humanity. I mean every child has potentially so much more than they've had the chance to explore. . . . I have worked with wonderful people who have become stars; now I also work with people who are stars of the streets in London, and they too have played out the anguish of their lives. Some of them can't read or write but it's marvelous what they do.

INTERVIEWER: You're still doing this?

LITTLEWOOD: Yes. I was doing this all last Summer with about fifteen-year-olds—kids called delinquents. Some of the actors were fabulous, and I asked them to do it, their particular "thing," not more than once.

INTERVIEWER: Where are they from?

LITTLEWOOD: Just from outside my old theater in east London. On the streets.

INTERVIEWER: So it's the East End again. And they're working-class children. Do you improvise with them?

LITTLEWOOD: Well, they've seen a lot of things happening. They've seen the days when we might have gone bursting out onto the streets out from the theater. And they were helping me make a play space for younger children. And they started to do a trial, without much help from me. And they did a trial which lasted for four nights, and found themselves guilty. They knew all the protocol and language of law, better than the adults, because they'd been in it, you see.

INTERVIEWER: What happens with the improvisational method? Is it possible for that method to be over-used? In other words, can you depend upon it too much so that the whole play is gone?

LITTLEWOOD: You use it for different purposes; people always did. It has become a vogue word, it's passé now. You use it for different purposes. You might use it to change identities in order to get people to understand the opposite person. And then you see things done as an improvisation and it's the most set, Brechtian thing that you've ever seen. It's a word that ought to be dropped.

INTERVIEWER: What about the mixed media that's so popular in New York now—the use of electronic lights, electronic sounds, projections and so forth?

LITTLEWOOD: But don't you think that goes even further back? You see, the kinetic boys were in 1910 starting a lot of this. And again, if you use a voguey trick to the exclusion of the human expression, you're going to be tricksy and you're going to be in the art magazine and you're going to dazzle everybody with your new gadgets. Sure, use gadgets, use anything, use bawdry and lyricism together, use all the human conditions, all the human techniques, but in the end the problem of communication between man-to-man, woman-to-man, whatever you like, is still the greatest problem.

INTERVIEWER: We are sort of moving away from the theater altogether. Does youth go to the movies? They say, "You've got nothing to say to us." What do you think of this?

LITTLEWOOD: Movies are getting better and better techniques and having less and less to say. The stories are dwindling; they're not much fun either, are they? I think people have got to find how to invent their own fun.

INTERVIEWER: Do you think the playwrights today have something to say to capture the imagination of the people?

LITTLEWOOD: I don't think they do. Let's open the door to lots of talent where we think it doesn't exist. Let's get lots of things happening that people enjoy and then you'll get a new kind of poetry, a new kind of playwright, a new kind of theater. For the moment, it is that next child that you meet on the street.

INTERVIEWER: Is your project now being sponsored or subsidized?

LITTLEWOOD: No it isn't. I'm subsidizing it from myself, because I'm back to where I was when I was twenty; they don't know what I'm up to. But theater's got to be for free, like bread and wine should be really. How are you going to subsidize that?

Interviewed by MARGARET CROYDEN, 1969

PHILIPPE DE BROCA

Philippe de Broca is very serious about comedy. To the young French director, who made his first film when he was only twenty-five, the genre is a personal way of looking at tragedy. Preferring the laugh to the tear, he gift wraps his comic statement in an excessively ribboned box of bonbons rather than forcing his audiences to choke on moldy crumbs left at the bottom of a kitchen sink. De Broca's world is light, fanciful, stylish, where frustration and pain are carefully masked behind the faces of Beautiful People. The slight, sandy-haired director completed his first film ten years ago, just as the New Wave was beginning to have an impact on international movie making. Today, at thirty-five, de Broca is preparing his ninth comedy, in which the traditional de Broca hero, a man not unlike de Broca himself, takes an upside down look at the absurdities of the animal kingdom and, with a sly wise grin—drops out.

De Broca—ultra-Parisian in that unavoidably blasé French manner, reflected by Jean-Pierre Cassel in the director's first three comedies, The Love Game, The Joker, The Five-Day Lover.

De Broca—the irrepressible romantic, tripping headstrong down the Champs Elysées or through the glass doors of Orly Airport with the insouciance of Jean-Paul Belmondo in That Man From Rio.

De Broca—wistful, the saddened sophisticate, alienated from the sane world, from Us, trying to keep from smothering under society's crazy quilt, like Alan Bates, the bewildered soldier in King of Hearts.

How do the pieces of this de Broca puzzle fit?

"When I was nine, an age when little boys want to be doctors or lawyers, I wanted to be a director. My parents thought this was a funny joke. But I couldn't have lived without making films. My family sent me to the Ecole Technique to study photography. During the army, I spent two years as a newsreel cameraman, then stayed on another year shooting a documentary on the elephant trail. It was Algeria that shifted my interest to comedy. I decided the real world was just too ugly.

"I came back to Paris. I knew that *now* I had to break into film production. So I walked up and down the Champs Elysées knocking on the doors of every film office. Every secretary knew me! I said I would work for nothing. Then, the New Wave hit—and it was a lucky moment. France was suddenly filled with bright young directors. I got a job as assistant on François Truffaut's first film, *The 400 Blows*. Later I worked as assistant director to Claude Chabrol on *The Cousins, Le Beau Serge* and *Leda*. After that I said to myself, I cannot be an assistant anymore.

"It was a fantastic period. Today in France it would not happen so quickly. But then . . . everyone was young and enthusiastic, and the first directors to succeed immediately helped their friends. Chabrol himself produced my first two films with his profits from *The Cousins*.

"The idea for my first film, *The Love Game* (1958), came from its leading lady, Geneviève Cluny. She was a pretty young actress well known in Paris for her toothpaste commercials. It was about a young couple who live together in happy immorality until the girl decides she wants a baby—and selects their best friend to be the father. Geneviève Cluny took the idea to Chabrol, who turned it over to Jean-Luc Godard and me. We were supposed to work on the story together—as collaborators—but obviously Godard's viewpoint is totally different from mine. We could not work together. I went ahead with my version and Godard later did his own, *A Woman is a Woman*. I didn't like Godard's and he didn't like mine. But I've never been a favorite with *Cahiers du Cinéma*, although they praised *The Love Game* and *The Joker*. Those were my most personal films until *King of Hearts*."

In The Love Game, *de Broca's star—Jean-Pierre Cassel—*
makes a virtue of frivolity, cavorting like an infant until his
playmate-mistress insists on expressing her maternal urge. This
makes him grow up at last—a not-so-happy ending. The de
Broca hero—a clown, a misfit, a stormy non-conformist in a
fantasy environment—was again enacted by Cassel in the
director's second feature, The Joker (1959). *More bitter than*
his first film, it presented Cassel as an athletic modern Casa-
nova, joyously scampering over roofs and walls in quest of his
latest conquest. Love makes him try to reform, but the girl
finally realizes he prefers irresponsibility and will never really
change. The pieces in the de Broca puzzle begin to come
together.

"Jean-Pierre Cassel in *The Love Game* was really playing
two sides of myself—first the fantasist who is crushed when
he's forced to acknowledge reality, then the farceur who simply refuses to succumb. Cassel is an excellent comedian who
did three films for me and I remember telling him, 'I'll make
all my movies with you.' Of course I did not. But for those
first movies, he expressed exactly what I wanted. When I
worked with Truffaut on *The 400 Blows* I was impressed by
the rapport between Truffaut and the young actor who played
the lead. It was as if Truffaut were directing himself. That
must have been in the back of my mind when I chose Cassel.

"My dream would be to have a troupe, like a repertory company, and then I could always use the same actors. Most
painters, I suppose, always use the same basic color. Actually,
I don't like to direct actors. An actor has a voice—a body—a
style. He brings himself to a role. I cannot tell him what to do.
But as a director, I can choose what voice, what style I want.
So the selection of actors is important.

"Belmondo *is* Belmondo. You can't change him. You can't
alter his personality. When he plays a drunk scene, he is
Belmondo drunk. When he plays a love scene, he is Belmondo
in love. Once a film is cast it takes on a certain form that
even I cannot change. So by the time we begin, I am the
slave—the servant of the film. I would like to be an actor
and make all my films with myself in them, but I'm not an

actor. And it is too difficult to direct *and* act at the same time."

The first phase of de Broca's career ended with The Five-Day Lover *(1960), a witty high comedy in which Cassel— again—decides to return to his rich mistress rather than work for a living to be with his true love—and de Broca implies that the lad is not necessarily wrong. It was his last film with Cassel, his last small production. As director of a particular specialized genre that eludes American directors, de Broca proved that he could be past-master of the form.*

"It was written in two weeks, filmed in five . . . and I remember nothing else about *The Five-Day Lover.*"

De Broca's international reputation was achieved with That Man From Rio *(1964), which won the New York Film Critics Award for best foreign film of that year. Typically, that bubbly modern chase brought him less acclaim in France than anywhere else in the world. Now he speaks of its popularity with some embarrassment.*

"I made *That Man From Rio* for political reasons. To be free, to have the money to make what I wanted to. To do this, I needed a very big success. Even so, there were problems. No one wanted to produce *Rio*. It took me six months to find a producer and then five months to write the script. That kind of adventure story always seems very easy, but it isn't. I had the opening: Belmondo sees his fiancée kidnapped, he follows her to Orly, gets on the same plane with her—but she's drugged, she doesn't recognize him. Suddenly they land in Rio. Now what can he do? I have to invent a story. I had certain scenes I wanted in . . . Jean-Paul escaping on a skyscraper and running through the jungle . . . but the problem was *how*. It is a very naïve film. I think that is why it worked. It won awards but I was not in love with it. It was the kind of movie I wanted to see when I was fourteen.

"After *Rio* I had my freedom, which is vital to a director. In France we have formed a society of directors because we want even *more* freedom. When I say I want to make a film, that means write and direct and edit. There can't be another way. A Hollywood producer called me and says he has a project. Everything is ready. Kirk Douglas will be the star. Dalton Trumbo will write the script. Can I come over and direct? But what does all that mean? If I direct a film, it must be *my* film. I will do the selection, otherwise there is no freedom. In America, I think, they will soon have to do as we do in France—then there will be more personal films like *The Graduate*.

"There will also be more original films. I hate adaptations. I love Stendhal but if I ever tried to film one of his books, it wouldn't resemble the original. I have to feel completely free to change anything to suit the medium. A book can be the beginning of an idea. But I prefer to find my ideas in painting or music, not in literature. In Hollywood they always buy the bestseller. They are afraid, that's why. Can you imagine a novelist like Faulkner seeing a film and then saying, 'I think I'll adapt it for my next novel?' You laugh, but it is the same when directors buy books and plays for the screen."

The third—and current—phase in de Broca's career began with King of Hearts *(1967), a stylish exercise in bitter comedy in which the hero was a sane intruder into a world of madness. The film, set in World War I, starred Alan Bates as a British soldier sent on a secret mission, behind German lines, to a provincial French town. There he finds the inmates of an asylum romping through the sacked village, oblivious to danger and possible death. Instead of returning to his regiment, Bates chooses to enter the asylum, severing himself from the war-ravaged "real" world. This preference for the irrational has been a consistent de Broca theme.*

"In *King of Hearts* there is the real world, represented by caricatures of soldiers, and there is the mad world—gay and imaginative people playing costumed roles and applauding the battle as a performance for their amusement. Which is more real? It is tragedy seen comically. The conception came from a story I read in *France-Soir*. It was just a short item about the commemoration of fifty French mental patients who had been killed by the Germans. Their hospital had been bombed and they wandered through fields dressing themselves in the uniforms of dead American soldiers. When the Germans saw them, they thought they were Americans and shot them. It is a terrible story. Another director might take the same material and treat it realistically—a moment of horror from war.

"It was the first film made exactly as I wanted to. And then what happened? It was not successful in France. But the Americans liked it, which means they understood what I was trying to do. I want to continue making these "comedies" because, for me, the only way to meet the tragedy of life is through comedy. I'm afraid of the world. I'm frightened. The comedy is a mask. Brecht is a comic playwright, although he is usually presented very seriously. The seriousness lies behind the humor. I'd like to direct Brecht once, to show that he is comic."

A recurring motif in de Broca's movies are nutsy gargoyled houses—as in The Joker—*which becomes the hospital in* King of Hearts *and a hotel in his latest film,* The Devil by the Tail.

"These buildings are symbols. Because I'm afraid of what I read in the newspapers—Czechoslovakia, Vietnam, Biafra. So I prefer to enclose my films in my subjective world . . . a micro-world. The hotel is a haven for gangsters, aristocrats, clowns—all types of humanity. I guess there are personal reasons too. I'm lonely. I'm nostalgic about having a family because I have none. I would love to live with the family in *The Joker.*

"But I'm a big boy now. So my heroes will probably change. Perhaps I will make *The Joker* again, but next time he will be older, wiser. They say my heroes are always de Broca, but I do not think so, really. I am the eye of the story."

Interviewed by PAUL GARDNER, 1969

JULES FEIFFER

Jules Feiffer likes to talk in his work room, overlooking New York City's Hudson River. He is surrounded by large photographs of Humphrey Bogart, and LBJ as Superman, and posters of productions of his plays. After this interview took place, Feiffer withdrew God Bless *because of its implications in the repressive Nixon era. His later play,* The White House Murder Case, *dramatizes the more immediate problems of consensus politics.*

INTERVIEWER: When critics want to put down your plays, they often say that they're cartoons. Is there a relationship between the graphic image on the page and the stage thing you're creating?

FEIFFER: The forms are quite different and therefore my approach to them is quite different. But my approach to a cartoon isn't basically that graphic. It's not really a struggle between a graphic approach and a theatrical approach. What I find most amusing about the charge that my plays are really cartoons is that for the first six or seven years of doing cartoons, people used to tell me these weren't cartoons at all. To be recognized as a cartoonist, I had to start writing plays. I think that cartooning is the need to categorize, to pigeonhole; you've got to hang a handle on something. If I were a plumber, a lot would have been made of Kenny spending a lot of time in the bathroom.

INTERVIEWER: Is there any parallel between the two forms, for you? The tactics that you use?

FEIFFER: They're my people, but the forms are very, very different. There are very few things in the plays I've done that I could put into cartoons. Because in one case I'm dealing with stereotypes and in the other I'm trying for people, although *God Bless* is, in a sense, deliberately a political cartoon, so the people there are archetypal figures. But because of the time that one is allowed in the theater—much more than in a cartoon—I etch them much more deeply; in terms of detail, relationships, in expressing ideas. They can't really be similar approaches. I'm working in a different medium, but I have basically the same thing to say. The reason I went into theater was that I felt the cartoon didn't give me enough room to say it. So I fooled around with writing a novel, found it took too much time and too much agony. Then I found I could write for the theater. I enjoyed it and it took less time.

INTERVIEWER: The facile dismissal of *God Bless* as a cartoon comes from a stereotyped attitude about what satire should be on stage?
FEIFFER: I don't even know if it's that. Satire is done so infrequently on stage that I don't think critics have much experience with it. The last satire we had on stage in New York was *Second City,* or maybe *The Committee.*

INTERVIEWER: Don't you think that something like *The Beauty Part* is satire?
FEIFFER: I think of satire as something much rougher, nastier than the world Perelman has; I've never really thought of that as satire. To me satire is an attempt to get at the root of a situation, and expose it to the extension of logic. Taking logic to the point where it becomes ridiculous; revealing certain truths about situations that otherwise might not be evident. That's not at all what Perelman tries to do.

INTERVIEWER: Satire is something which is fantastically ugly, and fantastically hardnosed? There can't be any compromises in terms of an audience?
FEIFFER: I don't know if it has to be ugly. I think when a piece of work is in balance, if it's true, labels like ugly, pretty, funny or sad don't pertain. That's why I'm puzzled by people who

say that *Little Murders* or *God Bless* take a despairing view. While that's what they may get out of it, that's not my view. And since I'm the writer and everything operates out of my view, I don't see these works as despairing.

INTERVIEWER: Do you see satire as redemptive? That if you can see these things, there's a possibility for survival?
FEIFFER: Right. One doesn't anticipate that the possibility will too often be picked up. But there is a hope in my plays and in my cartoons. By showing certain things, you can institute insights which later can lead to action.

INTERVIEWER: What happens when a play like *Little Murders*, which had such a short run on Broadway, turns out to be prophetic?
FEIFFER: I never thought of it as prophetic. I still don't. I thought that it was something everybody already knew. I am quite amazed that people who saw the play come to me and say: "My God, it's all happening." At the time I wrote it, it was already happening. The Kennedy assassination had already happened. There was a climate of random violence which I considered prevalent in the America of 1967 when the play was first done, and America in 1966 when I wrote it. This was the by-product of the frustrations of twenty years of Cold War, which I explored to a very limited degree in the cartoon and wanted space to explore it more. But the view I had, I had in 1964. Suddenly in 1968 people say it's true, but it was true in 1964. I think we're very slow in catching up with the obvious. And when we do catch up, we call somebody who saw it a year or two earlier, prophetic. Is I. F. Stone prophetic because he saw we were in miserable shape in Vietnam three years before Robert McNamara? It was just that McNamara was stupid. And misled by his own bullshit. I think one's ability to clear away the bullshit may be mistaken for prophetic powers.

INTERVIEWER: Having recognized the obvious and put it down, it must seem strange seeing the obvious compounded.
FEIFFER: I had that problem when I was in Chicago for the Democratic Convention—nothing happened in Chicago that I didn't expect. Yet when it happened I found myself so horrified

and so surprised that I discovered that there's an enormous difference between what you expect to happen and that thing when it finally does happen, because you really never do expect it. I never quite expect my satires to come true. And I'm terribly depressed when a Chicago happens, when a second Kennedy assassination occurs. So, while on paper—intellectually—I'm not surprised, in fact I'm horrified.

INTERVIEWER: You said that you couldn't resist putting *Little Murders* on Broadway—in front of the people it was about. I want you to talk about audiences witnessing satire.

FEIFFER: I did the *Little Murders* production on Broadway before I really got into the theater and it might have been a little fanciful to have that idea. It might be more of a literary notion. I still like the idea, but I don't make any guesses about audiences any more. I was quite disturbed about a critic in the *Village Voice* who said that this showed my contempt for the audience, trying to manipulate them into a position. But I think that's what theater is. It's certainly what the Living Theater does, trying to move you from one point to another point. The only real interest I have in theater is to create the drama between the actors, the stage and the members of the audience. So it's a two-way dialogue, not just between two people on stage, but between the two people and individual members of the audience, who are reacting to what's being said. Or, in *God Bless*, arguing back perhaps. I don't mean audience participation, but something much more interesting than that, which is internal participation. If you have said No in the theater, there is very little chance that you will say No outside, or even think about it when you leave the theater. But if you're arguing, or befuddled or angry in the theater, it will go outside with you.

INTERVIEWER: One of the criticisms of *God Bless* was that you took no position, that creating an ambiguity, using clichés of Left and Radical Left was cop-out.

FEIFFER: What was being said was that if I don't pick from packaged labels—A, B, C—well I haven't picked anything.

But I don't really think that the choice is between Richard Nixon and Abbie Hoffman. In *God Bless,* I really wasn't trying to show how everybody was rotten, how everybody was equally evil. What I was trying to show was quite obvious in the script, but it might have been less obvious as presented on stage. I was trying to show what our heritage of pragmatic liberalism has brought us in the last twenty years, using the framework of this century and even before. The liberal mentality that chooses to be affective, rather than woolly-minded, moralistic and idealistic. And where that affectiveness has brought us. Vietnam is one of its major betrayals. I found the reaction fascinating up at Yale. The reaction came only from the students at the Drama School. I am not too sure how to take their complaints because I could never get them to go into any detail. There was no chance of going beyond that surface attack. What disturbed me about this reaction was that most of the play is about Brackman. He has almost all the lines and is certainly the most interesting character. Most time is spent on him, and yet in all their objections, they never discuss him, only the two radicals. They're not quarreling about the play, only about my presentation of the two radicals. They don't see it in the context of the play, but simply as a mirror being held up to them. It may or may not represent a legitimate image of them, but they weren't discussing the play.

INTERVIEWER: Another criticism of *God Bless* is that it is an essay.

FEIFFER: The most interesting form today is probably the essay. It's what Godard puts on film. And it's in many ways what I try to do in the cartoon, and I suppose it's what interests me in the theater. To frame an idea or series of ideas within characters who will interact, and I hope that interaction will present the idea to the audience. I don't mean one of my characters being a spokesman for the writer. That's much too direct to mean anything to us, even if we take it seriously. But what can happen is that characters can stand on stage and argue from various fixed points, none of which is absolutely right. By listening, and you're forced to listen if the arguments are interesting enough—or if the points of view are interesting enough—we can get something for ourselves out of that. There's not a character in *Little Murders* who represents my point of view. But I hope that by what happens in the play, that point of view becomes evident. From the mail I got, lots of the audience did get it. That's what I find exciting about the theater.

INTERVIEWER: Do you find it a problem when the audience, used to television, is confronted with people, none of whom are telling the truth?

FEIFFER: It's not just television people, it's the critics themselves, who spend most of their time going to the theater. Some reviews of *Little Murders* said that my solution was to have people shooting out of windows.

I see nothing wrong in using the theater as an essay form. In *God Bless,* that's expressly what I am trying to do. To me the action is the arguments, rather than have something fake happen between the characters that's quite predictable. The action is in the language, the arguments between the people and the discoveries that people make about each other in the course of the play and everybody makes about ideas. The action of the play is simple; how Brackman can, very early in the play, be horrified by the barbarism of cutting off the ears of the Eighty-second Airborne, yet at the end of the play, in a very practical way, he's negotiating how many American cities are going to be bombed. And it's this escalation of barbarism overridden with humanistic terms that I'm trying to get at. To show the evolution from position A to position B is, I think, action enough, and I certainly think it's theatrical enough.

INTERVIEWER: It's not very American to have a debate. Physical action and plot have always been much more important to American drama, but this is something you're moving away from?

FEIFFER: Don't base this on one play—*God Bless,* because the next play may be very different. I know what I want to do, pretty much where I want to go, but haven't the faintest idea of how I want to do it. It will be very different from *God Bless.* The problem with *God Bless* was this: I wanted to do a political play, which was different from *Little Murders,* which is a political allegory—of the Cold War and Vietnam and how innocent people, nice people, right-thinking people can become murderers.

INTERVIEWER: And in their niceness, feed the very destruction?

FEIFFER: Yes, it's not overtly political. It's only political when you leave the theater and know it's a political play. Most critics just thought it was about violence in the streets. *God Bless* was overtly political. I wanted to write a play dealing with ideas that are in the air today. The main problem with a political play is it can very simply be just talk on the stage and that can be very, very boring. So I had to figure out ways of forcing the audience to pay attention. So the whole structure of the play is designed to keep things hopping. So they're hooked for some reason, something's always going on.

INTERVIEWER: Do you ever find yourself wanting to use the audience's response against itself?

FEIFFER: Well, I've done it both in *Little Murders* and *God Bless.* The radical drama students had a helluva good time with the play until the two radicals start giving a mutilation program in the second act. Then the play went all wrong for them, and that really interests me, excites me. To show various sides of a problem and catch an audience up when it's feeling too good about something.

INTERVIEWER: Despite the gunshots, they could think of *Little Murders* as a situation comedy, so you could count on that subliminal response?

FEIFFER: I saw *The Price* (Arthur Miller) and *Plaza Suite* (Neil Simon) on succeeding nights and I noticed (although I've been aware of it for years) that there's a whole chain of experiences that people assume to be real, but has nothing to do with real life. It has to do with theatrical and movie life. Confrontation scenes, in which everyone tells the truth, don't happen in life. But we're so used to it in the theater, that when it happens, we don't think of it as a device, we think of it as realism or naturalism. Nothing could be less real. So what I was trying to do in *Little Murders*, was take those very familiar devices and set them loose in the America of Vietnam. Set them loose in a country that's been living for a long time in a Cold War morality. It's fascinating because what you're dealing with is the audience. You're showing them something they know and they're familiar with and immediately relaxed with, and then showing them how it really is.

INTERVIEWER: Be more specific about other clichés of situation comedy.

FEIFFER: I'm working on a sex play. I've never seen sex handled in a real way on stage, even the world of a whore—especially the world of a whore. What is thought of as explicit and frank is crafted as if done by Busby Berkeley. It's boring or entertaining, but it has nothing to do with what's true.

INTERVIEWER: Is the piece you've done for Tynan's revue, *Oh! Calcutta!*, on sex?

FEIFFER: It's an exercise in that direction. I've tried certain things out. I guess Lenny Bruce came closest to what I'm doing, although I want to do it theatrically. Bruce would create little situations. There would be marvels of discovery. The audience would just hold its breath and laugh in a way which indicated that they were giving themselves away. That it had hit hard. It was marvelous to be there and be hit yourself. To have the air clarified. Lenny would say something that no one had ever said and suddenly the ghosts were laid and there was nothing to be afraid of. At least at the moment. It was a marvelous feeling. I want to have it come as a discovery at the end of the play.

INTERVIEWER: You want to free everyone from their intellectual baggage?

FEIFFER: It's an enormous ambition. In *Little Murders*, it's in the form of a parable, a concrete parable. A truth that you, as a member of the audience, discover for yourself will stay with you a helluva lot longer and mean more to you than if the writer comes right out with the meaning. It's leading you down the garden path to making that discovery that I find interesting.

INTERVIEWER: What do you think about modern American satire?

FEIFFER: There was a point in the fifties when we seemed to be developing some sort of school of American theatrical satire —most of it stemming from the cabarets: *Compass, Second City,* Nichols and May, Bruce and Mort Sahl. But that vanished about six or seven years ago. Actually it vanished as soon as The New Frontier came into being. That seemed to take the canker out, except for Bruce. So I don't see many things that are satire. Some Off-Broadway and Off-Off-Broadway is labeled satire, but I don't think it is.

INTERVIEWER: What do you mean by satire?

FEIFFER: It's what I want my stage to be, and I want somebody else to do it so that I can enjoy myself. I'm not making any definitions about what theater should be. Most theater is so deadly dull that I have not the slightest idea which direction it should move in. Most of the things today are as fake as the things they're replacing.

INTERVIEWER: What would you like theater to be?

FEIFFER: When I go to the theater, I like to be forced to think, to be taken out of the position I'm in. And be moved if need be, involuntarily. This threatens me, yet if I follow through, will lead to new perceptions and possibly even new truths. There must be many ways of doing this, but I don't see it being done today. I like some of the things the Living Theater does, but what I like has to do with theater and vaudeville, it has nothing to do with truth. And that's the area in which they're most lax and confused. Because when they talk about freedom, I find them most authoritarian.

INTERVIEWER: Do you mean absolute truth?

FEIFFER: I'm talking about individual truth. It's cosmic truths that are so dangerous. Any raw generalization tends to become hysterical.

INTERVIEWER: Satirists usually set their sights on particulars and use the absurdities around them. Are you consciously doing that with language?

FEIFFER: Not really. Except in *God Bless*, Brackman was a character who uses language in a very particular way. He comes from a classical school. It was great fun to write him. He's a nineteenth-century man, speaking the way that few people, besides Dean Acheson, speak. He's a man that takes pleasure in hearing himself tell a story. There's very little of that happening any more. I can't imagine Tom Hayden, aged eighty, taking great joy in his own language, because he almost has no language. In a way, language is an important part of *God Bless*, simply because that's one of the quarrels between the generations. In *Little Murders*, it doesn't play that kind of part. The language in *Little Murders* wasn't language, it was character. When you get into a character, he's going to speak in his own way, but unself-consciously. I never think specifically of how somebody is going to sound. You just get to the essence of a character and once you understand him, he'll speak in a certain way.

INTERVIEWER: Do you think that their selling pieces of her face is a device which is completely in keeping with the rest of *Little Murders*?
FEIFFER: Yes. It's how casually we're able to dehumanize. And turn something we felt love for, truly, to a market value. It's like the Kennedy children.

INTERVIEWER: How do you take a subject and turn it into a play?
FEIFFER: I get a theme, start making notes, and I find that even if it seems that I'm going far afield, that somehow once the idea has matured, everything I've written relates directly to the theme. I drafted *God Bless* in February, about thirty or forty minutes shorter, in which Eve, Brackman's wife, had no part at all, except to open and close doors. The play was all politics. I was nervous about writing more of a part for her because I knew which direction it would have to go—of her having had affairs with everybody on that stage. I was afraid it would become a subplot. But I had to start writing about relations with the various men on stage. I discovered all she had were political relationships. She is a power fucker.

INTERVIEWER: Are you discouraged with the theater?

FEIFFER: I'm only disenchanted with getting involved in productions, because I've discovered after being involved in two productions of *Little Murders*, and two of *God Bless*, that my presence adds absolutely nothing. A mistake that I'll catch in the second week of rehearsal, they would have caught by the third week anyhow. My being a cop on a production certainly doesn't help a production which is destined to be awful, as witness the London production of *God Bless*. When I'm writing a script, I know things, and what I don't know right away, I'll know by tomorrow morning. I have a feeling of certainty that I don't feel in a production. Since I want to continue to write for the theater, I find the best way is to write the plays and not go near them until run-throughs or previews.

INTERVIEWER: Can you tell me more about your definition of satire?

FEIFFER: Satire basically has to be antagonistic to the system within which it operates. Otherwise it has nothing to satirize. I don't think of Noel Coward as satire; they're pastiches, parodies. I don't mean that pejoratively. It's just that they don't fit into the basic meaning of satire, which is much more subversive.

And there are various levels of subversion; it becomes very easy and not necessarily uncommercial to operate on certain levels of subversion. That doesn't mean that you're going to get a network show, but you can make a helluva good living by being known to be anti-establishment. While in the McCarthy fifties being anti-establishment was enough because the rest of society was so repulsively conformist, today one has to investigate his own approach to his own particular subversion and find out if he can't dig still deeper. This subversion is simply a by-product of one's art. You're quite naturally looking for more, and you're always quite naturally dissatisfied with your current level. Not always; when you reach that level, you're very happy for a while. Since satire is the discovery of relationships in the society, it's always society you're looking at. What's going on in America today is really unprecedented. There's so much material and it's so easy to fall into chaos and miss particulars. It's almost impossible to analyze a large situation anymore, because of the changes and shifts. Nobody has any ideas, although we're all guessing, of what the next four years with Nixon will be like. What the Left's reaction to a Nixon administration will be like, what American foreign policy in terms of ingressive imperialism, future Vietnams will be like. It's all up for grabs right now. We won't know for at least another year. It's a very exciting time, a very puzzling time.

Interviewed by JOHN LAHR, 1969

JOHN HOPKINS

John Hopkins is at least as highly thought of as any television playwright in England. His most ambitious and considerable achievement at the time of this interview was probably Talking to a Stranger, *four television plays, each examining the same sequence of events through the eyes of a different character. George Melly in* The Observer *called it, "The first authentic masterpiece written directly for television."*

Hopkins made his reputation as a contributor to the BBC television serial, Z Cars, *short plays by various writers dealing with (fictitious) police cases in the North of England. He wrote scores of plays for the series, and has written many other plays for television, including* Horror of Darkness. *His first stage play,* This Story of Yours, *opened at the Royal Court Theatre, London, on December 11, 1968. It was directed by Christopher Morahan, who directed Hopkins'* Quartet *on television.*

John Hopkins lives in a flat on the top floor of a large house in Hampstead's Fitzjohn's Avenue. The room in which we talked was large, spacious, elegant and comfortably furnished. There were hundreds of books neatly arranged in bookcases, reproductions of French paintings on the walls, a drawer stuffed with scripts. By the door of the room was the playwright's desk, with typewriter and paper. Hopkins has the reputation of being a very hard worker. His output bears this out.

INTERVIEWER: May I ask you a very basic question first: what do you think constitutes a good television play?
HOPKINS: I don't know that . . . that's a very . . . yes, it's a *basic* question. It's a very difficult question. Difficult because

television is such an unformed medium. It should be, it's a very young medium. I think people try to group far too much under the heading "television play." I think people tend to feel that anything that goes on . . . well, which is not documentary and which is not news, is a play. I think that's disaster because there is a great tendency to encourage in television just its omnivorous appetite, which encourages a lack of attention to craft and form.

My definition of a television play is much the same as of any play: selection of material, organization, direction, a sense of purpose in the material presented. But, primarily, I think that one should recognize that the writer is creating something. For me, *Cathy Come Home*—while it is an extraordinary experience—is not a play; but then, equally, I'm not sure what is. I think that a dramatized documentary is so unformed, doesn't communicate directly enough with its audience in a sense of encouraging them to participate in the action, to learn, in a dramatic sense, from the thing that they see; but more to learn in a documentary sense, to suffer in a documentary sense. The suffering that one should endure, share, in a play should be enhancing rather than depressing, simply because it is a mirror of life. I think a mirror of life is always deeply depressing, because one's own life is often so depressing. I think drama can take, should take, the elements of life and present them in a form which is . . . while it may in itself . . . I mean, there is very little encouraging about *Horror of Darkness* or the Quartet, encouraging in the sense that life will be a brighter, shining tomorrow. But the fact that a writer should gather together that material and present it in that formed shape seems to me an optimistic attitude, to represent an optimistic attitude, rather than simply to say: "Here is this documentary about a family living in southwest London and, goodness, don't they have a boring, dull, rotten life," as Maurice Wiggin in the *Sunday Times* said. And if that were so, Maurice Wiggin would be right. But that is not the limit of the experience, I believe.

INTERVIEWER: You're implying then, are you, that the writer has a responsibility, if not a duty, to present his material optimistically? Not just by selection but by illuminating the experience he is writing about?

HOPKINS: Yes, that. I think the first part of your remark, to present his material optimistically, implies a light comedy approach; it could imply that. I think that you're not at liberty . . . I believe that a writer is not simply at liberty to present. I mean necessarily, because that's not his function. If that's what you are, you're a journalist.

INTERVIEWER: You're implying that the playwright has a responsibility to comment, not just to present his material and leave it at that? In your Quartet, I would say that you comment increasingly with each play on the lives of your characters, if only because they are seen in each play from a different, shifting standpoint; because each character is the protagonist in his or her own play. You're adding art to the basic situation.

HOPKINS: Absolutely, absolutely.

INTERVIEWER: Which *Cathy Come Home* doesn't do; it's almost artless, it goes to the other extreme. . . .

HOPKINS: Oh yes, but it is the most artful. . . .

INTERVIEWER: Yes indeed, because it's concealed. . . .

HOPKINS: In fact it's very self-conscious. I don't know whether . . . You see, there again it's very difficult to separate form and content, and to know where, in the case of a dramatized documentary, the writer is simply presenting his material; or whereas in the case of, for instance, *Cathy Come Home,* or *Up the Junction,* the director, who is a very conscious artist, shapes the material, which one of them is responsible for presenting what is in fact a very conscious art work. But not a play. The material has not been worked on. I don't want to keep using that . . . it's much too easy. But it is the formlessness of television which depresses me most. This is why, after the Quartet—which achieved a certain form, a certain satisfaction in form for me—the next play, in rehearsal at the moment, which is set in Africa, is a wholly different kind of play. Different in terms of subject, speech patterns, and characterization. Not as far removed as if I simply set out and said:

"Now, how can I write a play which is diametrically opposed?" But simply that having achieved a measure of satisfaction with my own work in the Quartet, in the African play I've been trying to develop a much more deliberately—I don't like the word stylized—but deliberately formal atmosphere within which to act out a drama which is much larger in scope, involving people's life and death, as opposed to the everyday concerns of the characters in the Quartet. And working out . . . using Africa deliberately because I find it an exciting starting point, a non-real . . . it gives one tools to use which do not hamper or restrict but rather enlarge and liberate the imagination. Not simply in terms of plot, but in terms of form. So that these people enact a much more formal drama than anything I've tried to write before, much more theatrical. But I think . . . there isn't a word, you see, for . . . televisual. There isn't a word which says theatrical for television.

INTERVIEWER: You'll have to coin one.
HOPKINS: Well, I think until someone does. . . . This has always been the problem with television, that it has inherited so many phrases, so many descriptive terms from the theater, from the cinema.

INTERVIEWER: But this is surely inevitable in view of the relative youthfulness of television?
HOPKINS: Yes, but it's good and time that television began to shape its own. And *Cathy Come Home* can very well be part of that, just as equally as the Quartet was and Duncan Ross' work years ago was. There seems to me to be a slightly disturbing lack of direction in drama.

INTERVIEWER: By playwrights?
HOPKINS: No, by television. There are lots of new playwrights. There always are, there always will be in television. There are new ways of packaging drama: we'll now do it as a repertory company, or we'll do it as Tales of Horror and Imagination, but there hasn't been a new form since the Wednesday Play, since BBC 2 sat down and said—and they don't any more—"we will present trilogies of plays on a related theme." This is the kind

of exploration which television can do with so much more freedom than the stage or the cinema because there is much less economic commitment involved. And it is the lack of that kind of adventurousness that I find depressing in television at the moment.

INTERVIEWER: Do you prefer to write for television than the stage because you feel it is more demanding technically? Therefore you have to work more as a craftsman than as anything else to get a good play at the end of it?

HOPKINS: Yes; in a sort of opposed way it's so easy to write for television. I don't mean that *I* find it easy to write for television: it *is* easy to write for television. You just have to watch the formless mass.

INTERVIEWER: Which is presumably why so many good writers won't or don't write for television?

HOPKINS: Exactly. And also why a lot of good writers who do write for television, and write well for television, are undervalued. I think this is now happily less so, but Peter Nichols and David Mercer have written for the theater, which is why Peter Nichols and David Mercer are valued now.

INTERVIEWER: But don't you think that some writers are basically television playwrights and others are basically playwrights for the live theater?

HOPKINS: I think some of us understand what television is about. Try to understand, anyway. But, I don't know. I would hesitate to make a separation. . . . Not that a writer should be able to work across the media. I don't think that is necessarily true, but I think that a writer should—just as a director should —choose the style for a play, find the style within a play, and so present the play, as Christopher Morahan does with my work, with Nichols' work; rather than coming to the play and saying: "Well, I'm Christopher Morahan and I'm now going to make this play look like a production."

I've three things that I plan to write at the moment. One of them is firmly and clearly a stage play. The type of idea, the way I want to work it out, the demands of distancing—perhaps proscenium arch, I don't know; something, some sense of the idea and the way that length of time, the pace at which I want to develop it, primarily the fact that I want to develop it in words, said that it's a theatrical play. I have another idea that is so clearly a television play I don't even have to think for a moment. I know that that kind of concept must be a television play. And another is a film. Those three stories came with labels on them.

INTERVIEWER: Do you usually think: "I now want to write a television play, or a filmscript, or a stage play," rather than when a subject presents itself to you you think: "This is right for television, or for the cinema, or for the stage"?

HOPKINS: It tends to come that way round. After I'd finished the Quartet and the stage play, *This Story of Yours,* what I wanted to write was a play about people whose concerns should be life and death. But the adventure within which they were involved should be large scale, epic somehow, in a way like nothing that I had written, nothing original that I had written thus far. And I thought of the African play, what became the African play, the idea of the two brothers, and it was a television play. When it happened, I thought: "That's what it is." Now, interestingly enough, the reason that it happened like that is because, although it is very visual and is demanding a lot of filming—filming in the sense of film work—at the moment I'd worked out the central confrontation between the two brothers in dialogue. . . . Now, since then I've written three, four films and I can see that I might have worked the idea out now, if it came along, entirely in film terms. I should be very sorry because the value I gained personally from working out in words the confrontation between these two men was immeasurably stretching for me as a writer. Ideally none of these things should be on the surface of your mind when you're at it, just as you should not be planning your life or planning the shape of your career. I think there is an area where . . . just as I left Z *Cars* after two and a half years because that was the end of it, and I didn't go on and do *Softly, Softly* because there wasn't any more for *me*—which is nothing about the program, simply about me—because I was getting . . . because one must, working under that pressure, develop self defenses. Just as someone like you meeting a lot of people, strangers, in your day, must work out short cut ways to a relationship so that you don't have to plunge into a deep human relationship with every stranger that you meet, because that would tear you into shreds, kill you.

INTERVIEWER: From your work it is clear, I think, that you are particularly interested in the relationship between people as individuals. You seem mainly interested, if you like, in two people in a room, what happens between them.

HOPKINS: Yes, and this I've just worked out in a film called *Time Out of Time,* which in essence reduces to the conflict between two people, a man and a woman, both in their late thirties, an Englishman and an American who meet in New York, an English man and an American girl, and putting them together, what happens between them, worked out entirely in personal terms.

INTERVIEWER: That's what life's about, dammit!

HOPKINS: Well, and that for me is what drama is about, and in effect that for me is what a television play is about. You can say anything and everything in human terms. David Mercer and I would never write the same play, because of our upbringing, our environment, and our basic personality patterns, the things that interest him don't interest me, and vice versa. But we both use human relationships as our drama, and we're both good dramatists in that sense; and Nichols too.

INTERVIEWER: As playwrights, I'd put you and David Mercer in the same bracket. You're working the same kind of area.

HOPKINS: I'm flattered, because I admire him very much. . . . The whole political thing that David seems to pursue—less now, but did pursue—is, of course, alien to me.

INTERVIEWER: As a writer, you're fairly apolitical, aren't you?

HOPKINS: Yes, almost completely.

INTERVIEWER: As a person too?

HOPKINS: Largely, I'm afraid. Although I hope that . . . I don't know that it's possible . . . I've always said that, yes, that's always been my rather flip attitude. I'm non-political surrounded by people who are very politically inclined. But, no, largely both as a writer, totally as a writer. . . . The whole of Z Cars, in fact, was the birth of a social conscience, or consciousness, which I had not really believed was there, or not really concerned myself with, which has since shaped everything that I've written.

INTERVIEWER: Was it to any extent because of your time on Z Cars that the central character in your new stage play is a policeman? Did you feel that "the policeman" is typical or untypical, representative or unrepresentative, of individuals in society?

HOPKINS: Of course it would be ridiculous of me to say, "No, it's quite by accident that I wrote a play about a policeman, having worked on Z Cars." But the predicament that Johnson, the central character, dramatizes is not solely a predicament that a policeman can find himself in; but, given that he is a policeman, the predicament then becomes tragic—no, tragic is a very strong word, like genius, that I'm loath to use. Tragic is a word that people should say about you rather than about your own work. The fact that he is a policeman dramatizes almost beyond bearing the flaw in his character, just as our need for policemen, our need for that kind of protection, and our need then socially to ostracize them if humanly possible, says a great deal more about us than it does about the police.

When I came to write This Story of Yours, yes, I had always intended further to develop in non-adventure terms my reaction and feelings about the police. And this is it, the dilemma that Johnson finds himself in seemed to me the right means, and also the theater, for me. I'd been frightened of working in the theater because I felt that . . . working as much in television as I have done carries a tremendous . . . creates a sense of inhibition about your ability to work in what you think of as a larger medium, you know? It happens about the cinema as well. Until you discover. . . . You see, you couldn't do the

Quartet on the stage or in a cinema; equally, you couldn't do *This Story of Yours* on television. I don't know, it would be an interesting experiment. . . . I don't believe at this moment that you could, because I don't believe that people would sit and be harrowed for two and a half hours. They wouldn't, so you'd have to bring it down to ninety minutes and the scope of development I wanted is immediately denied. And so you have to approach the story from a different point of view.

INTERVIEWER: But surely, apart from the length of time it would take to play, you could transpose it to television? It's not something that wouldn't work on television. The end of *This Story of Yours,* for instance, when Johnson begins to hear voices, seems to me something that someone who was not experienced at writing for television or the cinema would not have introduced. How you handle this technically is alien to the stage play.

HOPKINS: I can only tell you that listening to the sounds, or in a crude sense . . . no, listening to them even at the stage they've reached this morning—it's very frightening. . . .

INTERVIEWER: I'm sure.

HOPKINS: But it's a stunning effect. I think that I'm dangerously close to being a purist to the point of inhibition about what I think is and isn't television and cinema and theater. I think that's a bad attitude. I think it's a weakness on my part which I hope I'm breaking down. Even so, I think one must respect . . . I don't think it's possible to take a film and simply mount it on the stage. I thought that Peter Shaffer's *The Royal Hunt of the Sun* was a theatrical experience. . . . The sense that you might be watching a film is entirely delusory, because it is a theatrical experience. And when they do it as a film it will be a totally different experience.

INTERVIEWER: Or else it will be a failure.

HOPKINS: But what one saw was theatrical, not a film experience translated into stage terms.

INTERVIEWER: As a principle, this is beginning to be generally accepted, is it not? The film of the stage production of Olivier's *Othello* was a bad film. . . .
HOPKINS: Oh, yes.

INTERVIEWER: And to my mind, a brilliant stage production.
HOPKINS: The film had a certain validity as a record of a performance, of a production.

INTERVIEWER: But that's not a film as a film.
HOPKINS: No, any more than I think that the film of *Marat/Sade* is a film, whereas it's an absolutely staggering stage experience. I think Peter Brook must have felt that, because his approach to *US* was completely different, and in no way a record of his stage production, but a whole other thing involving many, many other different techniques and clearly, it seemed to me, an attempt to recreate the experience of *US* as a film, rather than to represent it as a stage play.

INTERVIEWER: As someone self-confessedly apolitical, did you find yourself moved by or involved with *US*?
HOPKINS: Oh, completely involved! But a hopeless audience because not able to respond with any clear knowledge of my own to what I was being told. In the worst way like the boy who takes as gospel what each person tells him. Therefore I'm not the ideal audience. Presumably the ideal audience for that is someone who agrees totally from a firm base of knowledge or someone who disagrees violently, equally from a firm base of knowledge, and then you have an argument between audience and stage. I think that my work . . . people agreeing and disagreeing with the characters in the Quartet sitting in the room facing their television screen, agree from a recognition between us—that's between me, the writer, and them, him, her, the audience—of shared experience, because we all share family experience; well, not all of us, there are of course exceptions, but in the main the family experience is a common denominator. And my generalization of the family experience is an experience that we all share and to which we all respond, either with loathing and contempt and boredom, or with ex-

citement, recognition and challenge, or argument, or simply
throwing up one's hands and saying: "Oh, my God, is it all as
awful as that?" Now, that's my political area, as it were. That's
the one area in which I begin to feel competent to write, just
about what people do to each other, for lack of love, or the
inability to love, or to express love, or, hopefully—and this is
again, for me, a major step forward in this film—a beginning.
It's a love story, and there is an area in it which is a direct
expression of love between two human beings, which I've
never actually, in an uncomplicated way, presented as a dramatist before. This minute examination of relationships is what
television is about.

INTERVIEWER: To go back to the beginning, why did you start
writing for television rather than any other medium?
HOPKINS: I don't really think I would have been a writer had
it not been for television. I suppose, yes, I suppose I would.
Television has a great deal to answer for in the number of bad
writers who have written because of it. I know that the demand
for television makes it possible today to be a professional writer
and make a living in a way that I don't think it's been possible
perhaps ever before. Actually, if you're not in the top flight
of writers—and who can say who they are?—but if you're not
a smash hit novelist, playwright, it's still possible to be a writer
today and to live comfortably, support your wife, your family,
because television demands such a quantity of material that
there is no end to the amount of work that one can do. I'm
not saying that anybody can sit down and write. . . . In fact
everybody feels they can because everybody can write a letter,
but not everyone can write plays. Not everyone would want
to. If they knew what it was like they would want to even less.
But I found when I worked in television as a floor manager,
and doing various odd jobs with Granada Television, that in
the course of time I was drawn inevitably toward being a
writer, helped on the way by the person I was mostly with,
which was very lucky for me.

INTERVIEWER: You hadn't written for other media at all?
HOPKINS: No, I had been going to be a director, for a while!

I had a sense of tremendous lack of purpose in the early part of my life, a sort of feeling of just wandering.

INTERVIEWER: When did you join Granada?

HOPKINS: I suppose I was twenty-six, twenty-seven. I had been at the BBC in sound radio, and then I went to Granada. I was there for a year and a half. And then I went to the BBC, as a writer, on their staff but a professional writer; earning a weekly salary so not actually making the break. But the crucial moment is involved in Z *Cars,* because up until then my sense of direction was fairly slight. And I finished on Z *Cars* two and a half years later: the only thing I can do is write. I was committed, in so far as I'd been committed to anything up to that point. It is interesting that with a growing sense of direction as an artist—and I don't mean that in a precious sense, but only in an awareness of what is involved in writing. . . . Giles Cooper wrote marvelous plays: they had such form, such iron strength. Some of them were difficult to penetrate but they had backbone: they were written by a man who could write. And I think *To the Frontier,* the last play we saw on BBC 2, showed a whole new area he was beginning to explore. It was truly a tragedy that he should die just then. The writers I admire are the writers that concern themselves with . . . the dual nature of writing, its form and content, but equally, one with the other; neither will function without the other. And Z *Cars,* in that it provided this mass of material, mass of stories, so that for a couple of years the one thing I didn't have to worry about ever was whether I'd actually have a story to tell. Stories became the least consideration because there were always so many, and if you ever ran out all you had to do was pick up a phone and talk to a policeman. Or, better, go up to the north and talk to them, and you could draw on several lifetimes of daily experience, just by saying: "Bill, tell us something that happened." We all did this a lot, and we all formed our relationships with the people we related to most easily; and very rarely actually went up saying "tell us a story," but just went up. I went up because I'm a southerner writing a program about people speaking with a Lancashire accent, and I had constantly to go up and replenish my feeling for the language. That again was very exciting, dealing with people who spoke differently, people who reacted differently. I as a person am if anything sensitive, and respond to things with a complexity of response, often making action impossible, and because one thinks: "oh yes, but, there are other things to be taken into consideration," to meet and live among people who thought all that was simply rubbish, and worked on a very much more direct line of response was very exciting, very challenging to understand, because it meant changing whole attitudes of mind; recognizing that it was not necessarily a good thing to be so thoughtful, that there were virtues in the simple response, not necessarily hitting someone, but simple responses. All this mass of experience at a time when my ability to write was something that I questioned all the time, created a seething mass of activity, external and internal, which produced in the middle of *Z Cars, Horror of Darkness,* which was the first time I wrote a kind of play that I could have written before *Z Cars* after *Z Cars.* And by the response that it had I had obviously externalized a private emotion and made it communicable to someone else, in fact to a mass of people outside myself, which is a step on toward *Talking to a Stranger.* Just as within *Z Cars* there are sketches of most of the things I've written since, most of the people who've appeared. It's like—I'm not making a comparison in terms of quality—the 100-odd sketches Picasso drew preparing to paint Guernica.

Interviewed by GILES GORDON, 1969

CHRISTOPHER HAMPTON

Christopher Hampton was born in the Azores in 1947, went to school at Lancing, wrote an unpublished novel at seventeen, came down from Oxford with a First in French and German, and had had at the time of this interview two plays produced in London. They had short runs but attracted a good deal of attention, and an important career in the theater was confidently predicted. The first play, When Did You Last See My Mother? *has been produced in a number of countries; the second,* Total Eclipse, *an account of the relationship between Rimbaud and Verlaine, will also by this time have been produced abroad.*

Mr. Hampton was working for a year as resident playwright at the Royal Court Theatre. I met him in the Circle Bar one afternoon and found him honest and stylish, like his plays. He has a gentle, rather academic manner, punctuated by flashing smiles.

INTERVIEWER: You've been resident playwright here for a few months now. What exactly does this entail?
HAMPTON: I'm in charge of the script department. We receive about twenty scripts a week and apart from myself there are half a dozen readers. I read about ten scripts as second opinion.

INTERVIEWER: How many of those might be produced?
HAMPTON: Well, in the time I've been here I've found three or four that might be worthwhile. I might discuss things with authors and suggest rewriting parts, and so on. We're going to open up a studio theater here, you know, which will make

it possible to put more new plays on. It has 100 seats. But
the policy is not definitely formulated yet.

INTERVIEWER: Do you go to rehearsals of your plays and get
involved in them?
HAMPTON: Oh yes, I like to discuss things with the director
and with actors. But I wouldn't overemphasize this; the director has his own job to do.

INTERVIEWER: You cooperate as much as you can?
HAMPTON: I'll cut if I'm asked to, that kind of thing. Usually,
anyway. But once or twice I've stood my ground, and wouldn't
have certain bits cut.

INTERVIEWER: Have you any interest in acting or directing
yourself?
HAMPTON: I took the main part in my first play when it was
produced by the Oxford University Dramatic Society. But no,
not now, it's too hard on the nerves! As for directing, time
would be the problem, although I don't think I'd try it now.
Perhaps later on.

INTERVIEWER: Critics have remarked on the compassion without sentimentality of your work, among other things. Have
they failed to notice things they should have, in your view?
HAMPTON: I found what the critics said about *Total Eclipse*
disappointing. They wondered why Rimbaud and Verlaine did
not show themselves to be geniuses, as if they should be hold-
ing conversations in blank verse or something. And the real
theme of the play—the problems facing the artist at that time,
and by extension, now—wasn't noticed. It was the relationship of the two men as artists that interested me, but it is a
fallacy that poets behave in an extraordinary way all the time.
In fact, I deliberately avoided using quotes from their poetry.
Only one or two phrases from each, I think, get into their conversation.

INTERVIEWER: In a more general way, are you bothered by
critics, or do you learn anything from them?

HAMPTON: I don't see how one can learn from someone who spends twenty minutes evaluating six months' work, but I must say I have every sympathy for them, since they're asked to do the impossible. Even a weekly critic doesn't have time to do justice to a serious play. I know, because I did some reviewing for a while on *Queen* magazine.

INTERVIEWER: A problem with many plays is that they take some time to have an effect, would you agree? Chekhov's plays were greeted with stony indifference at first; only later did they begin to strike chords. Ideally, I suppose, a critic should go back again to the play after a week or two, and then review it.

HAMPTON: That's one aspect of it, yes. There shouldn't be this emphasis on first night production. In any case the production tends to improve, alterations may be made, and so on. For example, on the basis of the immediate reaction it may be decided to take a play off after, say, two weeks. Yet at the end of that time the play may be doing well, have the potential of a good run. Something's been lined up to take its place, so it has to go.

INTERVIEWER: Both your plays are about homosexuality. Is this a coincidence, or are you particularly interested in the subject?

HAMPTON: It's simply that the first is really a sketch for the second. I'd wanted to do the Rimbaud play for some time, but the thought of all the research and time needed was daunting. So I thought I'd better do a modern play first. It was the book by Enid Starkie that set me off.

INTERVIEWER: I like Rimbaud's comment that what Verlaine calls faithfulness is merely nostalgia. And the typical exchange that follows: Rimbaud saying Verlaine's reluctance to leave his wife is weakness, not faithfulness. Verlaine says: "If strength involves brutality, I prefer to be weak." Rimbaud says: "With you, weakness involves brutality as well." Is this one of your main concerns, the question of what love means, and are you, along with Rimbaud, attacking the bourgeois world and its institutions, including marriage?

HAMPTON: No, not really. I was interested in the tremendous contrast between the two men, in the way they looked at life, and their attitudes to their art. I mean for Rimbaud art was a kind of alchemical key to existence, while for Verlaine it was much more a job of work. And the general attitude at this time toward artists. . . . It was a time of bourgeois affluence: at least, many people felt they had all the material things of life, and they expected artists to show them the way to something new, spiritual if you like. This is why Rimbaud felt the pressure to be completely original, so that as soon as he considered everything had already been done in poetry that could be done, he stopped writing.

INTERVIEWER: Do you think the attitude toward writers is similar today; is there a pressure on them to assume a role that doesn't necessarily belong to them?
HAMPTON: Yes, I think the decline in religious practice has contributed to this.

INTERVIEWER: There are some other interesting cerebral exchanges. Rimbaud shows Verlaine that he believes something because it pleases his aesthetic sense rather than something more likely to be true.
HAMPTON: This is an extension of the theme. I try not to be too cerebral. I admire Rimbaud, of course, and in many ways I can identify with him. But too rigorous an attitude means you don't do anything. And Verlaine went on and on writing, until the end, although his later work deteriorated. So, although he was a grotesque and impossible figure, perhaps I admire Verlaine more in the end.

INTERVIEWER: One or two of your techniques intrigue me, especially the one I think of as echoes, the repetition of incidents, but slightly altering them. There is the occasion of Verlaine placing his hands on the table for Rimbaud to stab them with a knife, as proof of his love. At the end of the play, when Rimbaud is dead, Verlaine relives the occasion, except that Rimbaud kisses his hands this time. Also, Verlaine's mem

ories of his first meetings with his wife Mathilde and with
Rimbaud are the same—they both turn away from a window
to greet him. Is this deliberate on your part?

HAMPTON: Yes. I think of them as patterns, and such things
are very carefully placed. I am very interested in the structure
of a play, and don't understand how *Total Eclipse* could have
been called rambling, as it was by one or two critics. Do you
remember the short scenes in the middle, ending with Verlaine's shooting Rimbaud in the hand? These are carefully
placed, and make a kind of curve in their relationship. If
this particular pattern doesn't emerge too clearly, perhaps I
cut too much out during the writing, perhaps one or two of
the necessary links went out with the cutting, and are only
in my mind.

INTERVIEWER: I find the structures of both your plays satisfying. My main criticism would be that the women are rather
shadowy figures. They are subsidiary characters, anyway, of
course. Mrs. Evans in the first play for example; her falling
for Ian is not very convincing to me.

HAMPTON: I think that's fair criticism. Perhaps their having
sex is not too plausible.

INTERVIEWER: And Madame Verlaine I find a bit more sub-
dued than she might be.

HAMPTON: Yes, though she does come out like that in her
memoirs.

INTERVIEWER: Of course this is well-trodden ground—why
great parts are not written for English actresses.

HAMPTON: Yes, it is difficult to say why it is; there's such a
long tradition of not doing so. It's what ruins most productions
of *Macbeth*. The one great woman's role being Lady Macbeth, she's always blown up to double her size. And who has
done anything recently? John Osborne's *Time Present* was
written for a woman, but it's not essentially a woman's role,
is it? It could just as well be a man. Apart from the accident
of similar themes for my two plays, my age may have some-

thing to do with it. I hope to know more about women when I write my next play!

INTERVIEWER: Could you sum up what you try to do in your plays? Do you want to educate people into feeling, as Osborne once said he wanted to do, or perhaps make people think, like Shaw?

HAMPTON: I want to write different kinds of plays, though like the work of most writers, everything may turn out to have the same theme. I try to produce a sense of realism, I mean I want audiences to see the thing as it is, no sentimentality. *When Did You Last See My Mother?* may not seem like that, perhaps.

INTERVIEWER: You had your tongue in your cheek.

HAMPTON: Well, that play is really a melodrama. But if I do choose emotional figures, I try to treat them in an objective way. And I like patterns, as I said before.

INTERVIEWER: Would you agree that plays should move you first, and make you think afterwards?

HAMPTON: Yes. That's why I think playwriting is a very difficult thing to do. You can have fifty dud pages in the middle of a novel and it may not be noticed, but a play has got to hold the attention all the time.

INTERVIEWER: What do you dislike most about present day life? What makes you angry?

HAMPTON: Advertising, the easy things, television.

INTERVIEWER: Why don't you like television?

HAMPTON: It is intelligence directed to a patronizing end.

INTERVIEWER: There are one or two good things though, aren't there? Will you write for television, do you think?

HAMPTON: I may do. It's that aspect of it I don't like.

INTERVIEWER: Which playwrights have influenced you?

HAMPTON: I used to like Anouilh a lot. Chekhov. I like Albee at his best. David Storey. As for influence, modern authors do everything to avoid being influenced.

INTERVIEWER: Do you go to the theater much?
HAMPTON: You know, I don't like going to the theater all that much. Let me see, I liked Arthur Kopit's *Indians,* although there were some faults in the production. I like films—I'd like to direct films, later on.

INTERVIEWER: What about novelists?
HAMPTON: I like some American novelists now writing. Most of the writers I like are dead.

INTERVIEWER: Are you involved at all in politics—demonstrations for instance?
HAMPTON: Not actively, no, and I've found no satisfactory way yet of getting politics into plays. I support the anti-Vietnam demonstrations, but I'm not the sort of person who goes around organizing these things, like Michael Rosen, who is still very active in Oxford. I'm all for the views of Feiffer —I saw his play at the Aldwych last night—but I didn't like the play.

INTERVIEWER: Are you writing a play at the moment?
HAMPTON: No, I have a few ideas for plays which I may work out later. Mainly, I'm turning over in my mind an idea for a novel. I'm a little restless at the moment, but I shall be moving into a new flat this week and will be more settled.

INTERVIEWER: You haven't decided to commit yourself to the theater then?
HAMPTON: Oh no, it all depends on the idea.

Interviewed by BRENDAN HENNESSY, 1969

JORGE LUIS BORGES

This talk with Jorge Luis Borges took place in Cambridge, Mass., where he was Charles Eliot Norton Professor at Harvard for the 1967–68 academic year. We spoke in his unassuming, rather tidy apartment on Concord Avenue. Borges, of course, especially since he lost most of his sight some fifteen years ago, sees most of the world inside himself. In the tradition of Homer and Milton he sees what other men are blind to. This aspect of revelation, which a few critics have mistakenly considered "playing games" with reality, also emerges in an almost secretive way in his conversation. We must remember that neither Borges nor his art would work properly if he were not himself so gracious and modest.

INTERVIEWER: Now I wonder, as you can't see so well now, how can you write a screenplay, which is a visual art? It must confront you with difficulties.
BORGES: Well no, but I've written only the dialogue. Besides, I can imagine. I've seen hundreds of thousands of films in my time; I can imagine a film.

INTERVIEWER: I know that you've written some film criticism.
BORGES: Oh yes, I'm very fond of films. Of course, in Buenos Aires people go to films far more than they do here. In Buenos Aires every day, well I suppose you can choose between forty different films, and those films, well most of them are American but you can also have ycur pick of Swedish, English, French, and Italian films, or even Russian films.

INTERVIEWER: Well, why don't you tell me something about the plot of your movie, *The Invasion?*

BORGES: Yes, the plot is, well the central plot, no? Should be that a city is attacked and then—the whole thing is rather fantastic—the authorities take no measures whatever.

INTERVIEWER: Take no notice?
BORGES: No, no, the city is about to be invaded. The invaders are very ruthless and very powerful and then the city is defended.

INTERVIEWER: The invaders, who are they?
BORGES: Well, you don't know. The invaders, you see them and you feel that they are very ruthless and very efficient and many. And, of course, you have a conflict. All this has no political meaning. We were not thinking, say, of the Communists, or the Fascists. And then the city is defended by an old gentleman and his friends. Now his friends are very halfhearted; they are very skeptical about the whole thing and they are bound by circumstances. For example, a man has to go and save his country, but he can't do that because he has to go with his wife to a party or because he has a bad cold, no? And yet somehow those people in their halfhearted, skeptic, unbelieving way, defend the city. And then in the end, the city falls out of the hands of the enemies, and you know that they will go on fighting, somehow. That's the story; not a very impressive story as I tell you, but it makes quite a good film. And then, you see those people are rather helpless, some of them are even figures of fun, and yet somehow they get away with it. And they defend the city successfully. And, of course, the whole thing has many adventures, because you have these people rushing to and fro.

INTERVIEWER: There seems to be an epic quality about the film.
BORGES: An epic quality yes, and at the same time, the whole thing is rather desultory. Those people may, for example, when they are in a great hurry, have a poker game or a card game and they'll be losing time over that, or a man may have an assignation with a girl and may forget all about the invaders; I think it's quite a good film. Of course, as I tell it to you, it doesn't sound like a good film, but—

INTERVIEWER: No, it does. I can visualize it and it seems like a very metaphysical kind of film.

BORGES: Yes, but I think it should be a very amusing film also, because you have all those kinds of characters, the characters are quite unlike each other and there are, well for example, there *are* some epic moments. For example, there is a man who's a coward and he is one of the defenders. And the others, they accept him, they're all friends. And they say, "Yes, so and so, well he isn't too good, no? I don't think we can count on him, no?" Because they know that he's a coward. And then, there is a moment when one of them has to get himself killed. Well, they have to send somebody, and then this man who is a coward says, "Look here, I want to go. Yes. After all, you are very efficient men, you are brave men, you *can* be helpful. What can I do? You have been very kind to me, all of you, but I know the way you feel about me and besides, what is more important, I know the way I feel about myself. The only thing I can do is to die. So let me go." And then the other says, "Thank you" and then he shakes hands with him. And then another is just about to shake hands with him, but then he thinks better of it because he feels that if he shakes hands he is acknowledging that the other is right, that he will die, and then the man does go off and get killed. And there are many moments of that kind, no?

INTERVIEWER: Yes, I see.

BORGES: Yes, but that's a good moment, no? When a man says, "The only thing I can do is to die. After all, I'm not very good at fighting but I have one advantage, I can get myself killed as well as anybody precisely because I *am* a coward." And then one of them pats him on the back and then they all feel very uncomfortable and then they say, "Oh no, you'll do fine, we wish you luck." And then he goes off grinning and they know he's going to die. And there's a love interest also. There is a man—he's in love—and he doesn't want his lady to know that he is risking his life. So he invents all sorts of excuses. Sometimes she takes him to task, and says, "I feel you are really more in love with those schemes than with me." But he says, "No, you know that I love you," and they make plans. But in the end, it comes out that she knows all about it, but she doesn't want him to be worried thinking that she knows. I mean full psychological detail of that kind. I think it's quite a good film. I'm telling you those two episodes; they're the ones that come to mind, but there are more. And, of course, as I was saying to Santiago, it's quite unlike any other Argentine film.

INTERVIEWER: Do you know anything about this director, Santiago? Is he a prominent director in your country?
BORGES: No. He's been working in Europe, but in quite a minor capacity, for seven or eight years, and he's a personal friend of a very famous English director. I can't recall the name. He knows a lot of the technical side. And he evolved the plan. And the central character is based upon a friend of mine named Fernandez, a humorist, but a metaphysical humorist. I think it should be quite a good film, but if they muff it, well you never can tell, no? Now I'm rather worried because he says that he's found the most wonderful actress on earth and that he's also about to be married. But I'm afraid that he's about to be married to the most wonderful actress, and the most wonderful actress may be no good as far as I know.

INTERVIEWER: In other words, the main actress of the film is going to be his wife soon?
BORGES: Yes, that's what I'm afraid of because he says, "I've discovered the most wonderful actress in Paris." I don't like that because why should he discover in Paris a wonderful actress for a film to be acted in Buenos Aires? Of course, she may be Argentine for all I know. And then he says, "Also I want you to know that I'm going to be married." But, I'm afraid that both ladies may be the same and then in that case we'll have to put up with somebody merely because he's in love with her and she's his wife.

INTERVIEWER: And that makes her the most wonderful actress.
BORGES: Well, that doesn't do us any good, no? But of course if he found a fine actress, and he's married to another lady, then that's all right, no? Because I mean he may afford to be partial about it.

INTERVIEWER: Have you ever been interested in acting?
BORGES: No.

INTERVIEWER: You're not an actor?
BORGES: No, I'm not. I wonder if I told you, when I read O'Neill, I was hardly impressed by him. And then I went to see *The Great God Brown* and I was overwhelmed. Because when you don't *see* the masks they make no impression whatever on you, no? So and so puts on a mask, they take off the mask, the mask is left on the table. You think of all that as being rather silly. And rather childish. But when you see it acted, it is quite different.

INTERVIEWER: Also, O'Neill doesn't read that well because his ear for English wasn't too good.
BORGES: Yes, maybe I'm being unfair to O'Neill. It could be because I've read Bernard Shaw, and Shaw wrote his plays, published his plays, in order that they could be read as novels. In Shaw's plays you get long descriptions of furniture, even of the book shelves; you get long descriptions of the characters; you can imagine them. But in the case of O'Neill he says, "A comes in, B comes in." You don't know what to expect them to look like or what they are, no? No, he didn't make his plays for reading but to be acted.

INTERVIEWER: What about the theater of Brecht?
BORGES: Yes, he was a fine poet, a very fine poet. I wonder if you know that in his plays he speaks of Manhattan, of America, of Wisconsin, no? And he never strayed outside Berlin. He was always speaking about his travels and so on. But, the same thing happened to Walt Whitman, no? He traveled with his fancy.

INTERVIEWER: What about the plays of Lorca?
BORGES: I don't like them. I never could enjoy Lorca.

INTERVIEWER: Or his poetry either?

BORGES: No. I saw *Yerma* and I found it so silly that I walked away. I couldn't stand it. Yet I suppose that's a blind spot because . . .

INTERVIEWER: Lorca, for some reason, is idealized in the United States.
BORGES: I suppose he had the good luck to be executed, no? I had an hour's chat with him in Buenos Aires. He struck me as a kind of play actor, no? Living up to a certain role, no? I mean being a professional Andalusian.

INTERVIEWER: The way Cocteau was supposed to be, as I understand.
BORGES: Yes, I suppose he was. But in the case of Lorca, it was very strange because I lived in Andalusia and the Andalusians aren't a bit like that. But his were stage Andalusians, I suppose maybe he thought that in Buenos Aires he had to live up to that character, but in Andalusia, people are not like that. In fact, if you are in Andalusia, for example, if you are talking to a man of letters and you speak to him about bullfights, he'll say "Oh well, that sort of thing pleases people, I suppose, but really the torero works in no danger whatever." Because they are bored by those things, because every writer is bored by the local color in his own country, no? Well, when I met Lorca he was being a professional Andalusian.

INTERVIEWER: You met Lorca only one time and you never met again. And Sartre you also met one time and then never again?
BORGES: Yes, but Sartre is a more intelligent man than Lorca. Besides, Lorca wanted to astonish us. He said to me that he was very much troubled about a very important character in the contemporary world. A character in whom you could see all the tragedy of American life. And then he went on in this way until I asked him who was this character and it turned out the character was Mickey Mouse. I suppose he was trying to be clever. And I thought, that's the kind of thing you might say when you are very, very young and you want

to astonish somebody. But after all, he was a grown man, he had no need, he could have talked in a different way. But when he started in about Mickey Mouse being a symbol of America, well, there was a friend of mine there and he looked at me and I looked at him and we both walked away because we were both too old for that kind of game, no? Even at the time.

INTERVIEWER: When was that?

BORGES: Oh, years and years ago. Even then, we felt that that was what you call sophomoric.

INTERVIEWER: Lorca had no ideas about the world, but I think he had a gift for words.

BORGES: But I think there is very little behind the words.

INTERVIEWER: He had a gift for hearing words.

BORGES: Well, a gift for gab. For example, he makes striking metaphors, but I wonder if he makes striking metaphors for himself, because I think that his world was mostly verbal. I think that he was fond of playing words against each other, the contrast of words, but I wonder if he knew what he was doing.

INTERVIEWER: What about Pablo Neruda? You've met him, haven't you?

BORGES: I met him once. And we were both quite young at the time. And then we fell to speaking of the Spanish language. And then we came to the conclusion that nothing could be done with it, because it was such a clumsy language, and then I said that was the reason that nothing whatever had ever been done with it and then he said, "Well, of course, there's no Spanish literature, no?" and I said, "Well, of course not." And then we went on in that way. The whole thing was a kind of joke.

INTERVIEWER: I know you admire his poetry, don't you?

BORGES: I think of him as a very fine poet, a very fine poet; I don't admire him as a man, I think of him as a very mean man.

INTERVIEWER: Why do you say that?

BORGES: Well, he wrote a book—well, maybe here I'm being political—he wrote a book about the tyrants of South America, and then he had several stanzas against the United States. Now he knows that that's rubbish. And he had not a word against Perón. Because he had a law suit in Buenos Aires, that was explained to me afterward, and he didn't care to risk anything, and so when he was supposed to be writing at the top of his voice full of noble indignation he had not a word to say against Perón. And, he was married to an Argentine lady, he knew that many of his friends had been sent to jail. He knew all about the state of our country, but not a word against Perón. At the same time he was speaking against the United States, knowing that the whole thing was a lie. But, of course, that doesn't mean anything against his poetry. Neruda is a very fine poet, a great poet in fact. And when that man* got the Nobel Prize, I said that it should have been given to Neruda. Now, when I was in Chile, and we were on different political sides, he went on a holiday during the three or four days I was there so there was no occasion for our meeting. But, I think that he was acting politely, no? Because he knew that people would be playing him up against me, no? I mean I was an Argentine poet, he a Chilean poet; he's on the side of the Communists, I'm against them. So that I felt that he was behaving very wisely in avoiding a meeting that would be quite uncomfortable for both of us.

INTERVIEWER: You never met Miguel de Unamuno?

BORGES: No, but he sent me a very nice letter. He's a very great writer. I admire Unamuno greatly.

INTERVIEWER: Which works of his do you admire?

BORGES: Well, his book on Don Quixote and his essays.

INTERVIEWER: You'd say he's a good thinker, I mean as apart from his writing?

BORGES: Oh, he is definitely, yes, a great mind. What I said against Unamuno is that he is interested in things that I am

* Borges is speaking of Nobel Prize winner Miguel Asturias.

not interested in. He is very worried about his personal immortality. He says, "I want to go on being Miguel de Unamuno." Well, I don't want to go on being Jorge Luis Borges; I want to forget all about him. But, of course, those are merely personal differences. You might as well say that I like coffee and he likes tea, or that I like plains and he prefers the mountains, no?

INTERVIEWER: "The opinions of an author are wrought by the superficial accidents of circumstance." That's what you said.
BORGES: Yes, quite right, that's what I said, yes.

Interviewed by RICHARD BURGIN, 1968

ROLF HOCHHUTH

This interview with Rolf Hochhuth took place in my apartment on the upper West Side of Manhattan a few days after the New York opening of his play, Soldiers. *Mr. Hochhuth, a pleasant soft-spoken young man, was perfectly at ease as we drank scotch and talked politics. He answered all questions with intelligence and patience, and although he was at first a bit surprised at the controversial nature of the interview, he later was pleased that the conversation had been so challenging. He was accompanied by a press agent, and a British interpreter, Robert David MacDonald, who did more than his share of talking.*

INTERVIEWER: Mr. Hochhuth, would you care to comment about the banning of your play, Soldiers, in England?

HOCHHUTH: I think that the English will be of a completely different opinion when they get the chance to read the printed edition of the play. So far the only people who have had a chance to read it have been a small inner circle such as the Chairman of the Board of the National Theatre. The number of people who have forbade it is not greater than those who have wanted to see it produced, such as Sir Laurence Olivier and Kenneth Tynan.

INTERVIEWER: Was the principal person who objected to the play a member of Churchill's government?

HOCHHUTH: Lord Chandos is Chairman of the Board of the National Theatre and had Winston Churchill to thank for his entire political career; he was a very close friend and associate of Churchill's and was President of the Board of Trade during Churchill's time.

INTERVIEWER: Did the authorities give you a specific reason as to why they didn't want the production to go on?

HOCHHUTH: The Lord Chamberlain is not obliged to give any reasons at all for banning the play.

INTERVIEWER: You said in a *New York Times* interview: "I do not want to be involved in history or in war, and I think that is actually the reason why I write these plays." Is not this a contradiction in view of the subject matter of *The Deputy* and *Soldiers*?

HOCHHUTH: No. For I represent a generation who, to their great good luck, did not have to stand in the fire, who were thus not involved, but who have a tendency to write about such things.

INTERVIEWER: In *Soldiers* you imply that Churchill could not escape the consequences of the war. But you also take him to task for the bombing of the cities which is a consequence of the war.

HOCHHUTH: Churchill is not being taken to task. I am simply showing what he did, and that he did so in the firm and definite belief that by bombing German cities he would bring about victory much sooner. The Second World War showed, and no military strategist has disputed the fact, that the bombardment of residential centers was in no way strategically effective, and for this reason today, in 1968, nobody can continue to bomb with the same sort of good faith as Churchill —that is, in the belief that the bombing would be effective. And in my play, the audience is reminded that Churchill himself had, at the Bermuda conference in 1953, urged a convention for outlawing aerial bombardments of civilian centers. But this convention does not yet exist.

INTERVIEWER: But if bombing cities was not effective, didn't Churchill know this? Why then did he bomb the cities?

HOCHHUTH: Churchill did not know that at the time. There

was no justification for it then, but Churchill did not know
this. The destruction of Berlin in no measure influenced the
Nazis in their conduct of the war. Similarly, one cannot suggest that the North Vietnamese, for example, will be brought
to their defeat by the bombardment, by the terrorization from
the air upon the civilian population. Churchill himself, after
the destruction of Dresden, recognized this fact. There exists
a memorandum which expresses that this action of the English was very questionable. It [the bombings] had not the
slightest military effect, but when he gave the order for it, he
believed that bombing would have a military effect. But today,
twenty years later, President Johnson, for instance, cannot
believe this.

INTERVIEWER: But in the play, Churchill seems *personally*
happy when he thinks about Berlin on fire. When Lord
Cherwell draws a map explaining the bombing, Churchill
seems rather gleeful.

HOCHHUTH: The play takes place in 1943, when he was still
under the impression that the invasion of France could be
avoided if the Nazis could be influenced morally and materi-
ally by the destruction of large cities. In the play, the German
war criminal is in no way glossed over, and something that
must be taken into consideration when discussing Churchill's
actions is the nature of the enemy against whom Churchill
was fighting. He was fighting the man who had invented
Auschwitz, he was fighting against people like Werner von
Braun, inventor of the rockets which fell on London. The
people being bombed today may not possibly know where
America is on the map, and they have no possibility of breaking a single frame of glass in Manhattan. Any comparison
of the two wars, the Vietnam war and World War II, is
inadmissible.

INTERVIEWER: I'm not comparing them, although I know some
people have.

HOCHHUTH: I'm very unhappy that this comparison should
have been made. It is an appalling simplification and a falsifi-
cation. Ho Chi Minh is not a Hitler. Ho Chi Minh is a man

like Tito, a nationalist, a fighter for national liberation—a man whose country has been oppressed by the Chinese for over a thousand years, and he is basically as much against the Chinese as he is against the Americans. If the white nations—the West—had acted honorably with Ho Chi Minh, and allowed the country self determination as Geneva had guaranteed, then Vietnam today would be as big a bulwark against the expansion of China as Yugoslavia is against Russia.

INTERVIEWER: Do you consider bombings of cities in a just war to be criminal?

HOCHHUTH: When the primary target, or the primary aim of the attack is the city, the inner city, and the entire attack is mounted with a view to the demoralization of the population, then it is a crime. The American bombing offensive against Germany during the Second World War was of an utterly different nature. The Americans flew on target raids against German industries, against stations, ports, and exclusively against German military installations, and did decisive damage to the Nazis. If, during these raids, civilians happened to be killed because they lived adjacent to the railroad station or to the docks, that is a different matter. The difference is whether the demoralization of civilians is the primary target or whether one is flying target raids on military or industrial installations. And the fact that the Americans during their bombing offensive on Germany damaged the Nazi machine shows that it is possible to make the difference, *if you want to.*

INTERVIEWER: Mr. Hochhuth, some people were disturbed by Eric Bentley's remarks that your play, *Soldiers*, would encourage those who wanted to increase the bombings of Vietnam. Would you like to comment on this?

HOCHHUTH: Yes. I have already written to Professor Bentley. This is a senseless comparison, quite senseless. The war against Hitler was unavoidable and justified, and if Churchill had not led the English to war, Hitler would today still be in power. I am not a pacifist. In the play, there is a line that says that pacifists are those who let other people do the fighting for them. There is no question that if Russia had not defended herself, and if the British had not entered the war for Poland, then Hitler would be ruling up to the Volga. And when he had finished with the Jews, he would probably turn his attention to the Slavs, and to the shortsighted, and the tubercular.

INTERVIEWER: At the end of the play, we are left with the impression that you condemn all soldiers as "potential criminals." What about the Russians, English and Americans who fought the Nazis? Would you care to make some distinction here?

HOCHHUTH: At the end of the play the father says that soldiers are men who fight other soldiers, a pilot is a man who bombs bridges, railway stations and so forth. Then the son, an Air Force captain, says, "What about me, what does that make me?" At that point his father calls him a "potential criminal" because he, the son, as an Air Force captain, is playing war games in time of peace and working out strategies for the systematic extermination of cities, and *that's* potentially criminal. . . . The play really has a two-fold purpose—which is why it is called *Soldiers*—to re-erect certain taboos. The first of them is to demand inviolability at the hands of the soldiers and secondly to preserve the honor of the soldier who can only remain honorable if he fights other soldiers.

INTERVIEWER: In the prologue, the character of Dorland, the Everyman of the play, refers to his son as part of the "permissive generation." Is this justified in view of youth's protest against the Vietnam war, for instance?

HOCHHUTH: Dorland says this to his son because he is a young officer in the Air Force. We can't possibly hope that all young people are as politically alert as the young people in Columbia University and in Berlin. The others are all in other professions and don't think about these questions, particularly if they are in the military professions.

INTERVIEWER: Mr. Hochhuth, do you hold ordinary individuals responsible for wars?

HOCHHUTH: Officers have the duty in the Air Force to reflect on what they are asked to do with new weapons.

INTERVIEWER: I mean ordinary civilians.

HOCHHUTH: I do not believe that the man in the street in Germany in 1939 was in a position to get rid of Hitler, but they are nonetheless to blame. That they elected him in 1933 is their fault, for then it was possible to get rid of him. At the beginnings of these events, the ordinary citizen can do something.

INTERVIEWER: What about ordinary people being ordered to kill Jews, or concentration camp inmates, or to drop napalm bombs?

HOCHHUTH: That's another thing. When the individual is asked personally to do acts of murder, that is quite a different matter. You know that in Germany at the moment, war criminals are being tried. If it is proved that a man had committed personal acts of murder, he is convicted. The excuse of acting on orders is not accepted in court. Occasionally, it is used as mitigating circumstances, but it is never accepted as a plea of not guilty. Of course there is a problem because German lawyers and judges were almost without exception themselves Nazis—a number of people sitting in judgment today were Nazis. For the SS man and the man at the front there were many possibilities of skidding around orders like that. The difference between these people and the bombing pilots cannot be too strongly brought out. The SS man who was killing Jews in Auschwitz was able to save himself from being sent to the front because he was killing Jews in Auschwitz. The bomber pilot at all times risked his own life, and in many cases lost it, during the order to destroy cities. And this is a very important difference.

INTERVIEWER: In both *The Deputy* and *Soldiers,* the real Christian emissaries are defeated. Do you believe that Christianity as an ethic can no longer cope with the modern world?

HOCHHUTH: The Commandments and the Sermon on the Mount are still absolutely relevant.

INTERVIEWER: Mr. Hochhuth, some critics have said that you

have evaluated the historical facts without any regard for class or national positions.

HOCHHUTH: What do you mean?

INTERVIEWER: Well, for instance, some claim that Churchill's bombing of the cities was his excuse for not opening up the second front because he was afraid of the Bolsheviks reaching central Europe. He was content, because of his Tory background, it is argued, to bleed the Russians on the Eastern front while he bombed German cities as a token action.

HOCHHUTH: This is an absurd and improper condemnation of Churchill. It is simply a theory of Communist writers. Churchill, like Roosevelt, was very thankful for every German division fighting on the Russian front, for they were therefore not fighting British and American soldiers. That is quite normal and natural. Stalin was obviously just as grateful for every English division fighting in Africa.

INTERVIEWER: But this theory of Churchill's deliberate postponement of the second front was very prevalent during World War II.

HOCHHUTH: It was the opinion of the General Staff and Defense Secretary Stimson that it would have been possible to land in France much earlier. This was in opposition to the opinion of the British. Now that we know that the Normandy invasion succeeded, the tendency is to agree with the American staff. But it was absolutely impossible then to prove who was correct. On May 3, 1944, only four weeks before the invasion, Churchill said to Eisenhower that if their undertaking were to collapse, both their countries would be doomed. The idea that Churchill delayed the invasion in order to bleed the Russians is a gross libel.

INTERVIEWER: In the play, Churchill says, "The man who survives the tragedy is not the hero." Who then is the hero of your play?

HOCHHUTH: The heroes are the ordinary combatants sent to death. But the only people who can be shown in the play are the Poles and Sikorski, who is the hero of his own tragedy.

Despite the *bon mot,* Churchill himself had a lot of tragic characteristics. In a long monologue in the third act, he predicts that England will sink to a second-class power despite all the victories. That is, of course, a very tragic view of the situation.

INTERVIEWER: Did the character of Churchill present difficulties, since everyone remembers him so well?

HOCHHUTH: I fell under his spell the moment I read about him. The difficulty came with other characters. A dramatist has to bring his antagonists up to equal levels, otherwise there is no dramatic conflict. And this was difficult because Churchill was so colossal and masterful.

INTERVIEWER: The published manuscript is very illuminating with its scholarly references and beautiful imagery. We would love to have that all on the stage.

HOCHHUTH: Bringing poetry onto the stage bores people.

INTERVIEWER: I don't think many people are aware that you write in verse instead of prose. Why do you write in verse?

HOCHHUTH: Churchill was a figure of the Victorian age, almost a figure of the Trojan age; it is absurd to put him on the stage speaking the journalistic prose of our times.

INTERVIEWER: Some people claim that your documentation cannot be conclusive because your proof of the alleged murder of Sikorski by British Secret Service is locked away for fifty years. Does this affect the validity of your play?

HOCHHUTH: The play does not depend upon the evidence that is in the Swiss bank. This documented affidavit has no relevance to the play except that it was the spur that started me on the research for *Soldiers.* What is published in the printed version of the play is such a large collection of circumstances and evidence that one no longer can be in doubt. I wrote two long articles for *Der Spiegel* about this and I would like to reprint these articles unabridged.

INTERVIEWER: People feel that the choice of Sikorski as a sympathetic character was peculiar because the Polish government-in-exile, it is argued, were not as anti-Nazi as they should have been.

HOCHHUTH: This is one more indication of the tragedy of history, that people today can have such ideas of a man like Sikorski, particularly in America. Roosevelt and Cordell Hull stood by Sikorski in the face of British opposition. Let me tell you something about Sikorski. He was the only Allied statesman during the war who, on two occasions in public speeches, gave details of the German massacre of the Jews. No other statesman did this. The others were frightened that the anti-Semitic elements in their own electorate would hold it against them; hence they tended to speak only in general terms about the Nazi crimes. But Sikorski spoke in detail about that particular war crime, the killing of the Jews. He had earlier had a quarrel with the government of Pilsudski and during the thirties he lived in exile in Paris. There he wrote a book in which he predicted the re-emergence of the Germans. He urged the West to overcome its prejudices against the Bolsheviks and form an alliance with them before it became too late. That such a man should be so misunderstood is appalling. But he will probably find his justification soon.

INTERVIEWER: You said in an interview that you are writing an anti-capitalist play because the United States system of capitalism has led to war. Does that mean you favor socialism?

HOCHHUTH: I have raised the question rather than given the answer. I question any system that can only remain valid by making war. I don't know if this is really the case. But if it is the case, then should one not fight it? If a subject suggests questions, it is a good subject for a play. If it doesn't suggest questions, then there is no point in writing a play about it. In the beginning of my two plays, *The Deputy* and *Soldiers*, there were two large question marks.

INTERVIEWER: And what will be the question mark in your next play?

HOCHHUTH: The next question—the Marxist question—is whether the capitalist system does in fact lead to war. This question, though it is a Marxist one, and though I mistrust

Marx and on many points find him completely outdated, is a question that still remains, and has got to be asked again, for us, for our time, for our own generation.

INTERVIEWER: You mean whether war is inherent in the capitalist system?
HOCHHUTH: Yes, that is the question.

Interviewed by MARGARET CROYDEN, 1968

ARTHUR KOPIT

Arthur Kopit was born in New York in 1938. His play Indians *was given a world premiere in London by the Royal Shakespeare Company at the Aldwych Theatre on July 4, American Independence Day, the first of five American works to be staged in the 1968–69 season. It had a mixed reception from the critics, but most were agreed that it was a work of considerable ambition, excitingly produced (direction by Jack Gelber, sets by John Bury). In the framework of Buffalo Bill's Wild West Show, twelve episodes in his past life are enacted in vaudeville or circus style in a bulb-lit ring: Indians are painted red, Whites are painted white, and phony show-Indians have red and white patches. As well as turning the myth of the West inside out, the play shows the failure of the good liberal, Buffalo Bill, who sees the evil of what is being done to the Indians but is powerless in his intermediary role. More specifically, some of the episodes are his haunting dreams.*

Kopit first became known through his play Oh Dad, Poor Dad, Mamma's Hung You in the Closet and I'm Feelin' So Sad. *He had, however, already written ten plays while at Harvard.*

I met Mr. Kopit and his extremely attractive wife in the foyer of their London hotel in Kensington. He is well over six feet tall, with long sideburns. He is dark, youthful and very affable. The interview took place while he breakfasted.

INTERVIEWER: In a recent TV interview you said it would have been almost impossible to stage *Indians* in New York for economic reasons.* Were there any other reasons for wanting an English production?

KOPIT: The cost of putting on *Indians* in New York with its large cast would have been tremendous, as much as a musical, so that it would only start breaking even after a very long run. Who would take the risk when the first night review in the *New York Times* might kill it stone dead? But that's not the only thing. The price of the seats is so high that you've got to write not only a success but a smash-hit success. The Broadway audiences have a completely different attitude from those in England. If you've paid fifty dollars for a seat, it's got to be good, you demand to be entertained. Whereas here the seats are cheap, you get better audiences, you can put on a serious play and get a fair hearing.

INTERVIEWER: On the other hand, the non-commercial, avant-garde theater is in a healthier state in New York, isn't it? Are you involved in it to any extent?
KOPIT: Well, I'm not in New York much. Can't write there, you meet too many people; it's an exciting place at night, but not for writing in. This division of audiences is a fact—there's not much can be done about it. There will always be an avant-garde audience interested only in the new and unknown: when Ionesco became successful, his original following weren't interested any more. But you can't write with a particular audience in mind. The great thing about a place like the Aldwych is that you don't worry about the audience at all.

INTERVIEWER: If you don't write in New York, where do you write?
KOPIT: Oh, Vermont in the Winter, where I do some skiing. I like any holiday resort in the off-season: Majorca for example was very successful last time—a huge hotel almost empty.

INTERVIEWER: You're clearly not pessimistic about the future of the theater.
KOPIT: No. There's a new vitality returning to it, which curiously enough hasn't much to do with the writers. I mean activities like Peter Brook's experiments at the Round House,

* Since this interview, *Indians* has had a New York production.

with a—flexible audience. I think flexibility about what the theater is, that's important.

INTERVIEWER: I asked that because you do hear pessimism expressed in England. Actors and writers turning to films, and so on. You used to hear about the death of the novel, now it's the death of the theater.

KOPIT: I like the cinema; in fact writers for some reason prefer to go to the cinema. You can relax. You can say: "There's a very bad movie showing—terrible—let's go and see it," but have you ever heard anyone say, "Let's go and see a bad play"? But you can be moved in the theater in a way that nothing else can move you. As far as audiences are concerned, we haven't got exactly the equivalent in the States of your repertory audiences; the nearest equivalent I suppose would be our college audiences—that's where the hope lies. But you've got to be able to write for yourself. . . .

INTERVIEWER: You mean take risks, let yourself go?

KOPIT: Yes. You've got to be able to fail. To try it and fail, to see what's happened.

INTERVIEWER: So the fact that you're writing a film script at the moment doesn't imply any desertion of the theater?

KOPIT: Not at all. It's the money. Working for the movies provides writers with the money they need to do other things. Speaking for myself, I'm not involved, it doesn't mean so much to me. But I love the movies—I would like to direct a film now and again.

INTERVIEWER: You directed some of your plays at Harvard. Would you like always to direct your own plays?

KOPIT: Immediately after a play is written I am too close to it to see it properly. After seeing one or two productions, then perhaps I may want to direct it. That is what happened with *Oh Dad, Poor Dad*: I took over the direction of the Paris production.

INTERVIEWER: Your plays are mostly farces, or near-farces, but with a bitterness or sadness underneath the verbal stylization and fireworks. *Indians* has a strong liberal passion running through it. Do you find that you're increasingly concerned to put things over in a direct way? Or do you belive the play's the thing, rather than the message?

KOPIT: Well, I suppose I'm getting more serious as I age—I'm thirty-one. I have changed since I wrote those early plays at Harvard; I'm more serious, and that change in me is sure to be reflected in my work. But the play can be whatever the writer wants it to be.

INTERVIEWER: You don't mind it being written to contain a message provided it works as a play? Do you admire Shaw, for example?

KOPIT: Oh yes, Shaw's language and wit make them work. Yet Pinter is brilliant, and he is without any social or political message. The feeling is what matters. I'm not interested in any play that the writer hasn't cared about.

INTERVIEWER: The destruction of the Indians has obvious parallels with present day social evils in the States. Sitting Bull says ironically, "Yes, we'll live like the white man, as you tell us we must. We haven't seen a white man starve." Are you directly referring to present day racial problems and violence generally?

KOPIT: Oh yes. It was the parallels with present day evils that took me to the Indians, made me do it. I am now rewriting Buffalo Bill into a stronger figure. His fascination with his own legend should be emphasized more at the beginning. You know, there was a whole prologue to the play cut out, in which certain facets of his character, his good intentions and so on, were shown, and I think some of these will now have to be worked into the present play.

INTERVIEWER: That's interesting. Certainly there's a shadow cast over the play from the beginning in that we know he fails.

KOPIT: That's it. He's defeated too soon. At the beginning he must be made more positive. He must say, "I did what I had to do."

INTERVIEWER: In most of your plays there is humor, plenty of it, on the surface, overlaying fear and violence. Do you tend to see things as funny first of all, and then on reflection perceive the sickness underneath?

KOPIT: In the States, violence generally hides itself, pretends it is something else. Think of the southern man's smile. Violence can be the expression of a grim kind of humor.

INTERVIEWER: Are you concerned so much with the neurotic and psychotic because you find American society so sick, or even our whole civilization so sick?

KOPIT: It is certainly not entirely a matter of American society. But Americans have a special inheritance of violence. Nowhere else is there the emphasis on the right of the individual to protect himself, that derives from an ancestry of frontiersmen. You in England and in Europe have got used to the idea of others specially organized to protect you under the law. The fact that we can't get a law passed to regulate the sale of firearms is unique.

INTERVIEWER: Do you tend to be optimistic or pessimistic?

KOPIT: By rationality pessimistic, by nature optimistic. If you think about it, I don't see how anybody can be really optimistic now, when the means of destruction are total, and so on. On the other hand, there is still the frontier spirit in America, which is frustrated because there is nothing left to discover, and that is part of the explanation for the violence. It may be that the discovery of the planets, the exploration of space, will make use of this spirit, so in that there is cause for optimism, though of course it will be a long time before that will be possible except for the very few.

INTERVIEWER: The way you handle the theme of matriarchy in Oh Dad, Poor Dad—the husband's corpse in the wardrobe —suggests you find this an aspect of American life that is particularly disturbing. Is this so?

KOPIT: I see matriarchy as an amusing aspect of violence. Madame Rosepetal is rather motherhood gone berserk. Not confined to America, I should have thought; you find it in Italy after all. She intends to do good, like America helping

Vietnam today by bombing its cities. For Rosepetal read America if you like, and for the dominated son Jonathan read Vietnam.

INTERVIEWER: I've read that your Paris production of *Oh Dad, Poor Dad* was the most successful.
KOPIT: There are two reasons for that: Edwige Feuillère and the actor who played Jonathan. I said to Madame Feuillère, "Everything you do is right," and it worked beautifully.

INTERVIEWER: Do you share the general admiration of playwrights for Beckett?
KOPIT: Of course. You don't want me to say why? His control over his material . . .

INTERVIEWER: Which plays have you seen in London?
KOPIT: I was not impressed by *Rosencrantz and Guildenstern*. There were no surprises in it. I like a play that you want to go back and see again, to discover things in it you didn't see before. But there you are. It didn't work for me, but other people liked it.

INTERVIEWER: Your most recent play, *Snatch*—will there be a production soon?
KOPIT: It has a large cast, and three sets. So I hope the National Theatre or the Aldwych may do it.

INTERVIEWER: Do you want to say anything about it?
KOPIT: It has a freer structure than *Indians*. It is artifice, a recognized farce.

INTERVIEWER: Are you interested in writing a novel?
KOPIT: I left one to do *Indians*. I don't know, the pose is so different. The playwright is at a distance from his characters. I find the narrator's role, getting inside his characters, intimidating.

INTERVIEWER: Can you say what your hopes are for the future? Have you any particular ambition?
KOPIT: I'd like to write a play a year. I admire those who write

a lot: Osborne, Albee, and others. You're less vulnerable to
critics that way—no matter how one play is received, you've
always got another on the way. In any case, the important
plays come by accident. You can't sit down to write an important play.

Interviewed by BRENDAN HENNESSY, 1968

TOM STOPPARD

"Heads. Heads. Heads. Heads. . . . " The coin is spun by *Rosencrantz (or is it Guildenstern?) and each time, many times, it lands the same way up. British critic Irving Wardle has written of the play which brought immediate acclaim to Tom Stoppard, "It is probably the first play in theatrical history with a pair of attendant lords in the lead. Stoppard does nothing to fill out their blank outlines. Their blankness is the whole point. They exist only to be occasionally involved in great events. When they are not wanted they are left together in a bare anteroom of the palace, spinning coins and playing word games to pass the time until the next call comes. . . . But he manages to provide his two heroes with an existential development. They discover the letter authorizing their execution, and choose to continue the voyage and deliver it, so as to emerge from the shadows of nonentity for a single moment."*

Tom Stoppard seemed reluctant to have me visit his home. There would be little peace with the baby being put to bed, he indicated. The fact that he is a very private person comes out in the interview, which took place at lunchtime in my rather dark office in Covent Garden. The place and time may account for the somewhat muted effect. Mr. Stoppard certainly seemed more head than tail.

The National Theatre program for Rosencrantz and Guildenstern Are Dead *provides the following biographical information, in addition to what emerged in the interview. Tom Stoppard was born in 1937. He is married with one child. He lives in London. He began his career as a journalist in Bristol, subsequently freelancing in London. In 1964 he went to Berlin for five months on a Ford Foundation grant and wrote a one*

act verse burlesque, Rosencrantz and Guildenstern. *On his*
return from Berlin he started work on Rosencrantz and Guildenstern Are Dead, *which owes little to the one acter except*
momentum.

INTERVIEWER: I was lucky enough to see *Rosencrantz and*
Guildenstern Are Dead when it was done at the Edinburgh
Festival of 1966, before it was performed in London at the
National Theatre at the Old Vic in 1967. In Edinburgh it was
mounted by the Oxford Theatre Group in an austere and
slightly musty church hall in the Royal Mile, yet it seemed to
me that it was a better play there, for two reasons. First, because it was shorter, the right length for its material; second,
because it was more pointed. Seeing the highly professional
production in London, I felt that the argument was drawn
out unnecessarily. You'd made a joke, a witty remark, but the
effect was often spoiled because the dialogue pertaining to it
would carry on for a few lines beyond the denouement, after
the laughter.

STOPPARD: You're the victim of an illusion. The National
Theatre script was in fact a little longer than the Edinburgh
one but this was mainly because I wrote an entirely new
scene for London. At the same time I cut quite a few things
out of the script which was performed in London. I remember a meeting with Sir Laurence Olivier and Kenneth Tynan
which went on until five o'clock in the morning and quite a
few things went that night. Mind you, I put a lot of them
back later. It is also true that we didn't even attempt to
do the very last scene at Edinburgh; it was simply unstageable
in those circumstances, the circumstances being a stage the
size of a ping-pong table and a dozen actors instead of thirty-
five. The *production* in London certainly went on a great deal
longer because there was a great deal more of it. Anyway,
there is no question of there having been any extra lines beyond
the point where we reached a denouement in Edinburgh. Perhaps the Edinburgh audiences laughed at penultimate rather
than ultimate moments, for some gnomic Scottish reason. Not
that I heard them do it myself. I was only there for the first
two or three days of the production and the play was received,

well, politely rather than with hilarity. On the day I left—
it was a Sunday—Ronald Bryden wrote in *The Observer* that
the play was very funny and I understand that after that
people tended to laugh at it rather more.

INTERVIEWER: What struck me more about the play than anything else was that of any play written by a British playwright
since 1956 and *Look Back in Anger* it was the least personal.
One had the impression that nothing was revealed about you
as its author. It was objective rather than subjective. It wasn't,
in fact, autobiographical.
STOPPARD: That's quite true. It wasn't deliberate in the sense
that I take pains—or took pains in that play—not to reveal
myself, or that I take pains in my writing not to reveal myself.
Or should I immediately contradict that remark, because in
point of fact I am sensitive about self revelation. I distrust it.
I've written very little which could be said to be even remotely
autobiographical and I've been subsequently somewhat embarrassed by what I have written. On the other hand, I suppose
that that play, as well as almost everything else, probably has
revealed quite a lot about me without it necessarily revealing
it in autobiographical terms.

INTERVIEWER: Why do you distrust self revelation? Do you
think it tends to result in less good plays than might otherwise
be the case?
STOPPARD: No it doesn't, at least not from other people. I
think probably the real answer would lie concealed somewhere
in my history. I simply don't like very much revealing myself.
I am a very private sort of person. But there again one has to
distinguish between self revelation and autobiography. A further point is that of course autobiographical work would tend
to be on a realistic level since one's life is lived on a realistic
level, and it happens that I am not any longer very interested
in writing realistic drama. Now, do I not write realistic drama
because I don't like to reveal myself autobiographically, or do
I not reveal myself autobiographically because I don't like
writing realistic drama? I would say the former. I have after all
written a realistic play. I started by writing a realistic play and

really there is nothing of me in it, that is to say nothing of my life in it, just perhaps the odd stray remark that I have picked up and wrapped up and saved up and thrown up. I did one or two small things, a few unpublished short stories and a couple of published ones which sprang more obviously from my own life, but I don't much like them as short stories now. And I think probably that if I had written my slab of fiction about a young fellow born in Czechoslovakia, brought up in India, who went to school in England, joined a newspaper, started writing his first novel, I would probably hate that too.

INTERVIEWER: Why do you choose *Hamlet?* Why Rosencrantz and Guildenstern?
STOPPARD: They chose themselves to a certain extent. I mean that the play *Hamlet* and the characters Rosencrantz and Guildenstern are the only play and the only characters on which you could write my kind of play. They are so much more than merely bit players in another famous play. *Hamlet* I suppose is the most famous play in any language; it is part of a sort of common mythology. I am continually being asked politely whether I will write about the messenger in *Oedipus Rex,* which misses the point.

INTERVIEWER: But in a way it is difficult to see the point. It is all very well for you to say that, but it was brilliant insight on your part to see that you could—or someone could—write a play about Rosencrantz and Guildenstern.
STOPPARD: But as I said, they are more than just bit players in another play. There are certain things which they bring on with them, particularly the fact that they end up dead without really, as far as any textual evidence goes, knowing why. Hamlet's assumption that they were privy to Claudius' plot is entirely gratuitous. As far as their involvement in Shakespeare's text is concerned they are told very little about what is going on and much of what they are told isn't true. So I see them much more clearly as a couple of bewildered innocents rather than a couple of henchmen, which is the usual way they are depicted in productions of *Hamlet.*

INTERVIEWER: And this presumably is why you wanted to write about Rosencrantz and Guildenstern?

STOPPARD: Yes, it presumably is. I can't actually remember.

INTERVIEWER: This is why to the play-goer, at least to myself, the play is the first post McLuhan (if that means anything), post Beckettian drama, because the two protagonists are bewildered innocents rather than henchmen, and their anonymity is magnified to such an extent that they become positive people. Do you feel that either Rosencrantz or Guildenstern corresponds to you at all? What you were saying earlier about your distrust of self revelation seems to fit here.

STOPPARD: They both add up to me in many ways in the sense that they're carrying out a dialogue which I carry out with myself. One of them is fairly intellectual, fairly incisive; the other one is thicker, nicer in a curious way, more sympathetic. There's a leader and the led. Retrospectively, with all benefit of other people's comments and enthusiasms and so on, it just seems a classic case of self revelation even though it isn't about this fellow who wrote his first novel . . . . But of course the saving thing is that I'm the only person who really knows to what extent and at what points the play reveals me. There's a great deal, of course, which has nothing to do with me, which satisfactorily obscures the photograph.

INTERVIEWER: Nobody can write anything which doesn't reveal a certain amount about himself.

STOPPARD: That's perfectly true. It's merely the difference between reflecting one's experience and reflecting one's personality.

INTERVIEWER: Was *Rosencrantz* the first play you'd written?

STOPPARD: No, by no means. The first play I wrote was a stage play called *A Walk on the Water*, which has now opened in London under the title of *Enter a Free Man*. I wrote it in 1960. I subsequently wrote a one acter which has only been done by students, and I've written several radio plays—*The Dissolution of Dominic Boot, M is for Moon Among Other Things, If You're Glad I'll Be Frank*, and *Albert's Bridge*—and television plays, and another one act play which is going to

be done later. *Rosencrantz* was about the twelfth play I'd
written.

INTERVIEWER: Do you want to go on writing plays?
STOPPARD: I do really. I don't like the process of getting a play
on, and when one is actually in rehearsals or on tour with a
play, a career as a writer of novels becomes very attractive
indeed. On the other hand, I've written one novel, *Lord Mal-
quist and Mr. Moon,* published in 1966, and it didn't compare
in any way with writing a play—in terms of involvement, in
terms of excitement, in terms of satisfaction. It's a much colder
occupation, much less dangerous. When one writes a play one
is really exposing oneself to every rotten tomato on the horizon.
I think there's a certain satisfaction in the danger of commit-
ting the conceit of writing a play and having it performed at
the expense of some effort by quite a large number of people,
and then having it judged in one go. It's like having one's
novel read by all the critics in a room.

INTERVIEWER: Do you enjoy the actual work involved in putting your plays on the stage?
STOPPARD: Yes, I find much of it very stimulating. This is
only the second time I've had a play staged and in each case
I've been very closely involved in the sense that I turn up at
all the rehearsals and I suggest things and I give notes and
whatever. At the time, I don't enjoy it very much. There are
certain occasions when one goes home in the evening and one
knows that because of one's presence there that day something
in that play will be very much better when it's done. Of course
the director does a great deal more than I do. I hang about.
What one is there for is to prevent oneself from being misrep-
resented, because the first and real truth about having a play
put on is that with the most intelligent and sympathetic director
possible and the most accomplished and intelligent actors available you will only actually get about seventy per cent of what
you meant, because a script turns out to be a great deal more
obscure in its intentions than one could possibly imagine oneself. It's taken me a long time to shake the illusion that everything I write is self evident, that it's self evident in the way it

is intended to be performed, spoken, moved and so on. Not at all!

I write with a very dominant sense of rhythm in the dialogue, and to me the orchestration of that dialogue has a kind of inevitability. The words on the page appear to me to be able to be said in only one particular way to achieve an optimum effect. Of course one finds that not only is this way something that one sees privately and which is not at all self evident but also that there are other ways which often work better which one hadn't even thought of.

INTERVIEWER: Did you do a lot of rewriting of *Rosencrantz?* The words and nuances seem very precise.

STOPPARD: I rewrote a great deal before I reached a final draft, but having got to a final draft I did comparatively little, though I did change the ending. We worked a lot on the ending with the National Theatre actors in the last two or three weeks of rehearsal. And, furthermore, between Edinburgh and London I wrote the scene to which I referred earlier. It was suggested by Sir Laurence, who pointed out that I had omitted a key scene in *Hamlet.* This is the scene where Rosencrantz and Guildenstern accost Hamlet after he has hidden Polonius' body. It arose because Olivier pointed out that when Claudius came on and instructed them to find Hamlet, who happened to have killed Polonius, it was the one time in the play when they were given an actual specific duty to fulfill and it was a pity that it had been lost in the sort of cinematic cut we had then. So I wrote that scene. It's there, and I'm glad it's there.

INTERVIEWER: The only scene which reveals them in action.

STOPPARD: Though it's not very active for all that.

INTERVIEWER: Who do you feel you've been influenced by as a writer, or don't you feel it's important?

STOPPARD: It's not important to me, but I suppose it's interesting. Influences such as appear in *Rosencrantz,* and any play of anybody else's, are I suppose admiration that have been unsuccessfully repressed or obscured. I don't mean consciously! But, of the influences that have been invoked on my behalf, and they have been Beckett, Kafka, Pirandello of course, I suppose Beckett is the easiest one to make, yet the most deceptive. Most people who say Beckett mean *Waiting for Godot*. They haven't read his novels, for example. I can see a lot of Beckettian things in all my work, but they're not actually to do with the image of two lost souls waiting for something to happen, which is why most people connect *Rosencrantz* with *Waiting for Godot,* because they had this scene in common.

INTERVIEWER: Beckett's novels are mainly about one lost soul waiting for nothing to happen.

STOPPARD: I wasn't thinking so much of what they are about so much as the way in which Beckett expresses himself, and the bent of his humor. I find Beckett deliciously funny in the way that he qualifies everything as he goes along; reduces, refines and dismantles. When I read it I love it and when I write I just guess it comes out as other things come out. As for Pirandello, I know very little about him, I'm afraid. I've seen very little, and I really wasn't aware of that as an influence. It would be very difficult to write a play which was totally unlike Beckett, Pirandello and Kafka, who's your father, you know?

INTERVIEWER: What about your play *Enter a Free Man?*

STOPPARD: I have worked on it a bit over the last year. In fact I wrote a new scene for it about three weeks ago while it was on tour, but it is basically the play I wrote in 1960. I mean it is still a play about the same people in the same situation. There is some new stuff in it and I have thrown out certain things. There was some imagery which went bad on me as things do. I suppose about a third of it has been written in at various times over the last few years. It was done in Germany in 1964 and I put some new stuff in then, and actually I took some of it out again. So it is a play which has been around my consciousness and my conscience for longer than I like to think. Anyway, as you know, it opened a week ago and it was patted on the head until it was dead. I think it ought to have been done, if only once, because plays are written to be performed. On the other hand, I was scared about it, because plays go off like fruit. They're organic things; they're not mineral. They change their composition in relation to the time they exist, or are seen to exist, and in relation to oneself; they start to decompose the moment the word is on the page. A lot has happened since I wrote the play—to me and to the times.

If I'd written a page of dialogue last night—and I wish I had—this morning there'd be a couple of lines which I wouldn't be quite sure about, and this time next week there'd be a line I'd absolutely loathe, and in a month's time probably only half the page would still exist, and the other half would have been thrown away. Certainly there are things in *Rosencrantz* which for me have gone off, and the soft bits go first, as in fruit. Well, *Enter a Free Man* is now pushing eight, which is quite a long time if one is a young writer. I think that if one writes a play at the age of forty-five then it doesn't very much matter if it's not done until one is fifty-two, but if one writes a play at twenty-three, by the time one is thirty, one has changed a great deal, and I no longer think of it as the kind of play I would write now or would ever write again. But following it around on tour I've been somewhat heartened by the fact that the kind of audience response which I was hoping to get out of the play when I was doing it is actually coming back at me now, which in a sense surprises me.

INTERVIEWER: Do you pay close attention to the work of your contemporaries?

STOPPARD: I read an enormous amount, at least I used to read an enormous amount. Now I read less, but of the countless books I've read and plays I've sat through there are very very few where I feel that I've been given an experience which differs from all the other experiences one gets from books and plays. There are very few books which seem to me to actually get away from what everybody else is doing. I think that a book like Flann O'Brien's* *At Swim-Two-Birds* is going to influence writers for a century. It's influenced writers already. It's certainly influenced B. S. Johnson. How far back can one go? *Tristram Shandy, Ulysses, At Swim-Two-Birds?* Of

---

* Flann O'Brien is a pseudonym of Brian Nolan.

plays, of course *Look Back in Anger* had an enormous effect
on everybody but it doesn't seem as important now as some
others. There are plays which had much less effect at the
time which I actually prefer, mainly because of one's own
idiosyncrasies. I think James Saunders' *Next Time I'll Sing
to You* is one of the best plays written since the war, simply
because it's written like music. It's a most beautiful and brilliant
use of language.

INTERVIEWER: I have the impression, from *Rosencrantz* and
from what you've been saying, that you're more interested in
form than content.

STOPPARD: No, I'm not actually hooked on form. I'm not even
hooked on content if one means message. I'm hooked on style.

INTERVIEWER: I wonder if we don't mean the same thing by
style and form. Style to me is modish, more superimposed than
form, which is structural, integral. To me, *Rosencrantz* is
formal, and has style; *Look Back in Anger* has neither, though
it has a lot of other things.

STOPPARD: I think it has both. It is as formal as a quadrille,
if you can have a quadrille with two girls and a man—you
could draw that play on graph paper, with lines for Jimmy,
Alison and whatsername—Helen?—crossing and recrossing in
a formal construction. And although at first glance it has a
sort of freebooting, free-associating flow of a compulsive talker
with a certain wit and coherence, it is in fact constructed with
an intense and ever present recognition of the fact that it has
got to be done in front of an audience and work in a particular
way, and this concern for structure pops through to
the surface at key points. The way that, for example, you
end an act on a point where Jimmy and Helen, whom he
has despised for the previous twenty minutes, come to a clinch
—she hits him and he kisses her—Act! It's exactly the same
thing as ending a serial in a woman's magazine at a point
where the reader is intrigued to buy it next week. As for
style—the play seems merely emotional, but you can't really
talk like that in real life without feeling self-conscious. And

the reason you feel self-conscious is that you are aware that you are doing it with style, with just as much style as an Oscar Wilde character contriving to speak exclusively in epigrams.

Interviewed by GILES GORDON, 1968

DAVID MERCER

David Mercer received less than a paragraph in John Russell Taylor's guide to the new British drama, Anger and After, published by Penguin in 1963. He is now considered one of the most interesting British playwrights. He made his name with television plays, including A Suitable Case for Treatment (later filmed with the prefix Morgan) and In Two Minds. At the time of this interview his two recently performed stage plays were Ride a Cock Horse which starred Peter O'Toole and Belcher's Luck which was put on by the Royal Shakespeare Company.

Mercer lives in London, in a tall thin house between St. John's Wood and Maida Vale. His study is on the top floor, and when I was shown into his room he was at his typewriter. He stood up, poured me a whisky. I noticed the spines of a few of the hundreds of books: Shirer's Third Reich, Catch 22, Brecht, Osborne's Luther, D. H. Lawrence's Letters. On his desk were copies of the Penguin Dictionary of Quotations and the Penguin New English Dictionary, as well as a copy of the Calder & Boyars edition of Belcher's Luck. On the white walls were posters for productions of Mercer's plays, and photographs of apes and Russian revolutionaries. In the corner by the door on an easel was a largely red, unfinished portrait in oils. Mercer claimed it to be his last painting. When I commented on it he pointed out a drawing on the wall by David Storey, the novelist and now playwright. Storey and Mercer both come from Wakefield in Yorkshire. They were both at art college, Mercer at King's College, Newcastle. This was after he had begun to work at the age of fourteen, after he had been apprenticed as a laboratory technician, and after he had de-

*cided—after three weeks' studying—not to be trained as a
scientist. His father is an engine driver.*

INTERVIEWER: You were saying a minute ago that you think
that writers, artists of all kinds, are better at accurately ap-
praising their own work and its value than are other people.
MERCER: I don't mean that a writer is necessarily equipped in
any critical or academic sense to judge himself better than the
critics or whatever people are forming the public judgment
of a writer, but I'm fairly sure that most writers have an intuitive sense, if not exactly of their overall achievement, of
a particular piece of work. I think they have a fair idea of
where it stands in relation to other people's work, what's been
done and what is being done.

INTERVIEWER: How would you place your last stage play,
Belcher's Luck, in relation to what other playwrights are
writing?
MERCER: When I talk about a writer having this sense, I
think it's a very private thing. One thing I am sure about,
about *Belcher's Luck,* is that for me it marks the end of a
period in my work; and I hope that it marks the beginning
of a second period. I originally wrote television drama mostly,
and I fell into that rather by accident, simply because the
BBC did a stage play of mine adapted for television, and then
they gave me a virtual guarantee that what I wrote they would
produce, and they've kept that promise. The temptation to
sustain television plays was quite strong because to have freedom from the beginning is a remarkable thing. Anyway, in
the beginning—if one must put labels on things—I suppose
I was vaguely a social realist writer, with a lot of objective
social content.

INTERVIEWER: *Belcher's Luck* still contained quite a bit of
that.
MERCER: I know. But I think that another sort of stream in
my writing which developed was non-naturalistic, non-social
realistic, rather a vein of fantasy. To me, *Belcher's Luck,*
whatever its merits or demerits, to some extent unified these

two streams in the sense that although it had a social meaning it was a play of imagery as well, to me basically a play
of imagery although I wanted the imagery to have social significance. *Belcher's Luck* is almost a kind of résumé of forces
and directions in twelve television plays and three stage plays
and a film.

INTERVIEWER: Are you conscious of deliberately writing differently for the theater and for television and for cinema?
MERCER: No, I think it works the other way around. When
I start writing something I very quickly recognize whether
this thing makes sense in theater or makes sense in television.
There's a lot of preliminary drafting and thinking. I think
before I write the first page of the substantial draft of the
play that I know which medium it's appropriate for. And
actually I don't change much after that.

INTERVIEWER: You don't do much revising?
MERCER: I don't. I revise mostly in rehearsal. I think that,
for me, that's the time for revising.

INTERVIEWER: Once you realize what medium you're writing
a play for, are you aware of writing it in a different way from
what you would if it was for a different medium?
MERCER: I think that I've expended as much nervous and creative and moral energy over any given television play as I
have over a theater play or over a screenplay. As soon as I
realize that a piece is, say, for television, there's a kind of
available vocabulary of means of expression which I can use,
which I can play. And therefore, obviously, I will tend instinctively to use the medium to my knowledge of its maximum potential. There is that kind of difference. Obviously
you can take a television play anywhere, any time—all kinds
of mechanical devices can be used, and so on.

INTERVIEWER: You're not therefore writing particular plays
for particular audiences? The audience can take it or leave it?
MERCER: I think that's about it for me. I only write a play—
if you can talk about having reasons for writing, which I

think is a dodgy thing to talk about—in order to find out what that play is. A thing must come into existence before I can know what it is, and to know what it is is the impetus underlying the writing of it. So I don't think that I really write for anybody.

INTERVIEWER: Are you, in retrospect, a good interpreter of your plays? Can you look back at a play and say: "Oh, in that play I see I was doing such and such." Or does this not concern you?
MERCER: I think I've got a fair idea of what's been going but it's almost impossible for me to say, to be objective about it.

INTERVIEWER: I asked that because of what you said about *Belcher's Luck* being the end of a particular period, and your moving on to plays concerned more with fantasy. How much are you in control of what you're writing, and how much is it taking over from you?
MERCER: I don't think I'm much in control of it, not consciously. I think that you acquire and assimilate means of expression, but to me the writing of a play is a mystery, the origin of it is a mystery. I don't know where it comes from, or how it comes. I don't even know what it is. I don't mean this in a camp sense, this is a strictly neutral matter of fact for me—I do not know. I suppose the development, if one had a development in one's work, is a question of everything's being accumulated from previous writing. I wouldn't say that I learn anything in a conscious, rational way but each play that I write, I feel, uses everything that I've discovered in previous pieces of work. But it's in control of me, not the other way around.

INTERVIEWER: Do you take a particular subject you want to write about, and write a tract on it?
MERCER: No, I don't. I did it once, right back in the beginning. I was writing a trilogy of television plays which, it turned out later, were about three generations of socialism in England. In the first play I was completely unaware of this. I was simply writing a play about a family. Then I realized what

in fact the play was also about, about its social implications. The second play, *A Climate of Fear,* which was about protest and protest movements, but at a superficial level, I wrote at a time when I was very much involved in the anti-nuclear campaign and the Committee of 100. It now seems to me that that particular issue in the play is the most sort of . . . weakest one, really. I think this is unfortunate in a number of ways. One of the certain ways in which it is unfortunate is that the actual contemporary social texture of the piece automatically signals certain things to an audience. Therefore people who would be sympathetic to the assumptions of the play stay with it, and those who are naturally antipathetic to its assumptions disappear immediately. They have no opportunity to penetrate to the play behind, which is basically a play of human relationships, and again of images. This is where images began to grow in my work. So if you have this superficial skin, or outside texture of content, you can push people away from what might otherwise be an interesting play simply because they immediately disagree with its overt assumptions.

INTERVIEWER: Do you think, or have you ever believed, that a playwright can influence for the good politically, can do more than state his own political attitudes and convictions, can actively by being a playwright do something to improve —to use Jennie Lee's phrase—"the quality of life"?
MERCER: I think a writer can obviously do something to improve the quality of life in the sense that he can extend people's range of perception. I suppose the basic purpose of works of art is to generalize unique experiences. In that sense a writer can function in the way you mention. But politically I wouldn't say at all, except in a most indirect fashion. I think that there are plays which sort of percolate through a society. I think there are detectably different things in England today simply because *Look Back in Anger* was written. But they are not a consequence of *Look Back in Anger* as a play. *Look Back in Anger* also released quantities of energy and brought in its wake a lot of writers. Which I suppose, insofar as John Osborne is political at all, is related to some kind of anarchistic Left Wing rather muddled view of politics, I would say.

INTERVIEWER: This in a way, surely, is why his plays are as successful as they are, because politically they are rather muddled. They are sentimental and romantic rather than realistic.

MERCER: Sentimental, romantic, nostalgic, I think.

INTERVIEWER: Those were precisely the three adjectives I'd applied to *Belcher's Luck,* which incidentally I liked very much. I thought it was sentimental, romantic, nostalgic.

MERCER: How d'you mean sentimental?

INTERVIEWER: It's difficult often to differentiate between sentiment and nostalgia. In a way, the feeling of mourning for a certain England that was dying or dead. For me, the play didn't face up entirely to the reality of the situation insofar as the kind of England portrayed in *Belcher's Luck* no longer exists meaningfully.

MERCER: But the England of whom? The England of the old general . . .

INTERVIEWER: Yes, the England of the old general.

MERCER: I don't think I was sentimental about that. What I was at some pains to do was to avoid a crudely polemical view of that England, and when I created the character of Sir Gerald Catesby I in fact wanted to embody some of the positive aspects of enlightened nineteenth century liberalism, in relation to a kind of aristocratic and colonial and dominating set of assumptions about England's role in the world. I don't think I mourned the passing of that at all, and in fact the character of Catesby's son absolutely denies them both, in that he denies the old general and he denies his father, who is a kind of bawdy terrorizing bastard. Since I've been moving away from overt political statement, by the time I got to *Belcher's Luck,* which was my fourteenth play, I was almost pathologically concerned to keep the social-political implications of the play in the wings. This may have resulted in the opposite of what I wanted, which was to leave the play open to interpretations on many different levels.

INTERVIEWER: Would you like to say anything about what you are writing now? I've read quite a bit, and was deliberately not going to ask you about it for that reason, about how you've been influenced by the writings of R. D. Laing.

MERCER: I don't think I've been so much influenced by them as reinforced by them. What happened with Laing and me was that after about six or seven of my plays, most of which were concerned in some way or other with what people call aberration or neurosis or obscenity, Laing through a mutual friend asked to read the scripts of these plays; and I in turn began to read his books. He'd had the idea that in a purely intuitive, creative way I'd been on a parallel direction in drama, the kind of thing that he was trying to state in theoretical, clinical terms. When I read his books they instantly made sense to me as an intellectual structure which made sense of my own work. This has both its rewards and its dangers, really. I don't like to become too conscious of what I'm about. Perhaps this in itself is a kind of superstition. But that's how it occurred. I don't mean that I haven't got anything to learn from Laing. I've got everything to learn from him. But in terms of his work, and the world that he's writing in, and in terms of clinical psychiatry and political philosophy and many other things, I've nothing to learn from him as a dramatist.

INTERVIEWER: Did you find it exciting when you first read his books? This knowledge that at a given time, even in the same city, a number of people in different fields are working the same strata, quite independently and quite unknowingly of each other, and that there are important parallels?

MERCER: Yes. I was surprised and amazed and above all, I think, considerably reassured to come to realize that something which for me is purely intuitive and creative can make sense in intellectual terms, because I don't see myself as an intellectual at all. I'm just not an intellectual. That was the amazing thing: he was going on one track and I was going on another track and they were complementary in their meanings, or they seemed to be to us. This began a kind of association, both personal and in terms of work, which I think has been nothing but good for me. At the same time I think that now perhaps the most abiding thing that I feel I have learnt is finally to trust the theater or the screen really as a world in itself, as a world where I can make exist what I wish to exist. I think this is a necessary development for me, because I've always been haunted and hedged about by what, I suppose, I would call my political personality, which is more or less neo-Marxist, whatever that means.

I think in the beginning, if you—this is a sort of fantasy too, in a way—if you associate a kind of structured political ideology, what can be an authoritarian political ideology, with the sort of super-ego part of yourself, and you associate the art of making something or creating something with the playful, more infantile part of yourself, I think that my political super-ego had always conspired against the playfulness and spontaneity and freedom of my actual creative writing. I now think I'm beginning to free myself, because I still felt in the first two or three years of writing, when I still had a lot of political content in my plays, a kind of submission and a deference . . . I don't know how to put this exactly. . . . I always felt history and Marxism and Communism there, and they were goals and objectives; however they've been destroyed and aberrated by revolution. They were completely real for me and completely valid and they remain valid. But I think it did have this, what I call, super-ego role in my writing, that I felt I couldn't really say "No" to Mother and Father. I think I've grown out of that. It's a late development but thank God it's happened.

This is one of the important things about the Cuban Revolution. I mention Cuba because I've just come back from there, from my second protracted visit. In the context of the Cuban Revolution it's possible for writers, without feeling hedged around and harassed, to write in that particular kind of way. What they are encouraged to do is to develop their originality and spontaneity, even if it appears to be superficially in conflict with the aims of the Revolution; whereas I grew up—I'm nearly forty—with a kind of dedication to revolution and Marxism, which was terribly deformed and basically very authoritarian, so that . . . you know, I think haunted is the best word . . . I was politically haunted as a writer; now I've stopped being haunted.

INTERVIEWER: Do you think that any writer so long as he's "politically haunted" is going to produce inferior plays, as works of art?

MERCER: I don't think that he will necessarily produce anything inferior. The quality of what he will produce is purely a function of the degree of talent that he's got. What I do think is that this political haunting can exist as a presence in a man's writing to such an extent that it actually obscures his quality and virtue as a writer. I think Arnold Wesker is a case in point.

INTERVIEWER: Yes. I think that if Wesker forgot for five minutes that he was a socialist he'd probably write an inspired play.

MERCER: I agree. I think Wesker could write a very big play indeed, but I think it requires some kind of development in him which will enable him to put down this haunting influence, this harassing presence in him, and to admit all the other aspects of what is humanity, and not to let them be covered by ideal notions of humanity or society.

INTERVIEWER: You said a few moments ago that you don't consider yourself an intellectual. "The intellectual" as a concept makes me squirm. I think it's one of the least defined words in the English language. What do you consider an intellectual is?

MERCER: I agree with you completely, the word makes me squirm most uncomfortably. It's almost impossible to use in the English language. I mean, in French or Spanish or German or Italian you can refer to the intellectual, and mean something fairly specific, and it doesn't have the ugly undertones and overtones the word has in English. In English it oscillates between denigration and snobbery. In fact this is one of the things which sort of upset me in Cuba this time. This was a cultural congress to which the Cubans had invited "450 Intellectuals." Now the discussion of the congress, the reference to those at it as intellectuals, was incessant in the Cuban press and in Cuban society. It's like talking about the workers or the peasants. It had a kind of neutrality as a word. It has no neutrality in English. But nonetheless I feel driven to use the word because it's useful. I suppose by an intellectual I mean somebody with an elaborately and profoundly well-informed kind of academic relation to a subject. George Steiner is an intellectual. Raymond Williams is an intellectual. Eric Hobsbaum is an intellectual. Arnold Wesker is not. David Mercer is not. John Osborne is not.

INTERVIEWER: By these examples I think you've put your finger on something: that hardly any good artist—whatever good means—is an intellectual, or historically has been an intellectual.
MERCER: This is true.

INTERVIEWER: You know, having an intellectual frame of mind or an intellectual approach almost denies the artist's role which is, as you were saying earlier, intuitive to a much greater degree than most artists are prepared to accept, however disciplined they may be in their work.
MERCER: I think that's absolutely fair. I've also known gifted artists—painters, sculptors, writers—who had a formidable mental apparatus, who were destroyed by their intellectuality. Intellectuality in all its complexity came between them and their spontaneous ability to create something.

INTERVIEWER: Robert Bolt seems to me someone to whom this has happened. He's got considerable talent buried there somewhere, and yet his intellectuality deadens all he writes.
MERCER: His talent is so encapsulated in a kind of bourgeois mind that I doubt if it'll ever come free.

INTERVIEWER: He doesn't seem to dare to let himself go.
MERCER: No. I think an artist has got to be crude, above all he's got to have courage. He's got to be everything that he's capable of being, and that involves violence and brutality and outrage and despair and love and all kinds of things. Otherwise, you're trapped in a kind of conceptual structuring of the world that makes experience. . . . If you haven't broken out of it by forty you probably never will.

INTERVIEWER: It's a terrifying thought, the responsibility of the artist to be irresponsible. He's got to let himself go. But he's got to have had a fair amount of conventional success to be able to do it.

MERCER: I don't think it works like that though. I think it's an absolutely personal, emotional affair. I think a genuine talent is more robust than that. If the talent can be defeated by the mind then it probably isn't particularly worthwhile in the first place. These are wild generalizations but I think there's a lot of truth in them.

INTERVIEWER: The stock final question: which playwrights do you most admire of your contemporaries?

MERCER: In England, I think John Arden and John Osborne. In France, Arrabal, though he's Spanish. Beckett is the greatest of them all. Beckett is the incomparable master of the last fifty years and of the next fifty years probably. Beckett is the sort of Shakespeare of the twentieth century. One has only to think of Beckett to feel that there's nothing more to be said.

Interviewed by GILES GORDON, 1968

ELLEN STEWART

This interview with Ellen Stewart, founder and guiding light of the New York based Café La Mama (now the La Mama Experimental Theater Club), took place at London's International Theatre Club. Miss Stewart was in town watching over her traveling Repertory Troupe which spent half its time performing in Europe. While the Troupe was on the road, other associated artists kept the Café's home fires going.

INTERVIEWER: This is the La Mama Repertory Troupe's third annual European tour and yet, even with London's being the theater capital (maybe) of the world, you haven't performed here on the past trips.

STEWART: Well, the explanation is this. Although we are known in the Scandinavian countries, which is where I'd say we are best known, we were not until recently talked about a lot in the English speaking world. However, England was responsible for our being invited to Experimenta II in Frankfurt, which was really fantastic because the festival people from Germany paid our passage over here on the strength of the plays which we did in Nottingham last season.

INTERVIEWER: Have any of the regulations been a reason for your not being here in the past two years?

STEWART: Well, we didn't perform in the past because we weren't asked to. You, at the International Theatre Club, were the first to invite us.

INTERVIEWER: It's a strange thing to me as an American over here involved with the International Theatre Club seeing the two theater scenes. You have this tremendous explosion in New York today, but nothing corresponding to it at all in England. The International Theatre Club is virtually the only non-commercial avant-garde theater left in metropolitan London.

STEWART: I must tell you something. I don't know if you know how well thought of the Club is. But Henry Popkin— do you know him? The critic? Well, he's a good friend; and when I was asking him what to do he told me about Jean-Pierre Voos.* He said you're not well known but you are trying to do something. And that is what I believe in: somebody that is trying. You know, John Arden, who has been teaching a seminar in the States, visited Café La Mama, with his wife. They came often—and he liked our work very much, so much that he gave us a generous gift toward our coming here. He was especially impressed with the Troupe and with Tom O'Horgan's direction. I think this was a fantastically beautiful gesture because this 'man is not a rich man. He kept asking why there was no similar movement in England, just outposts.

INTERVIEWER: Yes, but outside of these outposts—and it gets lonely when there is no one to laugh with you at tradition-bound critics—there is nothing.

STEWART: What you are doing now is *something*. That's one thing. I hear the word *nothing* more in Europe than anywhere else. Considering now that I have been to Europe three times in the past nine months and traveling all over the place, I simply know that this is not true; because I see there are minds and hearts and bodies—it is not zero.

INTERVIEWER: But you have an incredibly volatile situation in the States with an affluence that can afford the luxury of bohemia. With the wealth of artistic chaos stewing in the Village you could form your own country.

STEWART: Just one moment. It took a lot of hard work. We got this little basement which was about the size of this room [twelve by sixteen feet]. That was the first La Mama. We

---

* Voos was Artistic Director of the International Theatre Club.

rented it in 1961, in September, and it took us until May before we had a floor in it because of all the dirt.

INTERVIEWER: How did you get the money to redecorate the place?

STEWART: That story is another reason why I feel some kind of affinity with London because there is a person living here named David Haas, who is an American, but I think he claims British citizenship. In 1961 when I ran this little basement he had been working for years saving enough money so they would let him stay here in England and he was torn as to whether he should really stay in America or should he stay in London. La Mama was very precious to him. This little basement had no walls. The ceiling had fallen through. There was no plumbing—nothing. Paul Foster and myself were trying to make it into a room with no money because I was unemployed at that time.

INTERVIEWER: But you have since then been supporting La Mama largely through your work?

STEWART: Well, yes. I'm a dress designer and use the money from that to support my theater habit. But a lot of people have helped along the way, like David Haas, who took out some of his savings because we were trying to put a floor in. Have you ever tried to put a floor in? Well, it was not working out. So by his giving me a little of his savings, and to me this was very big because I knew what this money meant, we finally got the floor in; and in July, 1962 we were able to give our first play.

INTERVIEWER: This beautiful dedication! Why? For whom?

STEWART: Now, La Mama was established because Paul was studying to be a lawyer at that time and my brother who had got his master's degree at Yale was going to be a playwright. Paul said he wanted to be a playwright and so La Mama was started so they had some place to show their plays. My brother never wrote plays. To this day he has not written a play and now Paul, who had never written a play, is going to have this major production put on in London.*

* *Tom Paine* performed by La Mama Troupe opened at The Vaudeville Theatre on October 17, 1967.

INTERVIEWER: But surely you didn't intend to play to family and friends? How did you manage an audience under those conditions?

STEWART: Well, at first we didn't really. After we got the place built in this tiny basement—and it had no outside lights —we realized it had a low overhang so that you had to go and crawl through the door. It took us a month to figure out why we could not entice anybody to come in and this was because it was so formidable, you know, to ask them to come down in this hole to see a play they did not think existed anyway. The East Village now is a big thing in New York, but in 1961 there was no such thing as the East Village. When we used to see a few people walking down the street, we'd stop them and ask, "Would you come in and see our play?" We had sometimes four to six persons a night and we played Friday, Saturday and Sunday. If we got ten people in one night it was a major celebration. And to keep them in there, you could not breathe—there was no ventilation.

INTERVIEWER: One of your purposes—one that we share— is to perform new works preferably by new playwrights. Where did you get your material?

STEWART: Well, in the meanwhile, Paul had begun to write plays and our first production was a Tennessee Williams thing, *One Arm*. We did not get a new original play until August, in 1962, and that first play was by Michael Locasio —he now has his own theater in Mexico. That was the beginning; we began to get enough plays to do a new play every week. We did not know anything about the technical aspects of the theater—about lights, music and sounds. And all the plays were written about a bed because all the space we had down there was just enough for a single bed. We had different plays about the bed: around the bed, on the bed, under the bed. And Paul's main duty at that time was to get killed because he couldn't act. He used to come screaming out of the john after slashing his wrists. It took from August until November before we had a breakthrough in the bed scene. Then Robert Seely wrote a play called *Big Cheese* and a friend who was a window decorator in one of the big stores came down to the basement and he looked. And he brought a big over-stuffed chair and he put a piece of cloth on the back wall and a painting on that and we scattered books around the floor and that was the first different set that we had in all those months.

INTERVIEWER: I understand you had another contact with England at this early stage.

STEWART: Well, we did Harold Pinter's *The Room*. It had never been produced. He was terribly angry when he came to find that La Mama was doing *The Room*. But I managed to win him over. He was really charming. He gave me the rights to the play until it was commercially produced, for which I have always been grateful. This was another breakthrough in using the basement—it had a fireplace so it fitted nicely into *The Room*.

INTERVIEWER: Music plays an important role in many of the La Mama plays, especially with the Troupe's productions. Has this been true from the beginning?

STEWART: Well, at the beginning, not having money for a tape recorder, we had an old broken-up wireless. It was concealed behind the bar we had made from an old shoeshine stand. So when the play started I would sit on the floor and dial a station and I had to stay very close to turn it off at the right time. Then we started to get composers coming in. The first composer was Garry Friedman and he made a composition which was just fantastic for one of the new plays and he put it on tape and somebody lent a tape machine and that was our first original music. He was one of the first to experiment with electronic music and the like, so on the whole we had that kind of music; the artists had their paintings hanging on the wall; and we played every night because it was all we could do to get started. Now we have reached the point where Tom O'Horgan, the Troupe director, received the 1967 *Saturday Review* Drama Critic Award for Best Incidental Music for his score composed for *Futz* by Rochelle Owens.

INTERVIEWER: At the beginning were there not other people trying to do the same thing with theater?

STEWART: Joe Cino was the first to have café theater; Joe died recently but Caffe Cino still goes on. They are in the West Village and La Mama is in the East Village. We were the only two for a long time to be doing the plays of new playwrights. In the past two years many many places have started. When you say there is no life over here, you must remember we had to create life; we didn't have too many playwrights or actors or directors and we certainly didn't have any public. But we all loved the theater and it grew from that. When I visited London in 1965, I took David Haas by the hand and we went out to Hampstead and rented a garage just like that. We had it whitewashed and tried to get everything started in just one week, but the authorities would not let us do it and I could not stay here to fight it through. I thought if the playing area could be gotten, and the same concepts that we had done ours with, and there were enough bodies around . . .

INTERVIEWER: Could you elaborate a little on what these concepts are? The idea of Total Theater . . .
STEWART: Total Theater means "total dedication." We don't operate on the star system. We don't have any stars. And anybody might be the person who has a walk across or moves the light switch up and down—he is as important as the person who has a fifty minute monologue. And these are what they call coffee house ground rules.

INTERVIEWER: And they all get paid the same amount?
STEWART: Nobody gets paid. You see, this was my big fight with Equity. Some of the very best actors in America liked to work at La Mama particularly because of the new scene. In one or two instances they had jobs on Broadway that they refused because they didn't want to give up that scene at the Café. And I had the union down on my neck. But it was finally conceded that what we were doing is a very good and worthy thing and so now the union is behind us. But that was a struggle too. There are a lot of talented people who want and deserve a chance. There are perhaps thirty directors and 700 actors to call from.

INTERVIEWER: Are all of these people professional?

STEWART: I hate that word professional. That's the dry rot of every place because a person can never be professional until he gets a chance to become professional. La Mama is not based on a success. I read and choose all the scripts that are done and if I think the playwright has potential I play his play. Now he may come on after some other play which has packed houses for ten performances, but I would play his play for the ten performances even if he got only ten people a night. His play runs because La Mama is dedicated to the playwright and those plays are put on for him. That's my interest. There could be a playwright with a little seed. But his play never gets done because it is not good enough and most persons don't want to do anything if they think it is not good enough. But you have to help with any art with a little soul too from the outside.

INTERVIEWER: I remember what you said to me when my plays were supposed to be going on in Sweden and we were wondering if people speaking our own language would ever see them. It was quite touching and true—that every artist, every writer, no matter how independent, needs just that little something behind him. A production, not even a success, but just to see it done—a platform from which to carry on.

STEWART: You write a play but you don't know if that play plays until you play it. You can't tell until you personally sit through that production yourself. And then you can tell better than anybody in this world. The first night you might want to kill yourself but you need this. It is the only way to know.

INTERVIEWER: You might want to kill the director.

STEWART: Well, sometimes you might, but secretly you look into yourself too. Now all these young playwrights, I know the things they have written and I put them on and I see the development. Now Europe is seeing exciting plays that would never have been done anywhere without that first chance. In America the critics used to give us a review once every two months. It meant that one playwright out of eight would get a review. So I brought all these plays to Europe for the sake of the critiques. This thing in New York was vicious for those playwrights who had potential. Publishers and other producers would not read their works without a critique. And you couldn't get a critique because American critics wouldn't come. And that's why we started touring Europe. Now you take Jean-Claude van Itallie's *America Hurrah*; the critics hated the parts we did two years ago. Then we took it to Europe and we had a marvelous success with it.

INTERVIEWER: Well, what about this mortal enemy of the playwright—the critic?

STEWART: I believe in critics. I don't say I will agree with what they say. But just as we have had to teach an audience to accept our plays, you have to have faith in the critics too. The critics are necessary because I think that the critique is part of the theater art. Perhaps it is outdated. Many people are crucified and that is very wrong. You, yourself, were like a guinea pig over here and you should know. Your plays *Freeze* and *Stamp* were the first of the new wave to be done here and you had to pay the price for it. But at least you got them terribly upset; that means they didn't understand and they wanted to. But you see what good it did. You were able to do another new American play at the International Theatre Club and then *America Hurrah* came and now the La Mama Troupe is in London. There is a big reversal.

INTERVIEWER: One of the most famous experimenters in the theater over here is Joan Littlewood. She found that after a while the offers that were coming in from the West End were killing the experiment. Do you have a similar problem?

STEWART: I think that the playwrights and the actors have a right to go to the commercial theater. We will survive because we don't have a little coterie. A vast number of persons are coming all the time and these people come because they know that sooner or later they are going to have a chance to work. But you know, our productions aren't for the most part that successful because La Mama is dedicated to the experiment. If I choose only the scripts that are going to be a success and there are many, and if I by-pass the person that has the potential, La Mama goes straight and stagnant.

INTERVIEWER: Where would you say you draw this audience from—people willing to see something new on a chance?

STEWART: They come from every place, not only the Village, even from the suburbs. Strangely enough we don't get too much of the student audience.

INTERVIEWER: I've noticed that's true here as well with students. The International Theatre Club, even though our students' membership fee is ridiculously low, gets very few students. But I'm sure most of the new experimental theaters have a role with the community at large who are tired of the "old square." Certainly the La Mama Troupe has now made such an impact internationally that there will be no turning back.

Interviewed by ED. B., 1968

WILLIAM INGE

*William Inge has spoken to theater audiences with a forceful
midwestern accent since his first hit,* Come Back, Little Sheba,
in 1950. In addition to dramas such as Picnic, Bus Stop, *and*
Dark at the Top of the Stairs, *Inge has written film scripts,
including* Splendor in the Grass, *which he coproduced with
Elia Kazan. He has received the Pulitzer Prize, the New York
Drama Critic's Circle Award and the Donaldson Award for*
Picnic, *and was an Oscar winner in 1961 for* Splendor in the
Grass. *Inge's most recent play at the time of this interview,*
Where's Daddy? *was produced in 1966.*

*A good-natured Kansas friendliness is about all that is not
quite urbane in Inge. Living in a comfortable modern home
in the Hollywood Hills, he leads a quiet, consistently productive existence. He hesitated at first to consent to an interview
because, as he phrased it, he felt in a "transitional period."
Naturally, my first question was what this phrase meant to
him.*

INGE: Well, I'm not really sure. I find myself kind of fumbling,
just as I was fumbling back in St. Louis after I had written
my first play in 1945. I think any creative person who is going
to survive more than a decade or so has to find himself anew
periodically because he has to change with the times. I know
that the kind of play that was being done in the fifties has no
audience now. And I know that I don't have the same kind
of approach to writing as I did in the fifties.

INTERVIEWER: What kind of change do you see in your writing?
INGE: I seem to be dealing with more metaphysical material.
For example, I've just written a short "pop play" composed

almost entirely of TV commercials; that was an idea that grew out of *Where's Daddy?* I'm fascinated by the ads on television. They repel me so; I feel that I have to do something about them. The reality that they imply, or that they *create,* out of American life is so appalling that I just had to show it. So I thought it would be fun to string a lot of them together and construct a whole play. I've just finished the rough draft and it's really absurdist—a weird kind of humor. It reminds me a bit of Andy Warhol's Coca-Cola bottles and Lichtenstein's work: it's so horrible it's funny. When you look at TV commercials in this way on stage they take on a pretty awesome meaning. Remember those dreadful commercials where a girl's whole success in life depends upon some new deodorant or breath purifier? The desperate *importance* that the commercial gives to this nonsense is fascinating.

INTERVIEWER: What's the play called?
INGE: *Bad Breath.*

INTERVIEWER: You mentioned a novel you are working on. Is this a reflection of your transition?
INGE: It's midwestern Proustian . . . very analytical, slow-moving, ponderous. It deals with . . . Well, I don't start a novel or a play saying, "I'll write about such and such." I start with an idea and then find out *what* I'm writing about. In this novel I find myself writing about the failure of American manhood. I'm exploring the reasons for it, the estimates of it, and the tragedy of it. I think that the American male is in a tragic position because he has no real mode of personal expression. I was brought up in a semi-primitive society— Kansas in the twenties. Culture was far away, and the American man was limited to being a breadwinner. It's just one place where forms of life are imposed on the man. I've written about 100 pages and will probably do another 200 or 300.

INTERVIEWER: Before you began writing for the theater, you taught drama in colleges and you were a theater critic for the St. Louis *Star-Times.* Was that experience of any value to you as a playwright?

INGE: I was misplaced in my academic background. I was *originally* an actor. I started acting as a kid at seven and kept it up until the age of twenty-three. Then one of those personality changes happened; I just found that I couldn't act anymore—I suddenly became too introspective. So I got a master's degree and started teaching. I really floundered as a teacher, and since I was beginning to write on my own, I took the newspaper job as a critic in St. Louis.

At that point I had been thinking about playwriting, but didn't have the courage to start—I had very high standards for myself. Then, seeing all the plays that came into St. Louis for three years . . . one, of course, sees an awful lot of crap if one sees everything that comes to a big midwestern city . . . it occurred to me that I had as much right to fail as any of them. I wrote my first play while I was still critic for the paper. Critic! I was a walking culture page—art, music, theater, you name it.

My first play, *Farther Off from Heaven,* got a production at Margo Jones' theater in Dallas, Texas. The production was successful, but the play wasn't really up to Broadway standards. I returned to St. Louis, now teaching and really hating it, and I wrote another play that was only half realized. One's first work always comes more easily than the later efforts. I wrote two more plays before I finished *Come Back, Little Sheba.*

INTERVIEWER: *Sheba* was a smash hit though, right?
INGE: No, it was successful, but moderately so. It was a hit as a movie but the play only got about half the New York critics. Happily, Brooks Atkinson liked it. It played for five months and could have gone considerably longer, but Shirley Booth and Sidney Blackmur left for other commitments, so we closed in New York. On the road, we had great success. The audiences were much more responsive and alive. Which made me believe from the very beginning that the best American theater would be regional.

INTERVIEWER: Regional, especially midwestern, life seems to be the main focus for your work. Any particular reason?
INGE: Sure, I don't know much about New York life. One *has* to write from one's background and I never saw New York

until I was twenty-seven. I wrote my first play when I was thirty-two. That's a little late for a writer to begin, so I had to stay rather close to my own background for quite a while.

INTERVIEWER: You also seem to be particularly a playwright of family life.

INGE: The American family does concern me. And I do have my own childhood memories to draw upon. One might say that our greatest problems stem from the family—I mean family problems often become national problems.

INTERVIEWER: A lot of critics talk about the influence of your Kansas boyhood. Do you think there is anything special about coming from that particular area?

INGE: I'm one of those people who grew up in Kansas feeling very superior to it. I felt out of place in that forlorn midwestern agricultural state. I had nothing in common with it at all. It was boring as hell and I wanted out. It wasn't until I got to New York that I became Kansan. Everyone there kept reminding me that they were Jewish or Irish, or whatever, so I kept reminding them that I was midwestern. Before I knew it, I actually began to *brag* about being from Kansas! I discovered I had something a bit unique, but it was the nature of New York that forced me to claim my past.

INTERVIEWER: New York, as an atmosphere, doesn't hold much stimulation for you now?

INGE: I'm afraid not. That's a serious problem in the American theater: it's no place to grow up in. New York wants the first flashy efforts, the sensations. It's sort of like going to the circus and seeing only the freak show. The artist himself, the way he matures and grows, is of no concern.

INTERVIEWER: Do you really think you're being fair to New York?

INGE: Well, every serious playwright I have ever talked to agrees with me about one point: there is something about the whole New York scene that makes you feel—no matter how good your play is—that, if it's a success, you've just been damned lucky. I cannot possibly account for the success of some of those dull musicals. They just don't strike me as good entertainment. Theater has to entertain. I'd rather watch a good tap dance than a bad translation of Bertolt Brecht.

INTERVIEWER: Do you feel that Hollywood is any better as a place for the writer?
INGE: No, not at all. A writer may be able to work here for a short time if he's got a unique idea with commercial possibilities. To spend your life just writing for the movies is like training yourself to become an expert secretary.

INTERVIEWER: What about your film *Splendor in the Grass?*
INGE: That was my first film, written after I did *Loss of Roses.* We did the whole thing in the east. It was the first time I had the desire to write for films. I was so accustomed to the theater that is was hard for me to adjust to the freedom of the cinematic medium. But I wanted to write about the transition from the high financial prosperity of the late twenties to the Depression—the social transition. It was something I had lived through. I couldn't get it on stage and was having real difficulty conceptualizing it for film until I remembered Chris Isherwood's *I Am a Camera.* That's literally what I did: I identified totally with the camera.

INTERVIEWER: Did it reach the screen the way you had anticipated?
INGE: It was about 350 pages originally. But Kazan and I wanted to remain independent in production, and the studio would back us only if we stayed within two hours. So we cut my panorama script. The boy and girl were originally just incidental. They had this youthful desire for one another but as time passed, it was ironically lost, just as the golden prosperity of the twenties was lost. They had to face realities as real people. Unfortunately, the film came off a bit like saying, "If you don't give in to the sex urge, you'll go crazy." Which is not quite what I had intended.

INTERVIEWER: Didn't you get asked to adapt your plays for Hollywood?

INGE: I didn't want to adapt my plays for movies. I just wanted to learn more about writing for the theater. All through the fifties I dedicated myself to theater. Then in 1959 I was down in Florida where I wrote most of *Splendor* on vacation. I brought it back to Kazan, who was quite surprised because he thought I was writing a play.

INTERVIEWER: You write on vacation, too? Are your working habits regular, or do you sort of write when it hits you?
INGE: I write almost every morning, except after finishing something big. I have three Smith-Corona portables I work on. I think an electric typewriter would be wasted on me; I type too slowly.

INTERVIEWER: This is an awkward question, but how do ideas for plays come to you?
INGE: I think it's something like a geologist looking for oil. I don't know exactly how *he* goes about it, but I think he senses a spot of ground that he feels is productive and so he starts drilling. I start off writing with the feeling that I've got something I need to get out of my system—something to bring form to. I think Michelangelo would see an enormous hunk of marble and see a form there, which he would chisel out. That's really it: you start with an amorphous feeling that you would like to give shape and life to in your work.

INTERVIEWER: Can you give me any examples of this?
INGE: Well, *Come Back, Little Sheba.* I had this curious aunt and uncle. They were a childless pair, and she, my mother's sister, was really an eccentric woman. I used to think of her a lot and their relationship kind of fascinated me. The first thing I ever did with them was a little story, which had a closeness to me that nothing else I attempted did. And when I worked with it a bit, it suddenly began to grow into shape and the characters developed separate existences. They really became living people inside me who began to act on their own. It's a magical process that Pirandello writes about so beautifully in *Six Characters in Search of an Author.* You write a line for them that's wrong, then that character will

say, "No, that's not right for me. You have to give me a different line here." I guess any good novel or play writes the author.
He doesn't write it. Certainly there is a difference between an
organic play like that and a formula, craftsman's play.

INTERVIEWER: Did *Bus Stop* come to you that way?

INGE: Well, yes: I got the idea for that from an experience
I had teaching at Stephens College, which is in Missouri halfway between Kansas City and St. Louis. Sometimes I'd take a
weekend trip to either city on the bus. Once I got on the bus
to Kansas City and there was a young man, kind of a vagrant,
who was pursuing this girl. They were both alone, and there
were two or three rest stops between Columbia and Kansas
City. At each stop he'd sit next to her and try to talk her into
getting off the bus with him at Kansas City. I was attracted to
the situation, but the characters were my own.

Actually, *Bus Stop* is the closest thing to fantasy that I ever
wrote. It's pretty close to being a fairy tale. The town in Kansas was kind of an archetype. Boris Aronson's set was very
fanciful. The characters were types, but I was experimenting
a little, trying to give an example of each kind of love: the
earthy love, the purely physical attraction of the bus driver
for the woman who runs the restaurant. There's the corrupt
attraction of the old man for the young girl; there's a kind of
homosexual feeling the older cowboy has for the younger,
although I never thought of them as physical lovers. They all
kind of play into a pattern—the play was fun to write.

INTERVIEWER: Do you have a particular preference for any
one of your plays?

INGE: Not really, although right now I like my last play,
Where's Daddy? rather well. I thought I had taken a big step
in getting totally away from Kansas and writing about contemporary issues. I thought it was a good play. We all did—
until opening night. Everything went wrong and a year and a
half's work was bombed in twenty minutes.

It's sad that the entire American theater resides in one
man. You've got to please Walter Kerr or die. Sort of like the
Good Housekeeping Seal of Approval. One problem is that

there's no New York audience. The audiences are a group of transient tourists on expense accounts who want to see the play that's "in"—the show that's vogue. We really have an audience of sheep. The *real* audience of serious, reflective people is very small. It can keep a play running two or three months at the most.

Presently, we have a British theater in New York. The English drama is a product of centuries of tradition and now they're taking over New York because we can't compete with that kind of tradition.

INTERVIEWER: What do you mean that we have a British theater?

INGE: Just look. The only good show this year that isn't English is Albee's *A Delicate Balance*. We can't cast a play in New York anymore. Our actors are crummy; they just can't play continental drama. We don't train actors—we train personalities. They find an image they can convey and play it for the rest of their lives—look at Brando. Our so-called serious actors regard acting as some kind of group therapy. They still have no concept of what a *play* is. I wish someone would institute a class in dramatic literature for all actors. Then they could see the play as a work of art rather than a vehicle which they can exploit for their own personal problems.

INTERVIEWER: Where does some solution to the Broadway dilemma lie, as you see it?

INGE: I read somewhere, in Robert Graves I think, about a tribe which created gods in order to destroy them. I think that the instant a person becomes famous in America a machine is set in motion to destroy him. If you look at the personal lives of people in the theater in this country most of them are despairingly unhappy people. Some of our most talented actors are miserable. We have no future or security to offer them. We still think of our artists in the *La Bohème* portrait. America can't believe in the artist as a working man. He becomes famous, but he's not respected. I think it's time now that we get respected and quit being famous.

Interviewed by DIGBY DIEHL, 1967

JOE ORTON

Joe Orton's plays are funny. Before his untimely death (shortly after this interview took place), at the age of thirty-four, he was surely the nearest to a writer of farce working in the serious theater in England. Orton had style; he was not afraid of artificiality in dialogue, nor was he at all pretentious or "committed."

At the time of this interview, he had had two plays, Entertaining Mr. Sloane and Loot, successfully put on in London. Both were critical and box office hits, though when Loot was given a pre-London run in a much-truncated form a few years earlier, it got no nearer to London than Golders Green—which, in theatrical terms, might well have been Aberdeen. His first play, The Ruffian on the Stair, a one acter, received a Sunday Night production without decor at the Royal Court Theatre.

When I visited him, Orton lived in Islington in London, in what was probably termed a flatlet, though he had his own front door. His room had yellow walls and a red and gray ceiling. The walls were covered with innumerable color pictures extracted from magazines: he had created a Christian cross by cutting out reproductions of icons, plus a gorilla. There was a poster for Loot, and one for Seid Nett Zu Mr. Sloane. The room had two single beds, scores of records, a huge television set, some books, a pair of shoes under a bed. All very neat, very tidy. When I arrived, Orton was on the phone, giving Sheila Ballantine, the leading actress in Loot, instructions as to how to reach his house. It was extremely easy to find, but he also had given me complicated directions. He told her he must ring off, as he was being interviewed for the Inter-

national Review. *She replied that she had never heard of it,*
but that it sounded very grand. He put down the phone, then
donned a purple tie, saying he couldn't possibly be interviewed
not wearing a tie. The tape recorder was set up, and Joe Orton
settled into an armchair. . . .

INTERVIEWER: May we talk first about what I would call, or
rather what the critics call, art theater as opposed to commercial theater. Two of the most interesting plays put on in London in recent months, to my mind, have been your *Loot* and
Charles Dyer's *Staircase.* It incensed me, particularly in the
case of *Staircase,* that so many of the critics said that this was a
commercial play, intending the word in a derogatory, dismissive
sense; and adding that the play would not have been performed by a subsidized company but for the fact that it gave
two strong parts to two of the company's stars.
ORTON: I gather that *Staircase* was offered to several commercial managements, all of whom turned it down. I don't see any
reason why it shouldn't have been put on in the commercial
theater. Anyway, I think this whole thing of commercial and
subsidized theater is ridiculous. There are only good plays and
bad plays. I got the same thing on *Entertaining Mr. Sloane*—
people were always saying, "Oh, it's just a commercial play."
It always infuriated me, because it wasn't; there isn't such a
thing. It was a good play or a bad play.

INTERVIEWER: Why is it, do you think, that so many critics
and directors—and audiences, for that matter—insist on cate-
gorizing plays in these two ways, quite falsely?
ORTON: I really don't know. It's quite a snob thing, of course.
When you're put on at one of the subsidized theaters, you
do get an enormous snob audience. I think people like to feel
they're being entertained and also being cultural at the same
time.

INTERVIEWER: Do you set out to write a certain kind of play?
The three plays of yours that have been produced in London
all deal with the same types of characters, from a particular
segment of society. Are you conscious of this?

ORTON: In actual fact, the "class" of my plays is going up all the time! *The Ruffian on the Stair* began by being pretty grotty and criminal; *Sloane* moved up slightly, since the characters were lower middle-class. (Lower middle-class nihilism, I was told.) *Loot* has moved up one rung more because it's now a woman who leaves £19,000 including her bonds and jewels. I'm sure you can—though I don't know that I can, yet —write about very upper-class people and make them as interesting as lower-class people. I think *people* are interesting. I was very pleased that *The Times* in its first review of *Loot* said that if you can attribute a serious purpose to the play— and of course you can—it was a plea against compartmentalization. This pleased me very much as I've always been against compartmentalization. What I wanted to do in *Sloane* was to break down all the sexual compartments that people have. It didn't entirely succeed because it's very difficult to persuade directors and actors to do what you want. When *Sloane* had been running for a while, it had got into compartments, so that Madge was the nympho, Peter was the queer and Dudley was the psycho. Which wasn't what I wanted and which wasn't what I intended at all, but people *will* put things into compartments. It's very bad in class, in sex, in anything.

INTERVIEWER: Which brings us straight onto taste. Many people have said that *Loot* is in exceedingly bad taste. Are you aware of such a thing as good taste or bad taste?
ORTON: No. You see, the kind of people who always go on about whether a thing is in good taste invariably have very bad taste. I think the English have the worst taste of any people on earth. No, I don't think there's such a thing as good taste and bad taste. Some things *offend* me, but they're rather odd things. For instance, those translations of Aristophanes by Dudley Fitts. I think they're extremely bad. They sicken me, but this is just *my* thing. They obviously don't offend a lot of people.

INTERVIEWER: It's interesting how in *Loot* a number of people are offended in that so much of the action is centered around a coffin.

ORTON: I never understand why, because if you're absolutely practical—and I hope I am—a coffin is only a box. One calls it a coffin and once you've called it a coffin it immediately has all sorts of associations. In *Sloane* I wrote about a man who was interested in boys and liked having sex with boys. I wanted him played as if he was the most ordinary man in the world, and not as if the moment you wanted sex with boys you had to put on earrings and scent. This is very bad, and I hope that now that homosexuality is allowed, people aren't going to continue doing the conventional portraits there have been in the past. I think that the portrait of the queer in Peter Shaffer's *Black Comedy* is very funny, but it's an awfully conventional portrait. It's compartmentalization again. Audiences love it, of course, because they're safe. But one shouldn't pander to audiences.

INTERVIEWER: That's the great thing about *Staircase*. You don't notice that the play is about two queers, you notice it's about two people.

ORTON: Two *people,* exactly!

INTERVIEWER: Who happen to love one another. But apparently when the production opened in Brighton for a week prior to its London premiere, audiences were outraged that their Paul Scofield (he evidently comes from Brighton) should have been subjected to such a role. They saw the characters as queers, and were shocked. It didn't occur to them they were people, human beings.

ORTON: Yes, it's very odd. Of course on this subject the English are forever striving to be great liberals. I notice that even the great champion of liberalism, *The Observer,* always refers to homosexuals as queers. They would never actually refer to colored people as niggers. Even in quite serious articles they call people queers. If someone had written a play about West Indians *The Observer* would never say, "So-and-so plays the nigger." That I think is interesting.

INTERVIEWER: Before we switched on the tape recorder, you mentioned "schools of playwrights." Do you think that today there are such things?

ORTON: No, I don't think so. Playwrights, like people, are very individual. The fact that all sorts of things are written at a certain period immediately puts you into a school. You can talk about the Elizabethan and Jacobean playwrights, but they were all quite different. I think that if any plays survive from the fifties and sixties then their authors will be put into a school, but only because they were writing at about the same time.

INTERVIEWER: But I'd have thought that you, almost more than any other playwright today, have avoided being categorized along with others of your contemporaries?

ORTON: Yes, probably. I think that's because the people I admire aren't particularly modern. I admire Voltaire. Aristophanes, I read in prose translations. I prefer these because they're literal. You don't get anybody coming between you and the playwright. I'm very conscious of what's gone before. I like Lucian and the classical writers, and I suppose that's what gives my writing a difference, an old-fashioned classical education! Which I never received, but I gave myself one, reading them all in English, for I have so little Latin and less Greek.

INTERVIEWER: Do you admire particularly any playwright today?

ORTON: Beckett. And Pinter.

INTERVIEWER: Do you have "an ultimate aim" as a playwright?

ORTON: I'd like to write a play as good as *The Importance of Being Earnest*.

INTERVIEWER: You admire Wilde?

ORTON: Yes. I admire his work, not his life. It was an appalling life.

INTERVIEWER: Your plays and his have, I think, certain affinities, mainly of style and artificiality of language. I wonder if there's anything significant in that two of his plays are having all-star revivals in London at the moment?

ORTON: No. I think that's the tail end of the reaction in the theater which I hope we're finished with now. After the so-called "dirty plays controversy" the English have one of their periodic fits of morality, and I think we're seeing the end of it. We saw all those dreary Shaw revivals, and the dreary Wilde revivals, and I hope we've seen the end of it with *Staircase* and *Loot!*

INTERVIEWER: Both *Staircase* and *Loot* are highly moral plays.
ORTON: I hope so. I was quite serious saying in the program that I'm a puritan. I'm not sure that the word puritan is right but I think one can write only from that kind of standpoint. I would hate to see themes like those of *Staircase* or *Loot* done by people who . . . I don't know, it's rather pompous to say by people who haven't got talent as we have, but I would hate to see it done at the Whitehall with the kind of writing they have there, because I don't think much of Whitehall farces.*

INTERVIEWER: When watching *Loot* I had an uneasy feeling that you were extremely shocked by what you were writing about.
ORTON: No, this is quite wrong. That's like the woman who said that I only wrote about the police because I had a terrible time in prison. But in actual fact I did not have a terrible time in prison. I had a wonderful time and wouldn't have missed it for the world. It's a curious society, a pyramid, and I suddenly saw how comforting it is to be in a pyramidical society, like ancient Egypt must have been. I don't think you'd get any plays like, say, *Loot* from it, but certainly as far as living's concerned it's very comfortable. I wouldn't particularly like to do it indefinitely but it was most interesting. I certainly have nothing against the police. They're a necessary evil.

INTERVIEWER: Can we talk about the reason why you went to prison?

* I omitted at this point to inquire whether Joe Orton was aware that a number of Charles Dyer's previous plays had been produced at the Whitehall Theatre.

ORTON: Yes, libraries and library books. The thing that put me in a rage about librarians was that when I went to quite a big library in Islington and asked for Gibbon's *Decline and Fall of the Roman Empire* they told me they hadn't a copy of it. They could get it for me, but they hadn't one on their shelves. This didn't start it off, but it was symptomatic of the whole thing. I was enraged that there were so many rubbishy novels and rubbishy books. It reminded me of the phrase in the Bible: "Of the making of books, there is no end," because there isn't. Libraries might as well not exist; they've got endless shelves for rubbish and hardly any space for good books.

INTERVIEWER: Isn't this *you* deciding upon what is good, what is bad? Personal taste?

ORTON: Yes, I suppose so. But you can always say when some things are rubbish and some things aren't. I can obviously say Gibbon isn't. He said a very funny thing about books: when the Arabs took Alexandria they used the contents of the library to provide fuel for the baths and Gibbon thought that probably the books were doing more good being so used than they were when being read.

INTERVIEWER: Perhaps that's the birthdate of auto-destructive art. Didn't you deface photographs in library books?

ORTON: Yes. I did things like pasting a picture of a female nude over a book of etiquette, over the picture of the author who, I think, was Lady Lewisham. I did other things, very strange things. There was the business when I got the biography of Sir Bernard Spilsbury and there was an illustration which said: "The remains discovered in the cellar at number 23 Rosedown Road." I pasted over the illustration, which was a very dreary one of a lot of earth, David's picture of Marat dead in his bath. It was in black and white. I left the original caption underneath, so that it really did look like what it said, "The remains discovered in the cellar at number 23 Rosedown Road." This picture of the corpse in the bath had quite an effect on people who opened the book. I used to write false blurbs on the inside of Gollancz books because I discovered that Gollancz books had blank yellow flaps and I used to type

false blurbs on the insides. My blurbs were mildly obscene.
Even at the trial they said they were only mildly obscene.
When I put the plastic covers back over the jackets you
couldn't tell that the blurbs weren't printed. I used to stand
in corners after I'd smuggled the doctored books back into
the library and then watch people read them. It was very
funny, very interesting. There was a biography of Sybil Thorn-
dike in which there was a picture of her locked up in a cell
as Nurse Edith Cavell. I cut the caption from another picture and pasted it under the picture, so that it read: "During
the war I received many strange requests." One of the interesting things at the trial was that the greatest outrage, the
one for which I think I was sent to prison, was that I had
stuck a monkey's face in the middle of a rose, on the cover of
something called *Collins Book of Roses*. It was a very beautiful yellow rose. What I had done was held up as the depth
of iniquity for which I should probably have been birched.
They won't ever do that so they just sent me to prison for six
months.

INTERVIEWER: Was it the only time someone has been sent to
prison for defacing library books?
ORTON: I think so, but there has been a lot of it all over the
country.

INTERVIEWER: How old are you?
ORTON: Thirty-three.

INTERVIEWER: What did you start life doing?
ORTON: I had an ordinary sort of schooling. I left school when
I was sixteen, and went into an office. I had a number of jobs
because I kept getting the sack. When I was eighteen I went
to the Royal Academy of Dramatic Arts, where I did a couple
of years. I went into rep.—I didn't think much of rep. even
in those days—I met someone recently who knew me in rep.
and they said I was always moaning, even in rep., how awful
the theater was. This was in 1953. I gave it up after four
months and came back to London later on and did nothing
. . . got jobs . . . got a job at Cadbury's unloading things

in the warehouse; and I used to write. I was writing novels then. Of course before 1956 it was very difficult to think what you could write in a play. After then I was writing plays and novels. None of the novels were successful, none of the plays were put on. I was really occupying myself with these library books. It used to be a full-time job. I would stagger home from libraries with books which I'd borrowed and also stolen, and then I used to go back with them a couple of times a day. After I'd been in prison I wrote *The Ruffian*, which the BBC accepted, though it didn't come on until *Entertaining Mr. Sloane* had opened.

INTERVIEWER: Are you writing a new play?
ORTON: I've just finished a one act play. I'm having a rest at the moment, doing all my reading.

INTERVIEWER: You're able to live off your plays?
ORTON: Oh, yes! I was on National Assistance when *Sloane* started. They were going to send me to a rehabilitation center and I said, look, I'm having a play put on, and they said, well, we'll give you a respite then for a few months. So when *Sloane* came on I received a note saying, "We see your play has appeared, so presumably you don't want to receive National Assistance any more." Which was actually nonsense, because I'd only had the £100 advance. Anyway, it did so well I didn't have to work at anything else or have National Assistance. I couldn't work at anything else anyway. I was pretty useless at everything except writing. It takes me a long time to write plays. The one act play I've just finished—mid-November—I began in July. It doesn't just come out of my head as it appears to do; I've made about five versions of it. What I usually do is cut because I find cutting is the real thing. An awful lot of plays you could make much more brilliant by cutting, only there isn't anything there to cut. If you haven't a story and a plot you can't cut. I do all that myself, then polish and probably rewrite.

Interviewed by GILES GORDON, 1967

EDWARD BOND

Edward Bond's play, Saved, opened at the Royal Court Theatre, London, on November 3, 1965. The play hit the headlines immediately and appeared to enrage most of the critics. The Director of the National Theatre, Sir Laurence Olivier, wrote to The Observer *in defense of Mr. Bond's play; the Director of Public Prosecutions took the English Stage Society to court for showing the play not only to members. The play was directed by the Court's artistic director, William Gaskill.*

A handout from the theater had this to say about the play: "It is set in south London and shows the effects of an act of violence on a group of ordinary people. The act of violence is the murder of a baby by a group of young men, which is presented truthfully and therefore staged disturbingly. It is shocking and intended to shock but it is not, as has been suggested, sensational. The intentions of the author are unquestionably serious and, though he offers no moral solution, he poses the problem in such a way that one knows a solution must be found." The handout continued, "Unless we can use the theater as a platform on which to demonstrate the serious problems of today, particularly violence, we feel that we are not serving a useful purpose in society."

Edward Bond was born in 1936. His first produced play, The Pope's Wedding, *was presented as a Sunday Night production without decor at the Royal Court for members of the English Stage Society. Mr. Bond lives in Willesden, London, in a block of mansion flats off a main road, but would prefer to live in the country. Not being on the telephone, he is difficult to keep in touch with—a few hours before this interview took place I sent him a telegram. Before we began talking, Mr. Bond produced two willow pattern cups of tea; mine had two sugar lumps in the saucer. When he returned from making the tea he saw that I was looking at his bookcase. He told me not to think that the books represented his reading. They were connected with some particular work he was doing. Throughout the interview Mr. Bond, very quiet voiced, sat on a couch. At the beginning he seemed reluctant to say much, but after a while he spoke volubly.*

INTERVIEWER: I read in *The Observer* recently that you had spent years rewriting Chekhov. Presumably what they meant was writing imitation Chekhov?
BOND: I'm not responsible for what you read in *The Observer*. If you really read that it sounds a lot of nonsense to me.

INTERVIEWER: Do you like Chekhov? Presumably that's part of it?
BOND: Yes, I do. I'm a great admirer of Chekhov.

INTERVIEWER: That's one of the things that occurred to me when watching *Saved*; it's noticeably Chekhovian—if that's the word.
BOND: Yes, I like that, and I like it if it's true.

INTERVIEWER: I thought this because you seem to observe life, select your raw material without distortion, present it without comment. Would you agree with this?
BOND: No. It's impossible. Selection is in itself a comment, though the comment isn't "stuck on," it's implied in the development and so on of the play.

INTERVIEWER: How do you react to violence in the raw, violence if you come across it in everyday life?
BOND (*Laughing*): How do you mean, how do I "react" to it in the raw? I dislike it of course, and I really disapprove of all violence.

INTERVIEWER: I sometimes find violence on the stage much more horrifying than violence in actuality. You can see two drunken men fighting on, say, a tube platform when you get out of a train late at night and you walk past with your head averted. But when you see the same thing on the stage it seems far, far worse; partly because the play has been leading up to it and you are in a sense anticipating it; partly because you are a captive audience. Anyway, the violence comes over as being more shocking.

BOND: Could do. I expect it depends on how successful the dramatist is at portraying the violence.

INTERVIEWER: Do you think there's a risk that if violence features too often in too many plays most of the point of portraying it on the stage will be destroyed?

BOND: Recently somebody told me Oxfam shouldn't publish pictures of starving children because in the end one would just not notice them. I don't think this is true, and if it is true it makes nonsense of all human effort. One just doesn't turn away from facts because facts are frightening. There may be some people who can ignore things after they have seen them often but I wouldn't have thought that was so prevalent. Also, it's the dramatist's job always to make it fresh. Ezra Pound said, "Make it new."

INTERVIEWER: Do you think that among all the other ingredients in the play, because the violence in *Saved* received a certain amount of publicity which had nothing to do with the play itself, this may make people more aware of violence and lead them to try to do something about it?

BOND: The whole point about the violence in the play is that it was, or, at least I tried to place it, in a context. So it wasn't the act of violence that was important but the context it was put into, the consequences that came from this violence and the sort of society which the violence indicated. Just talking about the act of violence, I shouldn't think, would be much use.

INTERVIEWER: Do you agree with Ibsen that the function of the playwright is to state problems, not to solve them?

BOND: No, I don't think it's true. If a problem matters to you, you have a solution or at least you have feelings toward a solution. If you deliberately tried to cut yourself off from what you felt about it and wrote in a very dispassionate way, then I think you would probably be creating . . . well, phony art.

INTERVIEWER: But surely in *Saved* you have stated the problems as you see them and you have not gone beyond that? You haven't tried to impose a solution into the end of it, an easy way out?
BOND: No, but I think the play makes propaganda for the value of certain human feelings, certain human emotions.

INTERVIEWER: Very much so, but I still think you haven't refuted Ibsen's remark in the context of *Saved*.
BOND: I don't think that it's a true remark, as I said. It's certainly not true of Ibsen and I don't think it's true of any good writer. Or of me. Obviously, if you select a problem you have predetermined ethical ideas about the situation. This is why it becomes a problem. You're not indifferent to it. You've already got some sort of intellectual or ethical or even aesthetic suppositions about the thing. You write from that point of view. So even choosing the problem is itself a comment on the problem.

INTERVIEWER: But the treatment is obviously as important or more important.
BOND: Certainly. I would not like just to state a problem in bare terms. I think always one wants at the very least to imply certain moral values. Or intellectual values.

INTERVIEWER: What are your views, if you have any, on how language should be used in the theater today? The dialogue seems to me one of the most interesting things about *Saved*. It is much closer to some of the best poetry being written in English today; accurate and truthful, less rhetorical than in so many plays.
BOND: I like to think that. It's a very nice thing to have said. The dialogue in *Saved*, or any dialogue that I write, isn't tape recorded, though some people seem to imagine it is. It's a very highly selected and very carefully worked and reworked form

of dialogue. It has patterns of imagery and so on which re-
occur throughout the play. I would have thought it was
basically poetic but it is also, I hope, very true to life. In other
words, it's not the kind of phony poetry that you got in the
theater fifteen years ago or so, the sort of Christopher Fry stuff.
In south London they do talk a very virile and provocative and
adequate language. It can be very terse and epigrammatical; it
can be lyrical, it can be very passionate, and so on. There it is,
just waiting to be used; a real "doorstep poetry."

INTERVIEWER: I was amused to see, incidentally, that in a book
on graffiti by Richard Freeman someone refers to writing on the
wall as "the poetry of the underprivileged."
BOND: Yes, except that a lot of the poetry happens to be over-
literate.

INTERVIEWER: Do you think that plays such as yours are more
likely to get non-theater-goers into theaters than plays by writers
such as Christopher Fry, since you mentioned him?
BOND: Certainly. I think you could put on *Saved* at Blackpool
and holiday audiences would understand it and enjoy it. One
of the troubles with the theater at the moment is that its audience is too small and intellectual. Not that there's anything
wrong with that audience, it's just that other and larger audiences are needed too. The influence of the English Stage Society goes far beyond the people who've actually seen the plays
at the Royal Court: *Look Back in Anger, The Knack,* and so
on have had a very wide influence. Theater does reach out in
this way but the unfortunate thing is that very often it becomes diluted, gets served up in a half-baked version of the
real thing. I think one of the big problems of the Royal Court
is to try and get a larger reliable audience which will come
and see what they are doing just because the Royal Court is
doing it. It's curious that the plays which have in some way
been epoch-making, such as *Serjeant Musgrave's Dance* and
The Knack, all, at their first productions, had about twenty to
thirty performances. It's most odd, there's a sort of consistent audience that doesn't get any bigger than that. The critics have
a lot to do with this, of course. The present theater critics we've

got in London are absolutely inadequate. They exercise economic power, a lot of economic power, and they really could kill the modern theater movement in this country by their indifference, their hostility or their inability to respond or understand. Think of the Jacobean theater; obviously there were critical audiences, but there were no professional critics who had to write in the papers the next day or the next Sunday. The critics completely distort what is done in the theater. They completely distorted Ann Jellicoe's *Shelley*. *The Performing Giant* by Keith Johnstone is another example; what the critics wrote about it had absolutely nothing to do with the play.

INTERVIEWER: When I interviewed Arnold Wesker, he said about the critics, quoting Ibsen: "Their theories of theater will be formed in ten years' time by what I'm writing now."
BOND: That was true. Contemporary writers do have an influence on critics eventually, too late. The critics are always a decade behind.

INTERVIEWER: What's your alternative to the system, though? You're bound to have some kind of critics whether they're called critics or not.
BOND: It seems to me there's not much sense in letting the critics see the play beforehand, because although they wouldn't have to write their notices the morning after, I honestly don't think however long you gave them, that it would make any difference. You want to change them, get people who really know what's going on in the theater and then you'll get good theater criticism.

INTERVIEWER: Are you, as a dramatist, influenced at all by the critics?
BOND: I don't think there's a single contemporary critic I would agree with but there are a few who have a consistent point of view and who seem to know something of what is going on in the theater. I've knocked critics all over the place and I think one ought to, but there are obvious exceptions.

INTERVIEWER: You said recently that in the last 300 years the important things have been said in England by novelists rather than dramatists.

BOND: Yes. I think that's true. During the nineteenth century, the life, the guts, the testicles, if you like, went out of the English theater, and to a certain extent, though they were often emasculated, they went into the novel. I think that was partly because there were serious social and economic problems at the time and the sphere of literacy was confined to a small section of the community. The theater is always something which upsets people; they foam at the mouth if they don't like it. So in the potentially explosive atmosphere of the nineteenth century, when there was a great deal of economic injustice and a working class that really could have risen and cut the landlords' throats, I think there was a sort of tacit agreement not to do anything that might stimulate these things. So the theater became wet and wishy-washy and sentimental and goody-goody. It was a society safety valve.

INTERVIEWER: But do you think that at present more interesting work is being done in the theater than in the novel?

BOND: Yes, I do. You get an upsurge of scientific knowledge which changes the facts and the data and so on that one had about human nature and a result of this is to upset the orthodox image of what men ought to be and how they ought to behave. Curiously enough, this has in the past, I think, worked itself out in theatrical terms. It happened to the Greeks, it happened to the Jacobeans, and I think it's happening to us now. The theater really does seem able to go to the very heart of human experience in a way that the novel can't. You put people on the stage and they're actually *there;* they've got to move and live and *be* on the stage for a couple of hours and this in itself has to—it doesn't *have* to, you can have all sorts of theater, but the sort I'm interested in does—urge the whole experience to go to the very roots of human nature. This is the sort of thing that happens in *Lear* and *The Women of Troy.*

INTERVIEWER: Do you never feel that what you write in a play, the dialogue, becomes diluted in performance? Do you work closely with the director, for instance?

BOND: I think it's a very good thing for the dramatist to know a lot about the theater. I was fortunate because I did belong to the Writers' Group at the Royal Court for several years. In fact I actually appeared in a play at one time, a Sunday Night performance. George Devine said I was like a beacon flashing signals of distress. The first and only time I've ever acted, take my word for it! The point is, that working in a group we did tackle real theatrical problems in a theatrical way and this was immensely useful to me. It taught me a lot of whatever I know about the theater. I also saw every play that was put on in London for two years. It was quite an ordeal; it meant going twice most Saturdays. I saw absolutely everything, the lot, even the Moral Rearmament plays.

INTERVIEWER: Do you go to the theater much now?
BOND: Not so much, thank God! I can't afford to go a lot; it's very expensive.

INTERVIEWER: It needn't be. You can go to the National Theatre for three shillings.
BOND: That's true and of course it's what I used to do when I went every night and saw every show. But one gets sort of old and presumptuous and one doesn't want to. If you're earning your living as a writer, for instance, it's very difficult to find the time to queue for cheap tickets.

INTERVIEWER: How large were the audiences at *Saved*? Presumably it did quite well after it had received its publicity.
BOND: Well, to begin with it was like a great big empty barn. The slaughter by the critics just emptied the theater. After a while the word seemed to get around that it wasn't really the sort of play the critics had said and it picked up enormously toward the end. It didn't do too badly though it didn't last for very long, the usual twenty to thirty performances.

INTERVIEWER: Did you attend many of them?
BOND: I went to two or three. It's a very interesting thing to do and one learns a lot from it.

INTERVIEWER: You're writing a filmscript now?

BOND: That's right. I'm doing a film with Michelangelo Antonioni, about London.

INTERVIEWER: Are you enjoying that?
BOND: Very much.

INTERVIEWER: Do you find that, from the writing point of view, very different problems are involved?
BOND: The whole technique is completely different. The techniques that one uses on the stage are very often exactly the opposite of the techniques that would be appropriate in the same situation in a film. The sort of dialogue and movement and so on that makes for speed on the stage in fact slows down movement on the screen.

INTERVIEWER: Is this your first filmscript?
BOND: Yes.

INTERVIEWER: Were you asked to do it because of *Saved*?
BOND: I don't know.

INTERVIEWER: You distinguished in print recently between the new intellectual play and the new non-intellectual play and said that the intellectual play is all right with the critics—they'll back it up to the hilt—but the non-intellectual play, trying to do something new, they won't. How do you distinguish between the two?
BOND: The sort of intellectual play that goes down well with the critics prances around with glib, intellectual ideas, lots of references to other media and other writers, so that they can all tie up with things that the critics have read or seen before. This sort of play has nothing to do with what anybody has actually seen or experienced. That is the point: it's not an "experienced" play, it's an intellectual game. This goes down very well with critics because, of course, it's part of the critical activity.

INTERVIEWER: Yes, but isn't there some sort of dichotomy here? I suspect that *Saved*, a non-intellectual play, appealed to so-called intellectuals to a large extent, people who like to be able to say they have seen it, thus implying that they have experienced life.

BOND: I suppose that, because of the absurd performance of the critics, it did after a time become the "in" thing to see it. That's got nothing to do with the play, it's just part of the cultural prostitution that goes on in London.

INTERVIEWER: Do you think theater should be subsidized?
BOND: Oh yes, it certainly needs more money than it can get out of audiences at the moment.

INTERVIEWER: By the Government?
BOND: Yes.

INTERVIEWER: You don't think it should be able to stand on its own feet, financially?
BOND: It would be nice if it could. It can't. You can't put theater on without a lot of money. You're in a competitive field, so you've got to pay actors decent salaries to get them away from purely commercial enterprises. The theater is enormously important to the cultural life of the nation, to its life in general, its mental life. Obviously it ought to be subsidized.

INTERVIEWER: Have you any desire to write a novel?
BOND: I'm not really interested in writing a novel, although to a certain extent writing for the theater is a dispiriting thing, because of these critical morons who appraise what you do and then tell people about it and consequently stop them from going along to see it. The standards of criticism of the novel are much higher and so the novelist can write with much more intellectual and emotional honesty and reach a wider audience than you can do in the theater at the moment. That's why I knock the critics. I want to change the conditions of writing for the theater. Temperamentally, I'd rather not write novels. It was a disastrous thing that O'Casey had to do it. It was a theatrical crime that he couldn't make his living out of the theater.

INTERVIEWER: Do you think that the standards of fiction criticism may be higher (if they are!) because most novel reviewers are novelists themselves?

BOND: Could be.

INTERVIEWER: Do you think playwrights would make better dramatic critics?

BOND: I'm sure of it.

INTERVIEWER: I'd been hoping you'd say that without my asking. Do you make your living entirely out of the theater now?

BOND: At the moment, yes. Also out of films and journalism.

INTERVIEWER: And you received an Arts Council grant of £1,000.

BOND: Yes, it doesn't last all that long but it certainly helps.

INTERVIEWER: Will *Saved* be produced in America?

BOND: I'm told it'll be produced in America in the Fall. It's being produced in Vienna as part of an Arts Festival, been accepted by theaters in Holland, Sweden, Germany, perhaps France, Italy. It's doing quite well abroad. I've no doubt it'll do better abroad than it does in this country.

INTERVIEWER: Do you discuss the problems of writing plays with other dramatists?

BOND: No.

INTERVIEWER: Are you the opposite of gregarious by inclination?

BOND: I think by temperament I am; but I feel that it's an indulgence and one shouldn't be like that. I've just joined the League of Dramatists. I'll hope to make myself useful to that lot.

INTERVIEWER: Which of your fellow playwrights writing today do you most admire?

BOND: I'm interested in all contemporary writers. Wesker, Arden, Jellicoe, Keith Johnstone, Osborne, Pinter, that lot. But they don't really have any influence on me. The only dramatist

I've consciously been influenced by is Chekhov. I've been inspired, I suppose, by Euripides and Shakespeare (*laughter*) . . . and Chekhov.

INTERVIEWER: Which is where we came in.

Interviewed by GILES GORDON, 1966

ARNOLD WESKER

I interviewed Arnold Wesker at his house in Highgate, London. At the time, his play The Four Seasons *was on for the last week of its short run at the Saville Theatre. It had received irrationally bad reviews from the majority of the critics, and I expected to find Wesker bitter and resentful. Rather was he philosophical.* The Four Seasons, *a play for two characters and a love story, will, I believe, in time be recognized as the most important English play since John Arden's* Serjeant Musgrave's Dance.

Wesker's house is large, handsome and, inside, white throughout. I was told to go upstairs to his study on the top floor. On the top floor there were, I think, five white doors. No sound came from within any of them. The first two doors I attempted to open were locked. The third opened and I peered around the door. Wesker, on the telephone at a large desk, waved me in and held out his hand for me to shake as he went on speaking on the telephone. The window commanded a splendid view over Highgate. The walls were decorated with a number of pictures, photographs, drawings. Rows and rows of bookshelves were held up by piles of bricks. The day's newspapers were spread on a couch. Later I told Wesker in which of the day's papers his appeal for funds for Centre 42 * was reported. The following day he was mentioned at length in The Guardian *for having written to Kosygin requesting the release of a Russian student from an asylum. Wesker is a man in the public eye, yet above all, I would guess, he enjoys being alive.*

---

* Centre 42 was Wesker's short-lived but active theater that housed entertainments for the masses—plays, ballet, rock groups, art exhibits, etc.

*On more than one occasion during the interview he would strut
up and down the room, patting his chest and humming. He
is very small, very vital.*

INTERVIEWER: May we talk first for a few minutes about your
play, *The Four Seasons*? To start with, you were disappointed
that the critics didn't like it more than they appeared to?
Secondly, did it anger you that they discussed it, or dismissed
it in such a superior and rather patronizing fashion?

WESKER: Yes, I was appalled. It's difficult . . . on the one
hand I'm not sure whether I need simply to readjust myself
to the idea that a play of mine wasn't liked, because I have
been spoiled with high praise on my other plays, or whether
it's simply a question of accepting that perhaps it was a bad
play, or whether I really was annoyed because the criticisms
were snide and rude—just rude in many cases—and I don't
think I'm . . . well, I know—I won't stumble—I'm not the
kind of person who doesn't acknowledge criticism; on the con-
trary, I listen too much sometimes. I don't think it was simply
that it was criticized that angered me. It was as though they
were really talking about an image that someone else had
created and were attacking the image of me as a writer rather
than the play itself. And it was extraordinary that none of
them—with the exception of Mervyn Jones in *The Tribune*
and the anonymous man who wrote in *The Times Educational
Supplement*—seemed to begin to understand the sort of problems that I'd set myself as a writer or even to give me the
serious credit of having set myself problems. And I'd have
thought my previous plays, whatever their value, would have
earned me a sort of consideration from critics, that I was not
tackling something indifferently but had deliberately attempted
to explore new areas in theater as a means of doing what all
art does: recreate aspects of the human condition. But not one
critic paused to consider this.

INTERVIEWER: Did you in fact write *The Four Seasons* or think
about it in the first place because you wanted to write a play
which was different from your previous ones?

WESKER: No . . .

INTERVIEWER: Or because you actually wanted to write this specific one you did?

WESKER: No, I never decide deliberately to sit down and write a play in order to change the style or work out new forms. An idea for a play comes and when ideas for plays come they come accompanied by . . . they are tempered by one's experience of writing other plays and the new idea doesn't come and you can say, right, this is the new idea and I must work out a new form, but it comes at the same time as you have worked out other forms in your other plays so that you are prepared in a way for new forms. The two things happen at the same time and it seemed to me that the shape of *The Four Seasons* came inevitably with the subject.

INTERVIEWER: Did you originally envision it as a play? You had never thought of it as a poem or a ballet? . . . I'd have thought that of all your plays it is without doubt the one that could most easily be imagined of as working in another medium.

WESKER: Well, as a ballet. It only occurred to me after seeing the production that it could be a good ballet. Then it did occur to me that it could be set to music, but we all thought about setting it to music or at least giving it music but in a way I wanted the play to stand up on its own music, if it had any, and not rest on a composer's work.

INTERVIEWER: To go back to what I was saying a minute ago: the reason why you wrote it. As far as the form is concerned it is very different from your other plays, but were you also conscious of not writing a play about a particular cause, as you have done in your earlier plays, or did that not enter into it? Writing, in fact, a straight universal love story?

WESKER: The thing to remember about my other plays is that they were not written because I had an attitude or an ideal to expound but because I was concerned with the human beings in the situations. And the point of saying this is that primarily I am concerned with, preoccupied with, human beings. I was with the other plays and I was with this play but of course it did occur to me that in discussing, in recreating

love, a play about love, I was not going to be touching upon
social issues, and I had to ask myself the question: "Could I
do this? Is this valid in—not merely in theater, but is it valid
as part of a socialist concept of art?" And I believe I decided
it was, since if you imagine the millennium, if you imagine the
ideal state, you would soon be confronted with human problems. In fact I can make this much simpler. If I say that my
attitude to socialism, the reason why I believe as a socialist, is
not because I believe that a new economic order, when men
are not competing for survival, is going to solve problems, but
because I believe there is such a problem to being a human
being at all that to complicate it even more with economic
problems is to confront people with the wrong battle. So this
being my view of socialism it follows that once the economic
battle is over there is still the battle of being alive, of being
a human being. . . .

INTERVIEWER: Which is what the play is entirely about.
WESKER: Quite. So it didn't matter what the social background
was. And it's true that social background can affect concepts
of love and can affect marriages. The obvious example is
that poverty can help break up marriages. But it's also true
that personalities and temperaments and the very nature of
being male or female can affect marriage and love, and this is
what concerns me.

INTERVIEWER: Yes, but in *The Four Seasons* you threw over-
board all the accepted paraphernalia of what might almost be
termed a socialist play, certainly a realist play, which I thought
was very brave of you to have dared do after your previous
ones. You didn't, for instance, have either of the couple going
out to work in the morning. You showed absolutely nothing
except what was central to what you were really writing about,
how the love affair fluctuated over the year between these two
people, which I think was a very daring thing to do.
WESKER: Well, it wasn't that it was a daring thing to have decided to do, as it was perhaps daring to have let it happen once
it had started. The point at which the play begins is . . .
when people are unhappy in love a kind of depression sets in,

a kind of sickness in a way. One's been through a battle and one needs to recuperate and just as it's necessary to go away for convalescence or take a long holiday, so it seemed to me a logical and very natural thing to show two people just retreating in order to recuperate. Professors do go on sabbaticals . . .

INTERVIEWER: Some of us can't afford to.

WESKER: That's also true. Some of us can't afford to go on sabbaticals but people make their own sabbaticals, in a way, and I could have said: "All right, this is a teacher who can't afford a year's sabbatical, he can only afford a month's holiday," so one could have made it a month in a deserted house. But all . . . what you do if you make it a month in a deserted house, you take away the poetic image of the four seasons and you find something else, but you're still left with the confrontation of a man and a woman. Critics were complaining about things like the speech where he says, "One day a young man came from another country to be our guest," and so it's immediately assumed that Wesker was evading naming him; he was a vague foreigner. Well, all right, he was a Pole, but it doesn't matter. Does it increase one's understanding any more? But there was an extraordinary leap on the part of the critics to look for symbols and hidden meanings and looking at Adam as being a symbol of man. I just happen to like the name Adam.

INTERVIEWER: Perhaps it was unfortunate that you did select that name.

WESKER: I think it was unfortunate, but there are so many things one has to retreat from for fear of being misunderstood. What I decided was to plump for the simple and the straightforward, and this actually is very interesting for it ties up with other passages which were attacked, like, for instance, when she declares, in the middle of summer, "I have a golden eagle for a lover." Now people winced at that and were embarrassed, but apart from the fact that people do say this out on the Heath . . .

INTERVIEWER: Exactly, it's completely genuine and straight from life.

WESKER: Quite.

INTERVIEWER: That's not poetic in a sort of literary sense.

WESKER: Not at all. Quite. But even if I had to say to myself, right, so supposing people *do* say this, should one have it on the stage? Is it embarrassing? Is it convincing? I know lots of things that do happen in life but one decides not to present them because they just don't work. But the decision to let her say this, and to let her and him say many other things, was a deliberate decision not to retreat from just the bareness of it, the austerity of it, the simplicity of it. I could also have retreated from the simplicity of the image of the four seasons. It's not a subtle image, but it seems just too obvious to deny. We seem to be running away from so many things that are simple. . . .

INTERVIEWER: Simply because they are simple.

WESKER: Simply because they are simple. I think this is the evasion, this would be the evasion.

INTERVIEWER: I think when all's said and done probably the most alarming thing about what the critics said was not in fact what they said but their preconceptions. They went into the theater expecting to see a play by Wesker, therefore they expected to see XYZ on the stage but not seeing that they were knocked off their perches and had to start from scratch and couldn't begin to cope.

WESKER: What I can't understand is someone like Penelope Gilliatt whom, one assumed, would have had the sort of generosity—not only generosity—but the concern for development of writers to have allowed an experiment like *The Four Seasons*—but she went berserk.

INTERVIEWER: Did you write *The Four Seasons* before your other play which is so far unproduced, *Their Very Own and Golden City?*

WESKER: No, I wrote it afterward.

INTERVIEWER: Is *The Golden City* going to be produced in the near future?

WESKER: It was, but because *The Four Seasons* has been such a financial flop the management are not going to put on *The Golden City,* so we have to find other ways of putting that on.

INTERVIEWER: I have read it. I would say that as a piece of writing it is much closer to your earlier plays, though it combines some stylistic elements from *The Four Seasons.* I find it terribly sentimental.

WESKER: That's extraordinary, because I find *The Golden City* devastatingly hard and shattering in what it confronts.

INTERVIEWER: Perhaps there's too much in it. It's so much more than a play, more a universal concept of living. I can't really see it working on a stage.

WESKER: The play is not about a golden city, it's about a compromise.

INTERVIEWER: Yes, indeed.

WESKER: The idea of the city is a simple idea. It has only one essential idea that is different from the concept of other cities, and that is that the city should be built around its cultural institutions and not its administrative offices. That isn't what is important about the play, what's important is the tools that the people find in order to try and make it work and the extent to which they don't make it work. And the forces, the pressures, that make them compromise on each step.

INTERVIEWER: How do you divide your time, your life, between playwriting, and your other activities, principally Centre 42?

WESKER: It changes all the time. Before, with Centre 42 I found no time at all because of the festivals. Then when the festivals were over there was a long period of real bewilderment, because it had taken so much out of us to present the festivals that we were left in rather a battered numbed state—rather a different period in which I wasn't writing. But out of that period I began dabbling with *The Golden City* and as the routine of Centre 42 settled down just to being the routine of answering letters and working out ways of raising money,

I fitted in working on *The Golden City*. I would take off periods of three or four days to stay at home.

INTERVIEWER: You don't consciously sit down at nine in the morning and write for three hours?

WESKER: No. I must say I think I would like to. The older I grow the more monastic and disciplined I would like to become.

INTERVIEWER: Do you think in practice this isolationist approach to getting work written would work? I've always had as the ideal of my life to rush away to Cornwall and stay in a cottage and write for three months. I'm sure if I did it I wouldn't write a word.

WESKER: I think if I did that I wouldn't write a word but if the discipline is contained within one's own household this would work. In fact I'm sure it would work.

INTERVIEWER: Can I play devil's advocate for a moment and say that I see no reason why art should automatically be subsidized by anybody. Why shouldn't it, if it's good enough, pay its own way?

WESKER: There are two reasons. One is that there is too much evidence that even when it is good enough, economically it is impossible for it to pay its own way. Secondly because art should be taken out of the market. I think it should be recognized for being an experience and not a commodity, and an experience that enables a society to produce for itself, for its artists.

INTERVIEWER: Don't you think though that the risk is that people who have had little to do with art, who haven't been confronted with it and don't enjoy it or accept it as part of their lives, don't need it, will ignore it for this reason, that it is out of the market? For instance, the Ind Coope* exhibition of modern paintings which is at the moment touring some of the London pubs. Some of these are very modern paintings by

* A British brewery.

some of the most way-out British painters. Do you think this has any sort of effect on the people who go into their local to have a drink and are immediately confronted by these paintings on the walls?

WESKER: If your view of art is that the effects of it are immediate then the answer is no, it won't have an effect, it's of no value. But the effect of art isn't immediate, it's cumulative, it happens over generations. I think the idea of paintings hung in pubs, provided they're hung well and lit well, will just grow onto the consciousness of those who see them.

INTERVIEWER: I think it's terrific that a brewery is prepared to be a patron of the living artist in this way. But beyond that, if it's highly subsidized will people reject it because they don't consider it has any value?

WESKER: This has never made any sense to me at all. All the books I ever read I got out of the library free; my enjoyment of them was not hindered in that I didn't have to pay for them. What must be remembered is that you can't bring about any change on its own; it must be linked up with other things, more particularly education. You can't suddenly build, for instance, fifty Centre 42's in the country, unless you radically change the whole educational system whereby art becomes a much more important subject on the curriculum, conducted not by art masters or music mistresses but by the living artist, from the centers, which is incidentally one of the ideas of Centre 42.

INTERVIEWER: Do you think it is right that an artist should earn more than any other member of the community?

WESKER: I don't know that I can answer this except to say that every so often I sit back and realize, and am staggered, that in my eight years of being a playwright I have earned more than my brother-in-law, who is a farm laborer, will ever earn in his life. And that someone like Osborne probably has earned four or five times as much as me, and someone like Lionel Bart has probably earned ten times. No, I don't think it's fair, unless you work out another system. You must remember that, for instance, I have spent the last three years on two plays, neither of which is going to earn me any money, or much money, unless something marvelous happens abroad or something miraculous happens to *The Golden City*. The royalties from my other plays have ceased. Of course I am appalled at the amount of money that has come in and gone through, but what does happen is that suddenly when you come into an amount of money, you make up for all the twenty-odd years that you haven't had money and you gather all those things around you that you haven't had.

INTERVIEWER: I know, but even so there are millions of people who will never be in this position, who will go on working for ten or fifteen pounds or whatever a week and will never have the chance of earning a hell of a lot of money at some time in their lives.

WESKER: It's not that it's not fair that the writer should have earned the money but that it's not fair that others should be deprived.

INTERVIEWER: Would you like to see Centre 42 tied up with the Government in any way, assuming it's a Labour Government?

WESKER: No.

INTERVIEWER: Do you think it would begin to lose its identity, its individuality?

WESKER: No, it's not that. That isn't inevitable, though it may be true. The importance of Centre 42 not being an official Government body is that it can retain artistic independence. A play like *The Golden City*, for instance, which is as much a criticism of the Labour movement as anything else, is a play which Centre 42 should be able to put on without worrying about whether its subsidy is going to be withdrawn. On the other hand, I do think there should be a Minister of Culture.

INTERVIEWER: Yes. Do you think the Government should be taking more responsibility in directing the arts in this country?

WESKER: Organizationally, yes. I think we're going to have a Ministry of Culture anyway, that Jennie Lee's special responsibility for the arts in the Ministry of State, Education and Science will grow into that.

INTERVIEWER: Let's hope so. Do you write anything except plays?

WESKER: Not any longer. I used to write poems and short stories. I started a short story some months ago but I haven't taken it up.

INTERVIEWER: Why is this?

WESKER: I don't know. I enjoyed writing it. I can only imagine that wanting to write plays is just more important.

INTERVIEWER: Do you have much to do with other writers on a personal level? Do you see a lot of other writers and discuss ideas?

WESKER: No, I don't. I count people like Doris Lessing and Edna O'Brien as very personal friends, and close friends, but even Doris and Edna I see once every two months, perhaps. But there are no writers or artists who are part of . . . actually, as I think about it, apart from a handful of people I can't think that I have a circle of friends.

INTERVIEWER: And the idea of writers or any sort of artists meeting in a pub almost every night of the week is anathema to you, is it?

WESKER: No, it isn't. There are times when I would like to think that I was part of a kind of atmosphere where I could go into a pub or a restaurant and know that I would see so-and-so. The days of doing this sort of thing are in the past, aren't they?

INTERVIEWER: There seem to be a lot of people who do it. . . . Personally I disapprove—it must be because I'm Scottish or something, my Calvinistic background—I think so many artists and writers in London today waste so much time when they ought to be working, drinking themselves away evening after evening.

WESKER: I have my family also, three children, and these are very absorbing.

INTERVIEWER: Do you go to the theater a lot?

WESKER: Yes, a great deal really.

INTERVIEWER: Whose plays by your contemporaries do you

most enjoy? Do you like Osborne?
WESKER: Yes, I do. Best I think of all of us, and I've always
said this, although with the exception of just one play, none
of his works have been entirely satisfying. . . . John Arden
is the one writer I think who has the qualities of a major playwright. None of us is yet.

INTERVIEWER: Do you agree with the comment of an increasing number of critics, that the trouble with Arden is that however good a playwright he might be his plays in the theater are
boring? Which raises another question, doesn't it: how far
can a serious playwright go in the theater without being simply
entertaining in the worst sense; just keeping the audience
amused?
WESKER: "Engaged" is the word. When you use the word engaged you realize that he can't. He must engage an audience
all the time. There are passages of Arden which are boring
but I think they are only boring because what he's tackled
he's not been able to cope with. In *Left-Handed Liberty* he
didn't really resolve the problems of making theater out of
all that detail surrounding Magna Carta. But where he did
succeed he . . . soared.

INTERVIEWER: I'm a great fan of Arden's and always think,
good, I'm going to an Arden play, and then when I get there
I'm terribly bored. I except *Serjeant Musgrave's Dance* which
I am sure is a masterpiece.
WESKER: Yes.

INTERVIEWER: Anything else you particularly want to say to
the readers of the *Transatlantic Review?* You love them all?
WESKER: (*Laughter*) I don't know. I have a great temptation
to be arrogant about the critics and say: how *dare* they pit their
twenty minute considerations against an artist's work, and
really say what Ibsen did: "Their theories of theater will be
formed in ten years' time by what I'm writing now." But arro-
gance is a game actually, which one plays rather like Walter
Mitty.

Interviewed by GILES GORDON, 1966

FRANK MARCUS

Scene: the living room of a top floor London flat near Marble Arch. White sloping walls, brightly-colored furniture, a large somber painting of a building site by Auerbach contrasting with a collection of domestic trivia. Background noises are provided by three children and two cats. [Frank Marcus, interviewer, asks the questions and Frank Marcus, playwright, answers them.]

INTERVIEWER: Your play, The Killing of Sister George, has been described as "a true comedy of our time." It has also been suggested that you have used the freedom won by the avant-garde in a way which looks like achieving a great popular success. Is this a breakthrough?

MARCUS: I honestly don't know. I never tried to find a popular formula; I just wrote a play.

INTERVIEWER: But take your treatment of the problem of lesbianism—

MARCUS: My play is not about the problem of lesbianism. It concerns some women who just happen to be lesbians: a fact which neither surprises nor shocks me. I wanted my heroine to lead a socially precarious private life: I could just as easily have made her a Negress or Jewish or Irish. . . .

INTERVIEWER: I doubt if the Lord Chamberlain would have passed it, say, ten years ago.

MARCUS: He very nearly didn't pass it now! The fact that it was sponsored by a respectable organization (The Bristol Old

Vic) probably helped, and the fact that the word "lesbian" never occurs in the play.

INTERVIEWER: Weren't you taking rather a risk?
MARCUS: I was totally unaware of it. Just before I started to write it I phoned my agent, and she said: "Don't be silly, darling, it's perfectly all right. Lesbianism is legal!"

INTERVIEWER: Have you previously had brushes with the Lord Chamberlain?
MARCUS: Last year, when *The Formation Dancers* transferred to the West End from the Arts Theatre Club, all the "Christs" and "Jesuses" had to be taken out, and we had to find a more acceptable pronunciation for "La Rochefoucauld." There was also a prolonged battle over "piss off." When we proved that this term was used in *The Caretaker*, a lady from the Lord Chamberlain's office rang my management, and said: "You may reinsert 'piss off' "—but by then we had got used to "get stuffed."

INTERVIEWER: Why do you think your comedies are felt to be representative of life as it is lived today?
MARCUS: The very term comedy was ripe for re-definition. Until quite recently, it suggested laughter and a happy end and, unlike farce, an underlying seriousness or social criticism. "Happy end" usually meant the hero marrying the heroine; but that notion of happiness was demolished years ago by Ibsen. What is there to put in its stead? In the Macmillan era a win on the Premium Bonds* perhaps? Under Douglas-Home (the anarchist's favorite Prime Minister—a perfect example of non-government!) the sight on the horizon of a flock of grouse? And under Harold Wilson? "Let us raise our tumblers of Sanatogen**: the balance of payments crisis is OVER!" Slow curtain.

INTERVIEWER: But seriously . . .
MARCUS: Seriously, the only honest conclusion to a comedy

---

* Premium Bonds are like Government Bonds, but they are paid off like a lottery.
** Sanatogen is a tonic wine.

is the sense of life going on. What more *dare* one suggest? Tragedy is dead: there are no gods and heroes anymore, no destiny. In *The Killing of Sister George* the characters are drained of comedy until, right at the end, they stand naked and pathetic—as themselves.

INTERVIEWER: One critic cited *Love's Labour's Lost* . . .

MARCUS: My favorite comedy with a downbeat ending is Molière's *Georges Dandin*. I directed this play some years ago, and we made it look like Strindberg. The critics hated it, but I thought it was good. There is such passion in it: it seems to have been written in a hurry (it's in prose, not in rhymed couplets): Molière must have been bursting to get it out of his system! And the last despairing words: "There's nothing for it. If a man has an unfaithful wife, all he can do is jump in the river, head first." This at the end of a very funny comedy! In that sense, and in the sense in which I write my plays, comedy is the very last alternative to despair.

INTERVIEWER: Does this mean that you see yourself as a writer in the European tradition?

MARCUS: Very much so. I feel close—really personally close— to the great writers of comedy: from Molière, Goldoni, and Nestroy down to Chekhov, Wedekind, Schnitzler, Molnar, and Pirandello in this century. I share their attitudes, and I admire their courage. And the clowns, too, and those who could laugh even at Hitler: Lubitsch in *To Be or Not To Be*, Brecht in *Arturo Ui*, Chaplin, David Low. Using comedy as a weapon; laughing cruelty and oppression out of existence! The greater the menace, the more potent and important the function of comedy.

INTERVIEWER: What do you think were the major influences on you as a playwright?

MARCUS: Mainly, I think, a childhood spent in Germany under the Nazis—I still regard Authority as The Enemy—and all that is conveyed by the phrase "Berlin in the twenties."

You know, a few weeks ago I saw the Berliner Ensemble in *The Threepenny Opera*. I was delighted to see that the program contained a small facsimile of the program of the original production of 1928 (the year of my birth). It wasn't the cast list so much, but the advertisements! Hairdressers, wine merchants, and a literary magazine advertising in rhymes. It all came back to me—the flavor, the smell of it! I carry this little program in my wallet: it's my Identity Card.

INTERVIEWER: What else?

MARCUS: I had the same experiences as other playwrights of my generation. In fact—although I don't know them all personally—I think we are all rather similar sort of people. I expect most of us voted Labour last year (I should guess our favorite politician must have been Nye Bevan), and as a result of wartime austerity, I should imagine we are inclined to tell our children off when they play about with food. You won't find us laughing about war, or Fascism, or concentration camps. We're still inclined to be obsessed by Sex, but I expect that, in a few years' time, we'll all be writing about Power. Because, however hard we try to appear younger—standing uneasily in our Carnaby Street gear, smoothing out our wrinkles, or pulling out gray hairs—we'll soon have to face the fact that we and our friends are gradually moving into the positions of influence, that we're on the verge of being the New Establishment. And soon they'll be throwing brickbats at *us* and—poor decent sods that we are—we'll deserve them!

INTERVIEWER: Is there any single theme or obsession that is present in all your plays?

MARCUS: All my plays are about illusion and reality: about the impossibility of living either with or without illusion. There are, of course, other related themes. . . .

INTERVIEWER: In the same way as, in Anouilh's plays, the basic theme is the corruption of innocence?

MARCUS: In precisely that way. That's why I love the theater: because it's illusion made real—or is it the other way round?

Because there's a shape, a form, to a play that you cannot get in real life. "Happenings" and other experiments of the avant-garde are designed to bring the inconsequence and spontaneity of real life into the theater; my aim is the exact opposite. For better or for worse, a play should be judged as a work of art. After all, a Jackson Pollock canvas is an area of paint that can be viewed in a gallery; it's not an authentic mess on your garage door.

INTERVIEWER: It is said that your plays are sad and funny at the same time. Is this deliberate?
MARCUS: No, it's natural. That's how I see people and events. Sometimes it's a great effort to wrench myself away from a painful situation and force myself to see it from a detached (comical) point of view, but I'd hate to be accused of self indulgence. It follows that I am drawn to plays or films that have that bitter-sweet quality: plays like *Colombe* or *The Glass Menagerie,* and all those wonderful films made in France in the thirties.

INTERVIEWER: What is it in these plays and films that moves you?
MARCUS: Lovers parting, saying good-bye forever. Especially if the girl is pale and sad and sixteen—and slightly pregnant.

INTERVIEWER: Are you serious?
MARCUS: Yes, I am. I'm sorry, but . . .

INTERVIEWER: What of the future? What are your plans and ambitions? Has success made a difference to you?
MARCUS: It has made me more confident and, paradoxically, more anxious. But to a writer—especially to a playwright—success is a condition of work. The success of *The Killing of Sister George* means quite simply that the next play I write will have a pretty good chance of being staged. That, and no more.

INTERVIEWER: And your ambitions?

MARCUS: To carry on. And to go further; much, much further. . . .

He sips coffee from a ribbed pottery mug. The interviewer —as if by magic—has disappeared.

Interviewed by FRANK MARCUS, 1966

KENNETH TYNAN

London's National Theatre has its offices behind a long row of kiln-colored small houses near Waterloo Bridge. There's an archway in the middle of the row and approaching it I'd expected some monstrously imposing edifice to loom up on the other side. Instead of which I found a long brown hut, the sort building firms or advancing army divisions put up for their nomadic administrations, with small cubicles down both sides where directors, designers and the rest of the staff work. It was in one of these, three by three yards, at a generous guess, that I interviewed drama and film critic Kenneth Tynan, then Literary Manager of the National Theatre.

INTERVIEWER: Soon after I came to this country in 1957, I took a walk along the South Bank and I saw a big stone there. It was your foundation stone, apparently laid by the Queen Mother some five years previously and at first I thought it was a joke. I simply couldn't believe that this was all England had of a National Theatre. Why do you think it took so long? Was it really a distrust of state patronage and interference or just mean reluctance to shell out for the arts?

TYNAN: It has very deep historical roots. England has never had a ruling class or a monarchy to subsidize the arts. The Comédie Française was virtually created by a decree of Louis XIV and the German city states all had their civic theaters, but in England, though Queen Elizabeth went to the plays of Shakespeare, she never paid for them and though Charles II subsidized actresses occasionally, like Nell Gwynne, he never gave money for plays or playwrights or companies. The closure of the theaters by the Puritans under Cromwell left a permanent mark which it took 250 years to put right. It isn't an accident that Catholic countries have always had a more continuous dramatic tradition, because ritual, drama, song almost, the acting out of a rite, is part of Roman Catholicism, whereas it's the antithesis of Protestantism. And our Protestant background, coupled with the intense Puritan hatred of vagabonds, of painting yourself, of dressing up in other people's costumes, of anything that savored, as they thought, of the bordello, militated against official theater in England so that in the nineteenth century we were the only country in Europe with a totally commercial theater, solely concerned with putting on entertainments which the bourgeoisie would pay for after dinner. This meant musicals for the lower classes and Sir Henry Irving for the rest. Then as Irving made the theater respectable enough to obtain a knighthood in 1897, that was a breakthrough and people like Matthew Arnold and Shaw and Granville Barker began to instruct the English in the idea that the theater was a matter of public concern, not only of private profit. 1916 was the tercentenary of Shakespeare's death and everyone thought that was the obvious occasion for the opening of the National Theatre, but bureaucracy and the English being what they respectively are, it took until 1963 before public opinion could be convinced that the theater, if it was going to be really good, had to lose money and that this wasn't as near to paying for prostitution as they had formerly thought.

INTERVIEWER: Does the National Theatre in fact lose money, in spite of the heavy bookings?
TYNAN: Oh yes! At present we charge West End prices, but even if we charged ten pounds for some seats it would be very hard for us to break even. And since our job is to provide theater for everybody, we clearly can't put the prices up; in fact they're already much too high. In the first year, though we played to a very high capacity of eighty per cent, we had a loss, over and above our subsidy, of £60,000.

INTERVIEWER: Is it because rehearsals are much more elaborate than in the ordinary West End theater, or because you pay

your actors more, or because you have to pay a standing company, or what?

TYNAN: Partly because we have a permanent company. Our
object is to have a constantly changing and increasing repertoire and to do this you have to have a very large number
of actors permanently employed. Which means that if one
night we are doing Strindberg's *Dance of Death* with four
or five characters in it and the next night we have an epic
play which has a cast of sixty, on the Strindberg night there'll
be fifty-six actors paid without appearing on the stage. Similarly with the backstage staff and so on. We want to keep up
a high production rate, as we did with eleven plays in our
first year, any one of which in the commercial theater would
have had to run for about a year to show any profit. This
means that we'd have to have them running for eleven years
to pay off. And even if they're not immediate successes, we
want to keep them on the shelf for revivals which means
storage and this again costs money.

INTERVIEWER: You say that your aim is to provide theater for
everybody. Does this leave much room for experiment?

TYNAN: Yes, indeed. In the first year we did the English
premiere of a new play by Samuel Beckett and Sophocles'
Philoctetes, which had never been professionally performed in
this country. And we tried out a very ambitious play by Peter
Shaffer which demanded maximum cooperation from the director, a designer, a musician and a teacher of mime and it
could have been a disaster if anything had gone wrong. In
the future too there'll always be room in a year for one or
two experiments, which we won't expect to be smash hits and
will put in maybe for twelve performances each because they
are original works that ought to be seen.

INTERVIEWER: And what does the former audience of the Old
Vic think of your more ambitious projects? I heard that there
was some resentment.

TYNAN: Resentment perhaps of the fact that they couldn't get
in. You see we took over the old mailing list, thinking that it
would take us years to build an audience for this sort of com-

pany, and we never anticipated such an immediate and lasting rush for tickets. In the past, as Sir Laurence will tell you, during the so-called great days of the Old Vic in the twenties and thirties, they very often played to empty houses. There was a great sense of cameraderie and of fighting for art, but no audience came. Now we're not only fighting for art but also have an audience fighting to get in.

INTERVIEWER: What is your part in this? Are you anything similar to what in German theaters they call a *Dramaturg*?

TYNAN: No. The title is actually literary manager, which was a phrase coined by Granville Barker in his book on how the National Theatre should be run. He saw the job as one of planning in advance a repertoire drawn not just from the national classics, but internationally, so that at any time there'd be a balance of comedy and tragedy, ancient and modern, English and foreign in the repertoire. Also the literary manager's task is to seek out new playwrights, commission new plays or new translations of existing foreign plays, to try to save from extinction and bad translation many foreign classics which might otherwise be ruined by appallingly unactable versions which have laid waste great areas of European drama in English. Since his time, of course, a lot of other things have come into it. The theater has to have a spokesman and also someone in charge of its publications. We're publishing in the near future books about the Company's productions which I am editing and in part authoring. Also, I act as a resident critic. In a much less ambitious way of course than happened at Hamburg when the first of the great *Dramaturgs,* Lessing, was there, but acting simply as a man who'll sit in on rehearsals and then, say a couple of weeks before the play opens, write a long and extended review of it, in far greater detail than one would for a newspaper, pointing out what I as an intelligent member of the audience would think was wrong about the production in lighting, costume, interpretation, casting, everything. I act as a sort of early warning system.

INTERVIEWER: Which means that in that sense you've stayed on the same side of the footlights as before and haven't gone over to join the stage. But do you expect to direct at all? I mean you started as a producer.

TYNAN: Yes, but I found it was too much nervous wear and tear. I don't have the gifts of infinite patience combined with authority, the qualities of a chairman, in fact. I'm much too impatient, much too, how shall I say . . .

INTERVIEWER: Dictatorial?

TYNAN: Not dictatorial, but too incapable of the effort it takes to persuade people into a course of action, and, especially with middle-aged actors, I found it was too wearing for me and too wearing for them. With young people, as any director will tell you, it's different, they're not yet set in their ways. But for experienced actors I just haven't got the tact.

INTERVIEWER: This impatience of yours came out and was even perhaps useful in your drama criticism, which was trenchant and at times vitriolic. Don't you miss reviewing?

TYNAN: I just can't do it. I'd been for years, as a drama critic, plugging the idea of subsidized theater and of the National Theatre in particular and when Olivier was appointed director and asked me if I wanted to come in to help, it would have been a terrible act of cowardice if I'd said no. But it meant that I couldn't go on reviewing other people's plays without sooner or later being accused of unfairness.

INTERVIEWER: But don't you miss it? I mean do you feel, reviewing films, that you're as much in the thick of something moving and alive as you were in the theater?

TYNAN: I think that the film industry outside England is much more alive than the West End theater as a whole. In England the film industry is virtually dead, simply blocked by an economic situation which would require heavy legislation to cure, and the theater has more openings for someone interested in building something new. But I think if you're a critic and you want to be exposed to the best that's happening in European culture, then you'd better be a film critic.

INTERVIEWER: That's interesting because in 1954 you wrote: "It is a sad truth that nowadays our intellectuals go to the cinema and shun the theater. . . . Their defection is my opportunity."

TYNAN: I wrote that before the Royal Court and before the new English authors and actors arrived. Now I think in England, intellectuals are much more interested in the theater because the opportunities are there. Of course as soon as a playwright has any kind of a name, he'll be tempted, as Harold Pinter has been, to go into TV and films, but a young author would still think of the stage as his first opening. Europe is far more creative cinematically and a young Italian, if he is untrained and has an idea, would probably think of films. Or TV, where you'll find a lot of brilliant young authors and directors, because of the speed with which they can see their ideas translated into action. If I buy a new play here at the National Theatre, it would be hard for us to schedule it within a year, but in television, with its terrific appetite for plays you could easily say that it'll be on in twelve weeks' time. And there are contracted directors who will do it, whereas in the theater you'd have a problem of finding directors as well, because there's no school for directors in this country except that provided by TV. Young directors tend to go straight into television and from there to films, by-passing the stage altogether. This is a great handicap and I spend a great deal of my time trying to seduce people away from TV into the theater.

INTERVIEWER: Do you think it's true then, as was suggested recently (by Donald Baverstock) that if Brecht were alive he'd be running his own TV station? Would he regard TV as his medium and the medium of the future?

TYNAN: I'm certain he wouldn't, from everything he ever wrote about TV or films. Of all playwrights of this century he's the one who most demands a live audience reacting and judging what it's seeing on the stage, participating intellectually all the time. To deprive him of the theater would be to take away the framework of his art. I have no doubt that he wouldn't have objected to some of his plays being done on TV, but since part of his life's work was to break down the barrier between proscenium and auditorium, pointing out to the audience, "Look, we're just people, and you're people, we aren't real, we're only actors performing and telling a fable, don't be taken in, don't be deluded," it'd be impossible for him to go into TV, which is a great medium for persuading you that something is really happening. I should have thought that the realism and intimacy of TV would be the exact opposite of Brecht's anti-realism and dislike of intimacy.

INTERVIEWER: You mentioned that it was largely the work of the Royal Court which changed the situation in England. It has had a great influence, and Peter Hall and many of your own people have come from there, but what exactly do you think they have achieved? Haven't they as a group in some sense disintegrated and become part of a terribly clever establishment?

TYNAN: Now you see that is where I don't agree with Charles Marowitz. The point of a revolution is surely to succeed, to become the establishment and still remain fluid and experimental. Large-scale militant revolutions, like the Russian one, often turn out to be something different, but there's nothing in the idea of an artistic avant-garde which demands that as establishment it should become pompous and stale. I see no point in an avant-garde which has no ambitions beyond a tiny minority. What the Royal Court did I think was to open the door to let in an enormous amount of new actors and directors and new authors who have since spread everywhere and are working here and at the Royal Shakespeare and in TV and their influence has changed the whole cultural and theatrical balance of this country. Had they all stayed at the Court and worked for an audience of 700 people, that I think would have been crippling to their development. There's a natural desire on the part of the artist to reach a great many people and it doesn't necessarily harm his talent.

INTERVIEWER: No, but the thing was that at the time there existed a very large bulk of the English audience which Terence Rattigan and you after him called Aunt Edna, an audience that just would not take the sort of thing which the Royal Court provided, and this was why they were playing to a minority. Taste must have changed since.

TYNAN: I think it's a different audience. One of the failures of the commercial West End theater had been that it had never thought of attracting a young audience. It assumed that there'd be a permanently middle-aged audience coming to see permanently middle-aged plays. Then they began to realize, about ten years ago, that there were new young people, brought up under the Education Act during the war, who were much more literate and intelligent and open-minded and lively than their counterparts in the older generation had been and there was nowhere in the world of Terence Rattigan and Christopher Fry for these new people to go. But there was a great deal in the work of Osborne and Pinter and Arnold Wesker that they wanted to see. So the West End began to find this new audience being attracted to the new authors. Then with the arrival of the subsidized theaters, Harold Pinter went to the Royal Shakespeare with his work, Osborne has remained with the Court as a founder member and is also doing a play for us. By now the trouble is that the new authors and actors too have begun to desert the West End theaters, and if there's a young and intelligent audience, it's going to the Royal Shakespeare or the Court or coming here, and the commercial managements haven't yet found the authors and actors who are in step with the times.

INTERVIEWER: Do you think this new audience has opened the way for the political play, which was very much out at the beginning of the fifties?

TYNAN: I'm certain it has. Even if only in a negative way, because it would be impossible now to have a serious or even half-serious play which presented the working classes as jibbering comic imbeciles. That's no longer conceivable; but it was certainly conceivable in the Rattigan-Fry period.

INTERVIEWER: Yes, but that's more a matter of social attitude. I'm talking about the play of political ideas, political drama, which you yourself were very much against.

TYNAN: Was I?

INTERVIEWER: At the beginning of your career. Then you changed your mind around 1954 or 1955.

TYNAN: Yes, I did, simply because I'd seen good political plays for the first time, and by that I mean ones that aren't purely political. There could be no such thing as a good *purely* political play because politics are the microcosm of lots of forces, social and psychological, and having to do with morals and religion, which are crystallized in politics. Until I really got to grips with Brecht and saw that it was possible to write political drama which was on a human scale and yet involved social and economic forces beyond the individual, until I saw Brecht and his company at work, I hadn't realized this could be done. Now I think it can, but I still believe it requires greater powers of social analysis than most young authors have.

INTERVIEWER: What about something like *The Crucible,* which you thrashed in 1954 and the National Theatre produced last year?

TYNAN: When I saw it in New York for the first time, it was clearly a play that was directed for a specific purpose, to provide a parallel with the McCarthy situation, and I attacked it because it was not an accurate parallel. I mean there were Communists, but there had been no witches. Now, ten years afterward, when we can forget about the specific political situation that had engendered it, and see the play in detachment as a general study in hysteria, it becomes a much better play as the political relevance recedes.

INTERVIEWER: You've traveled a great deal in eastern Europe, and since we're talking about politics, do you think it's valid to regard Shakespeare as a contemporary in the particularly violent political climate there, the way Jan Kott seems to?

TYNAN: I think people who read Kott in eastern Europe, or indeed on the continent, may find his theories more surprising than we do, because Shakespeare has always been played with more reverence on the continent than he has been here. We've been doing Shakespeare in modern dress and Shakespeare with a political slant for decades. To take a single example, Tyrone Guthrie's *Troilus and Cressida* would have probably outraged a German audience, but it was very clearly angled here to be an attack on a pre-First World War generation of jingoists, and it was an anti-patriotic anti-militaristic production. One could cite other examples, like Orson Welles' *Julius Caesar*, which was the kind of thing you wouldn't have seen in Germany or Czechoslovakia. You might have seen it in Russia in the twenties or early thirties, but that's about all. So I think Kott's Shakespeare as the representative of a fundamentally nihilistic world, where there are no gods and the heavens are empty and blind forces clash in the dark and leave nothing positive at the end, isn't as novel here as it might seem. Of course part of the problem with Kott is that though his theories will work in many of the plays, especially *Troilus* and *Lear,* I think none of them apply to the comedies. You won't find anywhere in Kott's work the word pleasure, and there is such a thing as writing prose and verse to communicate a pleasure in words. Kott, because he doesn't speak any English, doesn't understand that though to him a speech in *Midsummer Night's Dream* may express the release of the dark forces of the id, we who know English find this inconceivable, because nobody who could write that Titania or Oberon speech could possibly have had anything like that in mind. The linguistic barrier is there when it comes to handling words and it enables Kott to create great structures of meaning which depend on one rivet of speech, but when you look at that speech the whole thing collapses, because you realize it's not iron there, only gossamer.

INTERVIEWER: Traveling in all these countries with subsidized theaters, what have you seen you'd like to have adopted here? I mean things like the chamber theater concept and so on.
TYNAN: I think it's a good idea, but I hope in our new National Theatre here we shall have a fairly large auditorium seating about 1000 and a slightly smaller one, differently shaped, and seating say 750, as opposed to the continental idea of a huge one with 1500 seats and a tiny one with just 400. That seems to me to perpetrate the wrong idea of the theater and split the audience into two artificial camps of those on the one hand who are capable of appreciating minority plays and on the other the general plush and gilt cupid public. I think that a play that's any good can appeal to 700 people and no play can possibly be heard and seen and understood by more

than about 1000. So we've borrowed the principle but changed
the proportions. Then I do feel at times in the subsidized
theaters of Europe that a certain staleness and sameness comes
over the acting and the directors too, which isn't only to do
with security, but with the fact that the great individual per-
former can very rarely find a permanent outlet in a standing
company. He's going to seem odd, the great exception. I'd be
in favor of a double system which allowed subsidized and commercial theaters to exist side by side, because the commercial
theater, for all its ghastly faults, has been the breeding ground
of the great individualist, the exceptional human being.

INTERVIEWER: Do you mean stars or directors?

TYNAN: Both. But more specifically great actors, particularly a
great comedian, without whom the theater would be vastly
impoverished and who has never come out of a subsidized
permanent company, because the sort of things he can do are
few but nobody else can do them; he's unique in the part. I
mean when Olivier in films plays a schoolteacher, he gives a
very good impersonation, but it's clearly a great effort and it's
not convincing. What he can play are the exceptional parts,
your Lears and Othellos and Macbeths, and there's got to be
a place in the theater for him and many other actors, great
non-teamwork talents, like him.

INTERVIEWER: When you were in Russia you wrote that in
what they regarded as the healthy outlook, there was always
a way out of our predicament, and this for them made pure
tragedy and pathos unthinkable. You also wrote that if that sort
of Utopia were realized, Salinger would have nothing to write
about. Later you attacked Ionesco for being a mere symptom,
instead of looking for ways to heal. What present day playwright in your view is showing us a way to heal?

TYNAN: I don't say that he has to present the cure, but just to
diagnose expertly, so that people are aware of their problems,
and give a possible answer. Not stating their only way out, but
offering them an opportunity of understanding their situation,
of being conscious of their ills and the horrors and ordinary
pleasures of their lives, so that they can do something construc-

tive about them after leaving the theater. It's part of the progress toward controlling your environment which is called civilization. And I think that Ionesco, brilliant conjurer though he
is, only increases the obscurity and the fog by playing on the
symptoms of the ills of civilization, the inability of people to
communicate, psychological barriers and so on. That can be
great fun, but what I said in my attack on Ionesco was that
this was not the main purpose of the theater, only an interesting diversion. I mean I wouldn't be without Ionesco and I
think until he became a serious playwright, he was a tremendously good one, but as a result perhaps of these debates and
other attacks on him, he has now become a playwright of ideas,
where he's lost.

INTERVIEWER: Does Beckett then, whom the National Theatre
produced, fit your categories of moral diagnosis?
TYNAN: Certainly. He's in a sense the most moral of all playwrights in that he forces the audience to confront the basic
fact of which it's aware subconsciously but doesn't like to remember, and that is that it's going to die. And that goes much
further than the other playwrights who merely reveal the social
ills behind one's life and the political ones. The ultimate
problem is, "What the hell am I bothering to talk to you for
if we're both going to die?" And Beckett at his best, as in
Godot, is the poet of mortality. "Why should I lift a finger to
help anybody when something apart from us both is going to
kill us both?" is the question he poses. I think that you have
to earn the right to that despair and you have to be a great
sufferer, as Beckett clearly is. And one wouldn't like all playwrights to be like that. The majority must concern themselves
with problems that are less basic, but the great ones will always
have that at the back of all the other problems. Take *Death
of a Salesman.* Apart from being a social analysis and a psychological one, it's also an analysis of the fact that you have
to die at the end of it.

Interviewed by PAUL NEUBURG, 1965

FEDERICO FELLINI

All over the civilized and in most of the uncivilized world the phrase "la dolce vita" has come to mean a wasted life of wild parties, drink, drugs and orgies. So it seemed a good idea to look into the home life of the man who put that label into currency: Federico Fellini.

Fellini is hard to pin down: the communists consider him a capitalist while most of the Roman upper crust consider him a flaming communist. (He's completely apolitical.) Writers consider him the guide to new directions in the cinema; other directors consider him "literary." Half the critics consider him an upstart, a maverick genius; the other half accepts him as an "old master." He is capable of leading interviewers up many a garden path, improvising whole private mythologies to keep a stupid journalist at bay. His mutability is the only constant thing about him. "The only time Federico blushes," his wife Giulietta Masina once observed, "is when he tells the truth." He is vague about time, but has a truly phenomenal memory for faces and names. He has been called a madman, an archangel, the power of evil, Svengali, a fool, a clown, a genius, a poet, an explosion, a clunk, and, as he points out, even "a good film director." He is the enemy of all that's pretentious and pompous, but respects ceremony and ritual. He has an unquenchable monkey curiosity about everything and everybody and loves crowds and busyness. He's a tall man and his leonine head gives the impression of a rather big man, but actually he's slim. He dresses casually, and often wears a soft black hat just like Giuseppe Verdi's. His eyes are strong; they burn, they look right at you. They have been called "Satanic" and "reptilian," and have led more than one person coming

under their light, their probing, to tell Fellini he is inhuman, a
visitor from another planet. I prefer to find them living de-
scendants of the big goo-goo eyes in the Ravenna mosaics.
(Fellini was raised in another Byzantine town, Rimini.) And
they remind me that the child Fellini ran off once with the circus; the adolescent Fellini made caricatures.

"Do you lead a dolce vita?" I asked him.

"Sure," he laughed. "Drunk all day and hashish fudge parties
at midnight."

But he invited me to come to his house for dinner on a
Sunday night to see for myself.

Although he has a grand apartment in the Parioli section,
Fellini prefers to spend most of the time in a small beach
house at Fregene, the beach resort just north of Rome. It
has a well-tended lawn with flower beds, is furnished in a
brightly-colored comfortable style. He amuses himself with
painting, and in one corner of the living room is a pile of
landscapes and imagined personages. A long table was set for
twenty-five people in the living room, while in the kitchen
Giulietta Masina was whipping up a sumptuous Abruzzese spaghetti with mushrooms and all. The guests began to drift in,
and made themselves drinks from a bar under the stair. Each
time someone came in, a cat would dart in with him, and
Marcello, the houseboy, was constantly under the furniture
to catch them.

"It's time for their dinner," said Fellini. "Come and watch."

The Fellinis have three or four cats of their own, but when
the summer visitors leave Fregene in the Autumn all the aban-
doned pets and strays gravitate to the director's villa. There
were about thirty-five cats. There was one big handsome black
tom, almost blind from cataracts. There was a scarred tough
named Wallace. There were six related oddly-marked black
and whites, a horde of tabby-striped animals.

The housekeeper Fortunata appeared with an enormous
bowl, which she held while Fellini and the houseboy fed the
animals. Truth to tell, the thirty-odd waving tails made rather
a spendid sight.

"Look out," said Fellini. "Feed Tiresias first, don't let the
others get his food. Look out, Wallace has gotten into the
kitchen. Look, there's a new one, where's she come from? In a

week, she's going to increase the flock. Patience, friends, stand back!"

Giulietta opened the kitchen door and put two interlopers outside. A third got in during the action.

"Catch that one! He's the one broke the bottle. Put him out!"

"Look, somebody stole Wallace's meat, give him some more."

Marcello dived and caught him in the kitchen.

Finally, when all the cats had been fed and a tub of water placed on the kitchen stoop for them, the two servants sighed deeply and settled down to their dinner at a kitchen table, Giulietta never leaving the giant cooking pot where she mixed the spaghetti sauce.

Guests continued to arrive, cats continued to get in, a young painter retrieved them all. Finally dinner was announced and with much musical chairs activity, everyone was seated. Dinner was delicious, noisy, animated, like a scene from some mad Fellini film. I noticed that Fellini drank nothing before dinner, ate little, hardly finished a glass of red wine with his meal. The French actress kept feeding scraps to her Pomeranian; Guidarino Guidi kept smoothing the back of a household cat furious to see the dog. The painter Anna Salvatore and producer Maurice Ergas were deep in discussion of a new film project starring his wife Sandra Milo in which the actress will wear a set of blonde curls and false buttocks, playing a lady known as *La Culandrina*.

But dinner was only the prelude; the great event of the evening was the series of charades performed by two competing teams: one headed by Fellini, one by Giulietta. Elaborate rehearsals took place, and trunks of costumes and wigs came out. With such an array of talent one could only gulp out an old saw: "You should charge admission!"

And who wouldn't pay to see, for instance, a pantomime of the election and coronation of Pope Joan with Lina Würtmüller in the title role, industrialist Alberto Guidi playing the papal mule, and a college of Cardinals composed of Fellini, several writers, a ballerina, a French princess, and a prizefighter? Followed by *Maison Tellier* in which the "girls" (oh, those wigs!) were impersonated by Sandra Milo, Edra Gale, Dany Paris, a Roman baron, a famous lawyer and his wife, and a Milanese

banker! With Giulietta Masina as Mme. Tellier. Followed by
a capsule version of *Around the World in Eighty Days* and
Carmen as it might be performed in a Norwegian girls' school.
To finish, Guidarino Guidi in scenes from the childhood of
Mae West. Nothing if not exhausting, but definitely gala.
Dessert came afterwards and more cats got in.

"Well, you see," said Fellini. "That's the dolce vita."

"It's hard work. . . ."

"Of course it is," he replied. "A good charade is lots harder
work than making a film. There are no retakes. You have to
depend on intangibles."

"And it's a kind of . . . busman's holiday, wouldn't you
say?"

"No . . . maybe this is my real work, and making films is
the relaxation."

"Very Pirandellian question, like some of those reality-illu-
sion problems in 8½."

"There weren't any problems in 8½; it was a film to amuse.
Why do you suppose people always talk about 'problems' in
my films? Problems, problems, problems! There may be jokes
or enigmas but no problems. And they ask, 'What does so-and-so
mean?' Just what you see, that's what it means!"

I remembered then, that, when he began shooting 8½, he
took a little piece of brown paper tape and stuck it near the
viewer of the camera. Written on it was: REMEMBER THAT THIS
IS A COMIC FILM.

"I've just read *Fellini's New Art of the Cinema* in . . ." I
began, but he interrupted me impatiently.

"Cinema is neither new nor an art," he muttered, then looked
up. "Cinema is an old whore, like circus and variety, who
knows how to give many kinds of pleasure. Oh, they've been
trying to wash her face and make her respectable, but it can't
be done. They've brought her in off the street and propped
her up in the parlor with a thick volume of philosophy in one
hand, and an *Introduction to Freud* in the other, but she's still
an old whore. Once a whore always a whore. Besides, you can't
teach old fleas new dogs."

"You said 'not new' . . ."

"Human beings have been staring into the clouds and im-
agining 'ifs' since time began. Now they have the cinema
screen with some 'ifs' already set up to trigger their own. Think

what a bale of memories and associations and all we carry about with us. It's like seeing a dozen films simultaneously. There's memory, there's memory that's been sorted and filed, what they call subconscious. There's also the cellar of the subconscious, a subconscious subconscious. There's a kind of idealized set of sketches of the dinner party we'll go to tomorrow night. And there's also what is happening around us, visible and invisible. Fiction imposes order and invents a manner to contain life, but cinema just picks up her muddy skirts and chooses a path through chaos. She just wants to give pleasure. She solicits memory or association as easily as she does daily reality."

"Is that how you make a film: choosing a path through chaos?"

"No, first I make a chaos. Somehow the camera finds its own path, like a marker on a ouija board. Images proliferate. I always find one character turning into two or even three, or changing sex, or vanishing completely. Just like, if you'll excuse the expression, in life."

"Ah, yes. Life. *That* old whore."

"Yes. Cinema is a kind of whore's whore."

"What new whoring do you have in mind?" I inquired. He laughed, pursed his lips, sighed.

"There are three ideas that prod my fancy. I'd like to make a film of Petronius' *Satyricon*—if not of *Orlando Furioso*—and I keep thinking what a wonderful film Jules Feiffer's *Passionella* would make."

"You've never made a costume film?"

"All my films are costume films!"

"I mean, you've never made an historical film."

"No . . . how can we presume to know how people thought or felt even thirty years ago? The past and the present are other planets . . . but the *Satyricon* and *Orlando* are both 'inventions,' not historical works. I'd like to try. . . ."

"Thank you for a glimpse of your dolce vita," I said, offering a leavetaking hand.

We shook. "Now, at least," said Fellini, "you've seen the truth about the dolce vita. Anybody can do it—all you need is thirty-odd cats and a big trunkful of wigs."

Interviewed by EUGENE WALTER, 1964

HAROLD CLURMAN

When Harold Clurman talks about the theater he literally cannot sit still; he paces, gestures, shouts, thumps the table, and generally performs with the same passion and conviction that has excited his audiences for over thirty years. The vigorous intelligence that was transmitted to readers through his weekly theater reviews in The Nation *and his freelance magazine articles is amplified in person by an impressive physical vitality. This personal energy also has contributed ten years of leadership to the Group Theater; two books,* The Fervent Years *and* Lies Like Truth; *and many Broadway productions.*

At the time of this interview, Mr. Clurman had been appointed executive consultant to New York's Repertory Theater of Lincoln Center and at the outset of our conversation I asked him what his function was in this capacity.

CLURMAN: Well, I facetiously describe my function as troublemaking, but actually what they expect me to do is to advise and help to direct the company in every respect possible. I suppose one of my chief values to them is my knowledge of world theater, and they hope that I will suggest plays to be produced from the modern and classic repertory. I hope that I will stimulate the writing of plays, that I will consult with playwrights and that I will supervise the education of the actors directly through regular conferences with them and indirectly through guidance of the teaching staff. I will direct some plays—although that is really a separate function—and I will make critical comments to the company about their work. In other words, I will be a High Priest on as many levels as possible. Of course, as with many High Priests, the communicants don't have to observe my injunctions—they can be blasphemous about it—but I am there to set down at least what I think should be the law.

INTERVIEWER: Who will have most of the artistic control then?
CLURMAN: The artistic control is in the hands of Robert Whitehead, the producer, and Elia Kazan, the director. But we frequently agree, and I try to make them agree with me even more frequently.

INTERVIEWER: From what you have just said, I see that this is going to be much more than another organization for the production of plays.
CLURMAN: Yes. This is an effort to develop a real theater. A real theater in my view, is not simply a production unit; it is a collection of individuals who work in common toward a goal which becomes more articulate and representative and characteristic of the community feeling as it develops. It resembles as a collective, or should resemble, the character which the individual artist hopes to develop: so that as the work progresses, the contribution of this collective becomes clearer and has more definite character as it goes on. In other words, it isn't just an eclectic body of people who choose any script they happen to fall upon at the time, but a group with a point of view that has social and aesthetic connotations, a point of view that they all share and that they hope to make the audience share as well.

INTERVIEWER: Do you think that this is achieving pretty much what you had in mind with the Group Theater?
CLURMAN: It hasn't really achieved anything yet, except that it has already attracted a great many subscribers. It is backed by a group of trustees who have already been apprised of the fact that if they sell out every ticket during the whole season they will lose $300,000. Making people realize that a theater such as this can't possibly make money and making them accept this as a reasonable thing rather than a mad artistic demand—this is an achievement. We have two theaters under construction: a temporary theater down on Washington Square which will be used for the next two seasons and the permanent

theater which is at Lincoln Center. In that sense there are
great achievements, but not artistic achievements. The true
character, its unity and cohesion as an artistic group, is not
to be expected before two or three years.

INTERVIEWER: Is it too early to speculate about what the
theater's point of view might be?
CLURMAN: It is a little too early, I think, to formulate. But
there are certain things that I feel strongly, and so far I
haven't been contradicted about them. Mainly, that the theater
shouldn't be a library full of masterpieces, that the plays
should have a particular pertinence to our time and to our
audience. There are many fine plays that I do not think
would be suitable for the Repertory Theater, either because
they are not suitable to the audience, to the period, or to the
company that we possess. That company, of course, will develop and expand, and perhaps some people will find themselves inimical to its aims, or to its disciplines, and we will
have to supplement the company with new people. I hope this
will not happen too often and that a large part of the company will remain for five, ten, fifteen years.

INTERVIEWER: Something bothers me. I haven't sensed the enthusiasm and excitement about this Lincoln Center project that
I have about other young theater groups like the APA when
they were out at McCarter Theater in Princeton, or the group
of players led by Brooks Jones at Cincinnati's Playhouse-in-
the-Park. It seems to me that the kind of fervor that you spoke
about in the Group Theater isn't evident because the people
don't seem to have the kind of pressure; they're too established. . . .
CLURMAN: I think what you are saying is partly true. I would
say that one of the reasons—one of the things I don't approve
of—is that the actors were not adequately prepared before
the company was formed. This is what was done by me in
the Group Theater. I called together many actors for over a
year and met with groups every week and spoke to them about
my ideas, so by the time we were ready to choose a company, the people who volunteered to be a part of it were

thoroughly imbued with the ideology and the spirit we wanted to carry on; therefore, it was a very strong company. For many reasons this was not done at Lincoln Center, but I found in my first contacts with the company that a spark can be ignited, and once this is ignited, I will keep applying the flame throughout the season.

INTERVIEWER: Will the acting be primarily Method?
CLURMAN: I don't even acknowledge the term Method. I would say the acting will have to be sound acting and I don't care how it is derived. To begin with the Method is a new term. When I became acquainted with the teachings of Stanislavski, from which this is all derived, I recall it as the System. I think that the transfiguration of the System into the Method was entirely American. The differentiation I make is this: the System is a complete body of technical advice and technical means for the production of any kind of play whatsoever, from Chinese to burlesque; it has nothing to do with the realistic play. It happened that historically Stanislavski lived in the time of the realistic play: Chekhov, Gorky, and so forth. And when the Group Theater took up the System, the need was for a realistic acting, a profounder realistic acting than perhaps had existed before. You obviously don't do an Odets play the way you do a Congreve play. But there is nothing in the System which makes it inevitably a system for realistic acting alone.

Now, there is one part of the System, an early discovery of Stanislavski dealing with the affective memory of emotion, which has been seized upon in America as if it was the end-all and be-all of acting. Somehow, because of the psychological needs of the American actor as an individual—not as an actor, but as a citizen of this troubled and practically uncultured society—he has taken up this because it deals with personal emotion. The actor feels as a citizen that his personal emotion is not allowed sufficient play in a highly industrialized conformist society, and so he takes to this like a form of prayer, or a form of therapy, a form of psychoanalysis. This is a distortion of the whole system and has made a false impression on actors, directors, critics and public who have discussed the Method. The idea that Stanislavski found something new with mumbling or with imitation of nature in the photographic sense is bosh, and anybody who thinks of the system in this way is simply ignorant.

INTERVIEWER: Do you think that the Repertory Theater will be patterned after some of the European repertory theaters?
CLURMAN: It's not going to be patterned after anything except itself.

INTERVIEWER: Well, what I mean is that from what I have read, companies like the Berliner Ensemble have presented cultural reflections in a fashion similar to that which you talked about previously.
CLURMAN: No, the Brecht theater has reflected . . . is reflecting an artist: Brecht. And since he was an important artist and had much to say that was relevant and had an enormous effect upon Germany and other countries, it is worthwhile. But what he said, and the way in which he said it, was specifically his own. Our aims at the Lincoln Center are different. We may do French plays and they will be done in a style that is our translation of the spirit of the French playwright in terms of our own people, and when we do Aeschylus, we cannot possibly become like Greeks nor can we produce the play in the Greek manner. If you produced the play exactly in the Greek manner, audiences would find it unintelligible and unimportant.

That we should even be discussing these questions results from the fact that the theater has been separated from cultural thought in general. We have culture for painting, culture for literature, culture for music . . . but somehow the theater is in a separate category, and things are asked about it that are never asked about other arts. So what we have to do is get theater back into the cultural world.

INTERVIEWER: I wonder if this lack of understanding about what constitutes theater in America isn't due to an isolation of theatrical elements. For example, Edward Albee has said that the playwright's vision of a play is to be interpreted through a director and a group of actors, and that the playwright's idea, and only his idea, of the play must be seen on the stage. A director who considers himself a partner in the development of the play is overleaping the bounds of his function.

CLURMAN: I certainly don't believe that the director or the actors should distort the playwright's work. But there is a profounder truth that Albee doesn't recognize mainly because, in my sense, Albee is not thoroughly educated theatrically, though he is a very talented playwright and I admire him.

When a play is produced, the directors or actors who take the play choose that play because it expresses something in words that they feel: not because it's the playwright's play, but because it's the community's play. The theater is not a series of words, but a composite work of art involving a variety of elements; if the script is well written, the other elements will form themselves around that structure, gather their inspiration from it, and carry it out to the best of their abilities. But if they were passive and merely instruments in the negative sense Mr. Albee suggests, they would give very bad productions of good plays. What Albee is complaining about is that with plays put on only for commercial purposes, they juggle around with the playwright's work. But for that matter, the playwrights and the directors juggle around with the actors' souls which are just as respectable as what the playwright has written. And the director becomes the slave of his producer, the producer is the slave of his backers, the backers are slaves to the audience, and so forth. In other words, there's chaos.

INTERVIEWER: Getting back to the Lincoln Center, what kind of audience will you be aiming the productions at?

CLURMAN: People like ourselves: unprejudiced. Too many people want the play to be an experimental play, a surrealistic play, an optimistic play, a funny play, a sad play. We hope for people who are educated, not necessarily in college, but in the theater. We want people who are receptive, who aren't cranks, who aren't committed to a particular cultish point of view.

INTERVIEWER: It sounds to me as though you are taking shots at the Theater of the Absurd.

CLURMAN: No, I think that Beckett, Ionesco, and Pinter are important and fine playwrights and I've written complimentary reviews of their work. However, I don't like the suggestion that their plays represent the truth about life. One critic said, "Beckett gives us the universal and permanent truth." It's his truth perhaps, but not my permanent truth, nor do I believe that philosophically it's any permanent truth at all.

INTERVIEWER: In your review of *Waiting for Godot* you said that you couldn't understand the confusion of the public, the reviewers and others who found Beckett so confusing, when really the symbols, the abstractions of the play, were almost too clear, too labeled. Do you think that this is true of other Theater of the Absurd plays?

CLURMAN: I am not sure that I would say the same things about *Waiting for Godot* now because I have seen it several times since then and I see within its simplicity and clarity certain ambiguities and shades of meaning that are more complex than I had thought at first. But those things which were clear to me at first are still so clear that they should have been immediately recognized by all those people who were confused. Beckett's recent work, *Happy Days,* is even clearer than *Waiting for Godot.* I don't think that Pinter is as clear, in many ways, in *The Caretaker* as Beckett is in *Happy Days.* There are actually all sorts of interpretations for that story which is really almost a parable, although it seems to be on a fairly realistic level. As a matter of fact, the one time in Pinter's play when the meaning is clear—when a character talks about the operation on his brain—is the time when it seems to me the weakest. It helps the audience but it seems to weaken the play by spelling out a meaning. People either get confused about what is obvious or they search for rationalistic explanations of everything they see: "Why do they wait? Why don't they go and get a job?" etc. The same thing has happened to Albee's adaptation of Carson McCullers' *Ballad of the Sad Café;* there are two reactions to it. One reaction says it is very poetic, very sad, very lovely, extremely fascinating . . . but I don't know what it means. That's nonsense. It has a certain meaning which can be deciphered and stated. I tried to, and at least my explanation is very simple and clear. On the other hand people want to know, "Why does she do this, exactly?" They want it spelled out like a bill of lading. They want everything to be unequivocably logical, rational and so forth, which just isn't true to life or theater.

INTERVIEWER: What about the idea of switching genres in *The Ballad*, from the novella to the drama?
CLURMAN: Generally, when I hear that a novel is being dramatized, I'm a little reluctant to read the play. I don't even like pictures to be made from novels or plays. Mr. Albee seems to me to have done a very good job, because the novel struck me as undramatic through its lack of dialogue, its very slender, unilinear structures, all suggestion. Albee did a good job and it was difficult, but I would much rather see him do his own plays than dramatize novels.

INTERVIEWER: How do you feel about the comparisons that several critics draw between the American playwrights of the thirties and England's Angry Young Men?
CLURMAN: Well, both were motivated largely by social change, but I think the historical periods are not at all comparable. In the thirties we suffered from hunger and unemployment in a prosperous country. But we still felt a basic freedom of opportunity and had a sense of classlessness that I don't think America has ever lost. In England now, however, things are much better than they were before the war, and the economic outlook has improved. But despite the fact that they have a type of welfare state, there is no great change in class consciousness; there is no great change in opportunity. The motivations of the Angry Young Men are more complex than just that, but that is one problem. Of course, the ideas are articulated in a much different fashion. Odets was a much more lyric playwright than Mr. Wesker is. He was much less of a socialist, despite what he was always saying. He was much less sure in his heart and soul that everything can be solved. The real proletarian or Left writers of the thirties were not very good writers and not very important, because they tried to follow a line which didn't inspire much creative work.

INTERVIEWER: An interesting thing about your participation in the theater is the sense of being both an insider and an outsider, in the dual role of producer-director and critic. Has this bothered you?

CLURMAN: It isn't because I'm a critic that I'm both an insider and an outsider; it has to do with my attitude toward the arts in general. For six years I wrote about the arts for a magazine called *Tomorrow* in a column entitled "Nightlife and Daylife." It helped me to see what was happening in the world as reflected through the arts: painting, dance, theater, music, fiction, films. Because of this broad view I am sometimes considered an outsider, because I am not enough of a specialist. It isn't a question of specialization to be professional in the theater. I consider myself more professional than most theater people. As a matter of fact, most people in the theater are very poor theater people because they have so few interests outside of the theater.

INTERVIEWER: Still, some people within the theater would insist that a man acting as critic has very little to contribute to theater because everything he says must perforce be after the fact.

CLURMAN: Yes, but there are also going to be facts after the criticism: more plays and audiences enlightened by the critic. George Bernard Shaw's criticism had great value for the English theater, George Jean Nathan's criticism had a great effect on American theater. Of course, these are men who did not simply state bald opinions; whether the play is deemed bad or good is really secondary in criticism. They illuminated material, stirred thought, challenged authors to re-examine their works. Nathan had a great value in making the public more receptive to Eugene O'Neill. I'd like to be the critic of a large circulation newspaper, simply to be able to influence the theatrical education of many more people.

INTERVIEWER: Well, that's what I meant when I asked you about the Lincoln Center audience. Do you think that you can change people's tastes?

CLURMAN: We're going to try. Either the Lincoln Center will begin to change its audiences, or its audiences will begin to change the Lincoln Center. It's like the way a group of conductors insisted on playing Mahler a few years ago, despite public and critical condemnation. When these conductors persisted in their belief that Mahler should be heard, the audiences began to enjoy and appreciate his music and now he is accepted all over.

The first response to Ionesco and Beckett in the average French journal was a violent rejection of everything they had to say. As a matter of fact, Mr. Walter Kerr was a model of receptivity and enthusiasm, compared to Jean-Jacques Gautier, who is the leading critic for *Le Figaro*. But the theaters persisted and the audiences approved, and now Beckett is played at the Théâtre de France, which would have been unthinkable earlier.

INTERVIEWER: One of the most distressing things about theater, if we accept it as the performed play rather than the written script, is its fleeting, ephemeral quality.

CLURMAN: Yes, it's ephemeral, but it has permanent values and lasting effects. I don't think we understand the importance of the present; there's nothing more important than what you are doing now. There's nothing more important than life itself—it's the guarantee of a continuation. The so-called ephemeral keeps feeding the future. We're all immortal because of the way that we influence each other. If it hadn't been for all those ephemeral people before us, there would be nothing now; the ephemeral has produced the permanent.

The idea that theater is ephemeral is really scholastic—if you can't label it, put it down on record, it's ephemeral. A rose doesn't cease to smell because you can't define its fragrance. Life is a constant chaos, a constant anarchy, a constant madness, an excitement which is completely meaningless and worthwhile.

INTERVIEWER: And theater tries to make a little order of it?

CLURMAN: Everything we do tries to make order of it. We are constantly organizing chaos; but that's the fun of life.

Interviewed by DIGBY DIEHL, 1964

CHARLES MAROWITZ

I met Marowitz in London in his Regent's Park flat overlooking the canal. He was as I had imagined him. Tall, stoop-shouldered, sallow-complexioned with an unruly lock of hair hanging from his chin. He was wedged into a mutilated leather armchair surrounded by pistachio shells and half-eaten graham crackers. His left arm was in a sling and a plaster cast which started at his waist and ran, in an unbroken line, down to his right toe. His movements were still those of a young man and his animated manner of speech belied his eighteen years. [Charles Marowitz is interviewing himself. At the time, he was co-director with Peter Brook of the Royal Shakespeare Company's Theatre of Cruelty Season and drama critic for The Village Voice.]

INTERVIEWER: In recent years, with the arrival of writers like Albee, Gelber and Kopit, the American drama seems to have developed a new muscularity and drive. What, in your opinion, is the taste of modern American drama?
MAROWITZ: It stinks.

INTERVIEWER: I wonder if you could elaborate on that a little?
MAROWITZ: It smells to high heaven—like an usher's instep or the locker room of the YMCA.

INTERVIEWER: Could you develop that point a little?
MAROWITZ: The American critics have been hungering for a national genius ever since they realized O'Neill just wouldn't fit the bill. After inflating the small-scale achievements of nonstarters like William Inge (Williams and Miller both having

been played out), they hit upon Edward Albee. *The Zoo Story* and *The American Dream*, two undergraduate exercises in other men's styles, became the height of American achievement in the drama. Albee was the name that glinted out of the glossy magazines and got bandied about at swami cocktail parties in the East Fifties. He fit the bill perfectly. Young, attractive, well-spoken, and undangerous. The man himself, catapulted from the Ivy League to the Big League, began giving lectures and lessons to other would-be parodists. Europe could summon names like Frisch, Dürrenmatt, Genêt, Sartre—and Greenwich Village, backed up by the grandstanders at *Harper's Bazaar* and *Esquire,* would counter with "Edward Albee." All because of one half-assed Ionesco parody and a forty minute conversation piece full of neon-lit symbology.

INTERVIEWER: That is a bit unfair, you know. Since those days Albee has produced *Who's Afraid of Virginia Woolf?*
MAROWITZ: Thank God for that. Otherwise historians, looking back on this period in the American theater, would have thought our critics had gone completely off their nut.

INTERVIEWER: I take it then you admire *Virginia Woolf?*
MAROWITZ: It's a genuine play; a musical play; a kind of scream and variations. Fluent and well-orchestrated up to the arrival of that makeshift telegram that announces the death of the imaginary son. From then on, it becomes another version of Albee's private trauma about unwanted children, and George and Martha just hang around till that wet Hollywood finish. But the play *is* hard, knobby and comic. I'll give you Albee.

INTERVIEWER: What about Jack Gelber? Surely you acknowledge Gelber as a major American dramatist?
MAROWITZ: As somebody, I think it was Harold Clurman, said of another writer: "He can't qualify as a major American dramatist, he hasn't had enough failures."

INTERVIEWER: *The Connection* was . . .
MAROWITZ: . . . an interesting Pirandellic peep hole, propped up with jazz and made exotic with drugs, and embarrassing

with "messages" piped in from the wings. It was a giant step forward on a road that ought to be closed for repairs: namely, social-realism. For me, the most distinctive playwright to emerge from the Off-Broadway cloisters is Jack Richardson. A writer who isn't frightened of a "grand design"; a language man and a true parodist.

INTERVIEWER: You have overlooked Arthur Kopit who . . .

MAROWITZ: Kopit is an over-rated campus comedian. His one opus *Oh Dad*—I won't go through the full rigmarole of that juvenile title—*is* better than anything else, gives you an indication of Kopit's sophisticated sense of humor, has all the density of a pancake and the relevance of a Klaw & Erlanger revue-sketch. It's the thinnest of all the drifts of whimsy yet inspired by that played-out, one-joke-to-his-name, middle European farceur, Eugene Ionesco. Just the sort of play that *would* appeal to Jerome Robbins, the man for whom a superficial premise is the ideal peg on which to hang a dozen theatrical gimmicks.

INTERVIEWER: What, exactly, do you think is wrong with the American theater?

MAROWITZ: Look, I've got a short life expectancy. I can't go into all that now.

INTERVIEWER: But you can't just throw out wild statements and not . . .

MAROWITZ: I'll tell you what's wrong with it. It's too rich and it's too poor. It's rich enough to build a Lincoln Center and subsidize the archaic Actors' Studio, but too poor to keep the Living Theater alive.

Broadway, in case you haven't noticed, is no longer in the hands of anyone even remotely connected with the theater. The dim, pot-bellied producers of old were, at least nominally, in the theater. But as time went on and prices got higher, they started being dictated to by the realtors who owned the theaters and hankered after "sure fire hits." Now even they are no longer in control. The new trend setters are the fat old ladies with fancy hats who organize theater parties and guarantee six or more months of block bookings if the fare is suitably cozy and mindless. Broadway has become an adjunct of big business. It caters to the business community for whom theater tickets are an item on a corporation expense account. A "show" has become an elaborately extended gin and tonic used to break down the resistance of out of town buyers. And just as business interests support the Great White Way, so does Broadway reflect their dollars and cents philosophy. There are always an endless stream of "business" comedies and musicals. *Seidman and Son, Come Blow Your Horn, I Can Get It for You Wholesale,* How *To Succeed in Business Without Really Trying*—all frolics celebrating shysterism, petty finagling and the triumphs of business success.

INTERVIEWER: But the theater is big business. In a city like New York, it can't be anything else. And of course, its plays are going to reflect this. But although the business community supports the theater, that doesn't mean they are in charge of it. The men who run the New York theater are not from the garment industry or Wall Street; they are theater artists of long standing.

MAROWITZ: Of too long standing. That's another part of the problem. The key positions are manned by loud-mouthed, varicose-veined hangovers from the thirties. Because of them, a whole new generation is now looking toward England, France and Germany for models and inspiration. Look at your Actors' Studio and your Lincoln Center repertory and then look at the world around you. Is that "today"? Are these plays about "us"?

Our world is fragmented, discontinuous, erratic and uncertain; our theater is pat, cohesive, arbitrary and consoling. The mainstream playwrights tell us comforting white lies, and those that are socially inclined tell us disturbing half truths, but nobody tries to correlate the tempi of our life with the clatter of its meaning. And no one *can* until there is some dynamic breakthrough in form. It would have been ridiculous to ask Ibsen to express the streaming ambiguity of human consciousness within the limits of the problem play; the convention simply didn't permit it. Today, the formats are just as restricted. Psychological case histories, whether by Miller or by Williams, only simplify complicated issues and in so doing, falsify them. It is as if our stages were fixated at four-four time and any attempt to introduce a more elaborate key signature fouled up the works. The theater is not geared for complexity, but this is the nature of our present world and it is this which we have to try and interpret. And the way to begin is to say quite flatly: the means at our disposal simply are not adequate. But the New York theater doesn't say that. It says, in fact, the opposite. It says: "This was good enough for us in the thirties, and once it's freshened up and streamlined, it'll be good enough for you. Here, take Sam Behrman, William Inge, Arthur Miller, June Havoc, warmed-up O'Neill. Aren't we good to you?"

INTERVIEWER: Whatever evils you charge Broadway with there is always the adventurous Off-Broadway theater which, in recent years, has become more successful than the uptown entertainment.

MAROWITZ: The Off-Broadway theater is a giant showcase. Everybody is trying to graduate uptown. And when they get there, they use "uptown" as a showcase for films. And when they get *there*, they try to get back to Broadway to raise their prestige in Hollywood. And when they fall on their faces on the stage because they've forgotten how to act with their minds and their bodies, they're about ready for the TV series—and that, kimasovee, is the last round-up.

INTERVIEWER: But in the Off-Broadway theater it is possible for experiment to . . .

MAROWITZ: Don't give me that experiment static. The Living Theater was "experiment"—what happened to that? Here is an indigenous Off-Broadway company; it establishes a permanent company, discovers new writers, struggles for survival and then gets bopped on the head by that vicious old philistine queer, Uncle Sam. When the Writers' Stage group introduces some interesting new talent and then flounders for lack of support, there's no one around to throw them a life saver either. Of course, there is always the upbeat postmortem in *The Village Voice*, and the chance of becoming a legend in Figaro's or the St. Remo, but it's cold comfort. What *goes* Off-Broadway is *official* avant-garde—a contradiction in terms if there ever was one. Ionesco, Beckett, Genêt—all the experimenters of ten and fifteen years ago. But what about the new avant-garde? The present day writers who should be exploring territory that Beckett and Genêt never heard about. There are only the Happenings boys. Ironically, they are mostly painters rather than theater people. To most people they are looked upon as some kind of beatnik comedy relief. If there is anything to be embraced, nourished and explored in today's theater it is the Happenings movement.

INTERVIEWER: Is the picture so much better in England?
MAROWITZ: Not *so* much better, but better. Hand me a graham cracker.

INTERVIEWER: These?
MAROWITZ: Yeah, help yourself.

Now in England, as everyone knows, there was a "new wave" six, seven years ago. In its heyday, it turned out some fine writing: the early Osborne, Pinter and Behan and sturdy one-shot items by Shelagh Delaney, Robert Bolt, N. F. Simpson and Peter Shaffer. As always happens, the message has finally got through to the Majority Audience, but now it's got to be reworded. Pinter, more concerned with films at present, is turning out Pinteresque imitations; redoing television plays like *The Lovers* and *The Collection* or refurbishing undergraduate novels like *The Dwarfs*.

Osborne promises a new batch for next season. The last batch suffered from tired blood. A skimpy double bill called *Plays for England*; one, an elongated revue-sketch all about his unconscious fascination with the Monarchy; the other, a kinky cross-talk act for fetishists—more bold than it was sound. As for *Luther*, the seriousness of the subject matter and the gothic style of Luther's own speeches don't make the play any less static or verbally hung-up.

Arnold Wesker may not have shot his bolt with *Chips With Everything*, but I can't say I'm tantalized with anticipation about his next. For me, he was always a turgid bore. A kind of delayed-reaction Odets turning out dramatic simplifications that occasionally worked as theater but invariably failed as argument.

N. F. Simpson has virtually stopped writing. A tactful decision. Bolt, in between filmscripts, turns out inflated trivia like *Gentle Jack*. Delaney seems to have dried up and Behan is dead. If it weren't for Joan Littlewood and the continuing work of the Theatre Workshop company, the English theater would have to tack up an Out To Lunch notice.

INTERVIEWER: But there has been a rash of new theaters in England recently, the Mermaid, the Nottingham Playhouse, the Peggy Ashcroft, the long-awaited National Theatre.
MAROWITZ: Oh, there's plenty of real estate operations. In that, England closely resembles America. A flurry of bricks and mortar is supposed to give the impression of a theatrical revival but of course, one thing has nothing to do with the other.

So far, the "long-awaited" National Theatre company lacks any semblance of style. Which, considering its age is not so worrying, but what is worrying is the fact that they don't seem to be in any way bothered. They continue to mount distinguished plays, assuming, I suppose, that exposure to the classics will mystically engender some kind of ensemble quality.

There are two antithetical elements in the company. One is the Royal Court nucleus—actors and directors who won their spurs at Sloane Square. The other faction seems to be the Olivier elect: established reputations and external techniques which look upon the National Theatre as some splendid extension of Shaftsbury Avenue—not as elegant, darling, but much more prestigious. There is no real aesthetic or social drive behind that theater. Only a desire to be as distinguished as a "long-awaited" National Theatre ought to be.

Right now, the Royal Shakespeare Company is more important. Not because it has revitalized the Stratford Company and made a good showing at the Aldwych, but because it has reopened questions which closed minds have neglected for over three decades. Questions about how Shakespeare should be played *today*; how actors ought to be taught their craft *today*; what experiments are necessary at this particular juncture in the theater's history. Peter Hall and John Barton have done more

Shakespeare in four years than the Old Vic did in fifteen. Michel St. Denis, by creating a studio in Stratford, has made the training and (what's more important) re-training of actors respectable; Peter Brook has tossed out the concept of "experiment" as a solemn, pseudo-intense milling about in obscure masterpieces. The Theatre of Cruelty season at the London Academy of Music and Dramatic Art was, if nothing else, wild hunches, outrageous attempts *and* fun and games: elements the theater ignores at its peril.

INTERVIEWER: What do you think lies in store?
MAROWITZ: Ulcers and internal bleeding.

INTERVIEWER: I mean for the future, in the theater.
MAROWITZ: My crystal ball is out being reglazed.

INTERVIEWER: I meant, had you any ideas about . . .
MAROWITZ: You want the portentous prophecy, don't you, as no interview is ever complete without it?

INTERVIEWER: Well, if you have any feelings about . . .
MAROWITZ: All prophecies are protracted wish-fulfillments. Khrushchev says the future is red; James Baldwin says it's black; Lyndon Johnson says it's red-white-and-blue; my queer friend from Mary's Bar says it's turquoise with flecks of amber. All right, you want a prophecy? Here's a prophecy.

What I think is brewing was referred to, ominously, at the 1963 Edinburgh Drama Conference as "the death of the word." (It's not that, of course; it never could be, but it was interesting to see the panic such an idea created among writers and critics.) As the Brechtian revival was anchored in the twenties, so this tendency seems to be connected to the surrealist and Dadaist experiments of that decade, inspired, undoubtedly, by the ideas —rather than the example—of Antonin Artaud.

It is preoccupied with form—but what trend hasn't been? It admires the experiments in discontinuity conducted by the *nouvelle vague* film directors. It learns from the techniques of action painting and collage. It feels at home with William Burroughs' literary splice-ups and the American existentialism of

Norman Mailer. It gets a charge out of Happenings and finds in their immediacy and sensation something the theater needs and has forgotten.

It's the sworn enemy of psychology and psychological realism. It runs a mile from the premises of the Actors' Studio and would like to boot Ibsen and his whole school solidly up the ass. It has no patience with stylistic consistency and straitjacket narratives. It bleeds at the mouth when somebody starts telling it "plots." The play that most typifies it is *The Death of Marat*, an astounding work which successfully blends the stagecraft of Brecht with the ideas of Artaud.

Its attitude to Shakespeare and the classics can be gleaned —only gleaned—from Peter Brook's *King Lear*, Planchon's *Edward II*, Jerzy Grotowski's *Doctor Faustus* at Opole, Poland, and the *Hamlet* experiment at the Theatre of Cruelty. Essentially it has an irreverent attitude to the arts and provokes the kind of outburst Kenneth Tynan made at Edinburgh when he described Happenings as "totalitarian and Apocalyptic."

It will probably claim to be more realistic—using prefixes like *hyper, super* or *ultra* to distinguish it from nineteenth century naturalism or early twentieth century realism. One thing is certain: it will be fought every inch of the way; defended by the wrong people for the wrong reasons; vaguely despised and largely misunderstood. The tax people will try to slap an injunction on it, and the Moral Re-Armament will call it "filth," *The Times* will "question its validity" and the Old Guard is certain to call it either "arrogant," "misguided," "juvenile," or "amateurish." After riddling it with contempt and booting it with disdain, the uptown boys will want to cut themselves in for a piece. Eventually, it will become fashionable and get coverage in *Time-Life* and *Plays and Players*. Around about that point, you—you parasitic crud—will ring up to ask for an interview. Get the hell out'a here, and put down those graham crackers!

Interviewed by CHARLES MAROWITZ, 1964

RICHARD BARR

At the time of this interview, which took place in London, Richard Barr, the American producer and director, was generally associated with the plays of Edward Albee. With his partner Clinton Wilder he was responsible for the successful Broadway production of Who's Afraid of Virginia Woolf? *In 1963 Albee joined Barr as a partner and their Playwrights Unit, a workshop for new writers, has since presented first or early plays by, among many others, Sam Shepard, Megan Terry, John Guare anad Terrance McNally. Mart Crowley's* The Boys in the Band *and LeRoi Jones'* Dutchman *had their first productions with the Playwrights Unit.*

INTERVIEWER: Mr. Barr, what is the most significant movement in modern American drama?

BARR: The Off-Broadway movement. It allows us for the first time to present plays Broadway cannot, or will not support. We can produce plays for about ten per cent of Broadway costs. This has opened up a whole series of theaters where the younger writers like Albee, Richardson, Gelber and Kopit have been presented. This has brought a change in the whole style of theater in our country—away from the romantic naturalism of Williams, Inge and Miller, to a much more classic form which in some cases imitates the Europeans, but is gradually breaking away from them.

INTERVIEWER: In what way "classic"?

BARR: Classic by direct presentation to the audience. The elimination of the proscenium, the naturalistic setting, the use of narration. . . . It's moving toward the Greeks more than ever before. The social and psychological elements predominant in Williams and Miller are being replaced by a real examination of the individual.

INTERVIEWER: And the modern writer feels he must cut away the influence of the romantic naturalists completely?
BARR: Yes. I would say so. But there is also a reaction against the European plays too—the influence of Ionesco, Beckett and Genêt. We have not taken up where they left off. They are European, and we, I believe, are struggling toward some kind of style of our own.

INTERVIEWER: Yet surely the progression of Albee, through to *Virginia Woolf,* is toward naturalism . . .
BARR: Don't be deceived.

INTERVIEWER: Why?
BARR: I know what's coming.

INTERVIEWER: What is coming?
BARR: Well, there's a play called *The Substitute Speaker* and one called *Tiny Alice*—they haven't been written yet—but when they are you'll see that he's not moving anywhere near to naturalism.

INTERVIEWER: Have you any idea of what this new style of American drama will be?
BARR: I have read approximately 1000 plays in the last three years—the ones which show the most imagination are influenced more by Brecht than other writers. Primarily because of his use of narrative, his didacticism and complete freedom of settings—the aesthetics, not the politics of Brecht's theater. I believe the style is moving toward myth and satire, using original and American legends. We shall begin to accept ourselves as a nation which has some historical background and some possibility as a unity, and the satirical comment will be on how we use our heritage.

INTERVIEWER: It occurs to me that Albee's adaptation of *Ballad of the Sad Café* fits this idea; the story has a myth-like quality.

BARR: Yes, that is so.

INTERVIEWER: And Updike's novel *The Centaur*.
BARR: And Purdy's *Malcolm*.

INTERVIEWER: Have you found any plays among these thousand you have read which give a clear example of exactly what is evolving?
BARR: Well, we have Monday Night readings you know, similar to London's Royal Court Sunday Nights. And we have presented two or three plays by unknown writers which have a very strong chance. A play called *Prometheus Rebound* is one: the title gives you a vague idea—Prometheus in an ordinary American family. And another play with a sort of Adam and Eve situation. But both writers are inexperienced; to say that this sort of play created a trend would be very pretentious. Still they exist, and there are more coming in. I can't judge at this point.

INTERVIEWER: Has the Happening, as demonstrated at the Edinburgh Festival, any real significance to this new movement?
BARR: None whatsoever. I honestly believe they are anti-art—but the proponents of the Happening deny this. I don't think it's going to free or teach or influence any aspect of the legitimate theater.

INTERVIEWER: What is the dominant theme of modern American writers?
BARR: Self examination—attention to the individual. I would call it American existentialism. There is an acceptance of responsibility, the stripping of illusions, the necessity of action, as opposed to being acted upon—they are absolutely away from what the Europeans are doing.

INTERVIEWER: What illusions are being stripped by, say, Albee?
BARR: The illusion of security. The false illusion of the ability or the lack of ability to communicate, the illusion about the

reality around one, so that one does not take what seems to be reality for the reality itself.

INTERVIEWER: This is preaching. . . .

BARR: Very strongly that. I would think Edward would think that was absolutely so. Certainly he thinks of Jerry in *The Zoo Story* as a teacher. I think Edward is mildly influenced by Brecht in this case.

INTERVIEWER: But Brecht was never concerned—in fact I think he disliked it intensely—with self examination, the cult of the individual. . . .

BARR: That's correct.

INTERVIEWER: And these plays are for the cult of the individual?

BARR: I think they are, yes.

INTERVIEWER: As you said before, American existentialism.

BARR: I would say so, although I think Edward would hit me on the head for it.

INTERVIEWER: Is he against existentialism?

BARR: I don't think he thinks of it. He expresses himself— I don't think he likes to examine where he is in relation to time or other artists or toward a philosophical movement. I know he doesn't.

INTERVIEWER: In one of his speeches at the Edinburgh Festival Conference, Albee used the phrase "art is accident." Is his work based on this principle?

BARR: Without speaking for Edward, I would agree with him. By accident I think he means that it springs from the subconscious, that as you move through the world and as you grow and as you absorb experiences your psyche changes accordingly and things come from the unconscious continually, and that as they spring into the conscious mind you either use them or not. Obviously the real talents, the great artists, use them well and have a more immediate ability to capture the unconscious as it springs out into the conscious mind. I think that's what he means by accident. You don't sit down at a typewriter and say, "Now I'm going to write so-and-so." I know he doesn't do this. I understand there are some writers who can. Edward walks and walks and walks; after he's walked for a year he has the plan and then he sits and writes. That's a matter of a very short time.

INTERVIEWER: Does he rewrite?
BARR: No. Not at all.

INTERVIEWER: Are the plays of Albee, Richardson and others reaching a wide audience in America? And with what effect?
BARR: I would divide the audiences in America. There is the Broadway audience and the only new play which has really made a dent is *Who's Afraid of Virginia Woolf?* And there is a new audience of younger people, not exclusively, all over the country—in smaller theaters such as the Arena in Washington, the San Francisco Theater, and in Dallas. This new audience is really fascinated by the new plays. Broadway is going to take a little longer.

INTERVIEWER: Do you think it will be possible to transfer plays from Off-Broadway to Broadway, completely and with no damage, when this new movement has become more substantial?
BARR: I think it's possible. It has not been successful so far— but I think a change is coming. Taking *Virginia Woolf* to Broadway was daring. A three and a half hour play, by a relatively unknown author, and although Miss Uta Hagen is a star, we did not cast it with stars in mind. It was daring and it worked.

INTERVIEWER: What about the current flooding of Broadway with English successes? Many of these plays—*Luther, Chips With Everything,* and some time ago *Taste of Honey, The Hostage,* etc.,—are products of the English new wave, if hardly avant-garde, theater. Yet they are on Broadway as commercial propositions.

BARR: I think this is because of lack of imagination in producers. This is not a comment against the English theater, it is a comment against the lack of daring in our own producers to produce plays written by Americans which are perfectly valid for Broadway. It is a sign of great laziness in the American producer.

INTERVIEWER: Or poverty of courage.

BARR: True. But it is too early to judge whether or not these English plays are having an influence. I don't think they are.

INTERVIEWER: Let's talk about this plan of yours for securing performances of new plays of younger writers.

BARR: Well, we have made a move this year. Last year *Virginia Woolf* occupied all our time. Now we are concentrating on Off-Broadway projects. We have a theater in New York which holds about 185 seats—the Cherry Lane Theater—which we have leased for five years. In that theater we will do our regular Off-Broadway productions, not letting them run as long as one does if one is lucky enough to have a hit because we want to present more playwrights. Then we have a playwright's unit in conjunction with the Cherry Lane, of twenty-five of the most interesting, in our opinion, playwrights we have read over the last three or four years. We are planning to take another theater and operate what we call a Free Theater in New York. The public will be invited, first come, first served. There will be two aspects to this theater. One will be simply a workshop in which the playwright can do a scene of a play in work, or a one act, or even a full evening, if it's possible. Then we will have a more fully developed aspect, similar to the Royal Court Sunday Nights. We will do full productions, invite the public and probably play for three or four nights or even a week if we can persuade the actors to stay, because nobody will get paid anything for this.

INTERVIEWER: How about finance?

BARR: Finance for this year is just jim-dandy. *Virginia Woolf* is making a lot of money for us—it's no secret. And we are plowing it back into the theater. From *Virginia Woolf* we can afford to support all these activities. I should imagine if we didn't have a big success running on Broadway it would be more difficult and we would have to go out and get individual private financing. But I think we could do it.

INTERVIEWER: When does this scheme officially commence?

BARR: We had our first big organization meeting the day before I left New York, and I am sure that productions have now been chosen.*

INTERVIEWER: Who are the new writers to be presented?

BARR: Well, Adrienne Kennedy is one. A young Negro writer who has a play called *Funny House of Negro*. Others are James Bridges and Lawrence Wunderlich. Ex-officio members are Jack Richardson and Arthur Kopit. Although they are accused of it, none of these American writers are imitating each other yet.

INTERVIEWER: Where are the new writers springing from?

BARR: All over the world. Primarily from the United States. Now that this organization exists, it has been made possible for younger and interesting writers to sit down and write because they feel there is an outlet. Formerly they were 150,000 hours away from the possibility of ever having a play done. We are getting scripts all the time and so are other theaters.

INTERVIEWER: One last thing: what influence have the plays of Albee and Gelber and the others had on the style of the American actor?

BARR: Well, as you know, in our country we have been seriously influenced by the so-called Actors' Studio and the Method, and the use of the Method in various schools that have been teaching actors. I deplore it; I think it's an imitation of what must have been going on in Russia, and I don't feel that it serves our theater at all. It has and did serve, I believe, to an extent, the—as I call it—romantic naturalist theater of

---

* Richard Barr was in Europe attending the premieres of *Virginia Woolf* in Stockholm (directed by Bergman), Venice (directed by Zefferelli), Berlin and Zurich. The play opened in London with the complete American cast early in 1964

earlier days. But what is happening now is that there no longer is a living room, a cigarette, rain outside or a coldness or equivalent, which they seem to use rather than the author's words for conveying their talent. What has happened is that they have to get on the stage now, speak out and perform the functions of an actor, as English actors do, who are, I think, much better trained. I think that the Method actors in the United States are going to find it extremely difficult to perform Gelber, and Richardson, who is a classic writer, and Albee. They are going to have quite a time, inasmuch as they must change their whole style. The facilities for training in the United States are very poor. Experience is usually the only real teacher and you have more opportunity here for the actors to go into rep. to get their basic training. The Actors' Studio doesn't teach, you know. It is a group of presumably professionals who get together for the exploration or development of their talent. They have been developing for over ten or fifteen years.

INTERVIEWER: But shouldn't the examination of the self, important to the Method actor, serve the inner examination of the individual of the new plays? In other words, aren't they both pursuing the same idea?
BARR: Well, I would certainly think so, but I haven't seen any results.

INTERVIEWER: What divides the two? An actor's as against a playwright's egotism?
BARR: Yes, absolutely. I think that one of the problems of the Method is that it has been ignoring the playwright, and the training that actors have had in the United States has made them concentrate on themselves and on their own psychological development, which has very little to do with what the author is trying to project. I think this has caused a great schism between actor and playwright and I think that this has got to be corrected.

Interviewed by BARRY PREE, 1964

ROBERT BOLT

Until the breakthrough in modern English drama in 1956, and for a while after, it was very easy to classify dramatists as either commercial or avant-garde. But since that time a fiercely-committed Arnold Wesker got an equal run in performances with Terence Rattigan; Alec Guinness appeared in Ionesco and could have kept Exit the King *running until every Guinness fan had been accounted for. The difference therefore between, say, a John Osborne and a Peter Shaffer is no longer a matter of money, although a number of English dramatists— including John Mortimer, Shaffer and Robert Bolt—are lumped together as a sort of "commercial" group as opposed to the committed faction exemplified by Wesker and Osborne and the more individualistic Harold Pinter and John Arden (though most of the latter have shown themselves, now and then, to be capable of earning a good amount of money). The word "commercial" then, is no more than a convenient form for those dramatists who serve an existing taste in English audiences, who change discreetly as the general taste changes, growing and developing in parallel.*

Many of the "commercial" playwrights are said to be in the Rattigan tradition, though almost all of them are, in fact, more ambitious in content. The plays of Shaffer, Bolt, the late John Whiting, and to a lesser extent, John Mortimer, do have certain similar qualities and attitudes; they possess a surface elegance of structure and language, they are all free of anything which can be called sensationalism, and the personalities behind the works are elusive. Each of them would strongly deny belonging to a "group"; each would maintain the importance of not being committed; each would say that their theater dealt with human values rather than social values.

This interview with Robert Bolt was an attempt in a very brief conversation to extract his ideas and attitudes, and perhaps thereby to penetrate closer to the personality of the "commercial" playwright.

Bolt was once a schoolteacher. When he first began to write, he experimented with radio plays, with novels, unfinished ("No, I will not try again"), and short stories. He wrote at night on an upturned box in the bedroom, away from the sound of the children next door. After the success of Flowering Cherry, *he gave up teaching, shifted his family to a quiet country house in Hampshire, acquired a well set up working room and produced* The Tiger and the Horse—*another West End success. After this came* A Man for All Seasons *and the filmscript of* Lawrence of Arabia. *His new play at the time of this interview,* Gentle Jack, *was his first play in the West End for nearly three years.*

INTERVIEWER: What is the theme of *Gentle Jack?*
BOLT: Well—I don't know whether I should . . .

INTERVIEWER: This will be published after the play has opened.
BOLT: Oh well, in that case. . . . Thematically it is very ambitious and difficult. It is the life of the mind, and morality, and social order, and control, which implies repression; against the life of the body, and spontaneity, and immorality, the natural order against the social order, which implies release.

INTERVIEWER: Is it treated as a comedy?
BOLT: No. By classical criteria—a tragedy.

INTERVIEWER: And have you broken any new ground with this play—as far as form goes?
BOLT: I use the same form I found for *A Man for All Seasons.*

INTERVIEWER: That form is said to have been influenced by Brecht.
BOLT: Brecht has influenced me only inasmuch as he shows you

a theater in which things are happening and doesn't try to create a realistic impression.

INTERVIEWER: So this form you have found (the introduction of the Common Man and the economic, non-illusory staging of *A Man for All Seasons*) is just a theatrical convenience?

BOLT: Precisely. Just a means of telling the story quickly.

INTERVIEWER: Do any other modern writers influence you?

BOLT: All writers, even bad writers. One reacts. And I'm no disciple of anyone. I like X for certain qualities, Y for others, Z I find irritating but fruitful. Some modern plays in which I have found attitudes I like are *Serjeant Musgrave's Dance, The Fire Raisers* and *The Lily White Boys.*

INTERVIEWER: Do you go to the theater much?

BOLT: Not much. I go. But not enough.

INTERVIEWER: And do you read novels?

BOLT: I have orgies. Musil for instance just now. And I've been reading a lot of Dickens lately. And Powell. But I can turn away with revulsion from them and say, "This is the product of a nasty vulgar mind" and things like that because I'm not trying to write novels anymore.

INTERVIEWER: What sort of press have you had?

BOLT: In England I've had only a very moderate press; even for *A Man for All Seasons*. We thought we'd have to take it off after a month, but word of mouth kept it going and . . . in New York it has been very different. *Flowering Cherry* ran for three nights. The curtain went up and there was no one there! With *Tiger and a Horse* it was a split reaction. I tried to get too much in that play you know. A bit like an emergency pack of intellectual food, and consequently inedible. But with *A Man for All Seasons,* the New York press was unanimous. We ran for nearly eighteen months.*

* The play was, in fact, one of the most successful English plays ever on Broadway. While enjoying this run, Bolt was at the same time filmscripting *Lawrence of Arabia*—an intellectual "biggie," widely, if diversely, acclaimed.

Working on *Lawrence of Arabia* was hectic. All rather like a
rugby scramble really. Both David Lean and Sam Spiegel are
terribly experienced and professional men. I didn't know what
I was doing, but I was kept under constant pressure and enjoyed it all. I came to learn that the problems of film writing
were very like those of writing plays: classical problems—such
as telling the story, economy of language, feeding the audience
here, starving them there, etc.

INTERVIEWER: Has this experience reacted on your ideas for the
theater?
BOLT: No. It has just confirmed what I've always felt about
the importance of telling a story. I don't want to be dogmatic:
it's what interests me most.

INTERVIEWER: Will you script any more films?
BOLT: Yes. *Doctor Zhivago* again for Lean and Spiegel. Films
pay so well. I mean, if *Gentle Jack* flops, and I've been working
on it for a year, there goes a year's income.

INTERVIEWER: You've made a substantial living from the
theater?
BOLT: Oh yes. But three-quarters of it goes to the tax man. Of
course one can flee the country or become some sort of business-
man. It's another kind of life then. But even when the tax
man takes this terrible fraction away from me, I'm still earning—spending rather—a lot more than I did as a schoolteacher.

INTERVIEWER: You don't want to flee the country?
BOLT: No. I'm content this way. In a way you know, it's a good
thing. It's not possible to become a millionaire anymore as they
did once. And it stops you from trying to become a millionaire and writing that way.

INTERVIEWER: About the same time as *A Man for All Seasons*
was produced there was a spate of plays with historical settings.
Why was this?
BOLT: I think there was a general feeling of wanting something
else than naturalism, or social realism, what the critics call "the

kitchen sink." Those plays were inadequate for what people were feeling, with the bomb and everything. The times were apocalyptic.

INTERVIEWER: And probably writers sought to explain this feeling by connecting with history? Was this the stimulus for *A Man for All Seasons?*

BOLT: Yes. But it's a funk you know. Dressing your characters up in costume is Dutch courage. And because you don't know how they really behaved and spoke—what they were like traveling on buses for instance—you can give them elevated language without embarrassment. But it does allow you to write grandly.

INTERVIEWER: What do you mean grandly?

BOLT: Well . . .

INTERVIEWER: In the classical manner?

BOLT: Exactly. Writers can write grandly by giving an implied importance to what is being said. . . . I believe in the terrible cliché that there is a human predicament and everyone feels it, even if it's a matter of getting on with your wife or lover, or getting to know your children or parents, although many people deny it, and ignore it as a lot of nonsense. And you have to think about this predicament with feeling. Philosophy with feeling is poetry. And because of this predicament one asks questions. I ask these questions in *Gentle Jack.*

INTERVIEWER: And do you answer them? Do you take sides?

BOLT: Well, one answer, the only answer, is that there is no human predicament. That is the Christian viewpoint. Because man does not belong to the earth but to. . . . To try and answer this problem of the human predicament is to try and find tranquility, and of course, there can be no tranquility with the problem.

INTERVIEWER: Has *Gentle Jack* been specially written for Kenneth Williams and Dame Edith Evans?

BOLT: Well, not especially. Naturally when I was told that they wanted to appear in one of my plays, I had them in mind.

INTERVIEWER: All of your plays have had star performers— Richardson, Redgrave, Scofield and McKern, and now Edith

Evans and Kenneth Williams. Has this influenced your work in any way?

BOLT: I love stars. I like the grand manner and big personalities. Working with stars has only confirmed this liking. And naturally when you have had this experience you write big parts for big actors. There's been much criticism against the star system and justifiably too, but the star is still important . . . O'Toole for instance. When he comes out onto the stage, you can't take your eyes off him. Perhaps there's another chap on the other side, probably equally as talented, and acting his head off, but you just don't want to know. In the cinema the star system is vicious. The publicity machinery is so powerful that it's possible to make a star out of someone who's quite untalented.

INTERVIEWER: But the big stars of the cinema today seem to be stage actors—such as O'Toole and Burton. Bogart and Gable too had appeared on the stage.

BOLT: And Brando. He's a genuine star. . . . It's a force that's almost repellent because it is so strong. . . . The bigger the personality, the more a writer wants to exploit it with the right material.

INTERVIEWER: Would you like to write for a repertory theater, to be attached to a theater such as the National Theatre in the same way as writers on the continent are sometimes?

BOLT: Yes. For the Aldwych people. I have a great respect for them. They had a lot of clobbering earlier on when the avant-garde critics got at them because they were being a commercial management and wanting to fill their houses.

INTERVIEWER: Have they asked you to write for them?

BOLT: Yes. But I just can't commit myself—to anyone. It's not as much money of course, but if you're lucky, it's still quite substantial. What I like about the idea is group theater. It creates its own style. This interests me more than anything else—more than questions of commitment, etc. Style cannot be taken for granted. It is the most important thing.

Interviewed by BARRY PREE, 1964

PETER SHAFFER

Peter Shaffer, the author of the highly successful plays, *Five Finger Exercise* and *The Private Ear* and *The Public Eye,* a double bill, is a comfortable-looking man in his thirties. The comfort look is immediate, but misleading. Behind his glasses, he can subject an interviewer to a look as piercing and as illuminating, for him, as a wartime searchlight. He lives in comfortable surroundings, totally without pretension. He seems to be preoccupied with his work in much the same way as any other man who is fond of his work is preoccupied. His two most frequently used words are "obsessed" and "tension": they are used with sincerity, rather than passion.

Peter Shaffer began writing with detective novels. After an untold number of these, he switched to writing television plays: "I write plays because I feel I have to. It is the most difficult thing to do, as well. Because things happen within a certain time and one concentrates all one's efforts into precise language to wring out individuality. It is less subtle than poetry, I suppose. But more difficult than the novel." Two television plays were performed before his stage plays. The first play in the double bill (*The Private Ear* and *The Public Eye*) was originally written for television.

I asked him if *Five Finger Exercise* was autobiographical. "All art," he said, "is autobiographical inasmuch as it refers to personal experience. This is so in both the plays and in the Inca play I have been working on . . . The torment of adolescence is in all the plays, as is the essential pessimism in the face of certain death. These tensions and obsessions are autobiographical. But of course they are dressed up as stories, myths. That is theater." The "Inca" play was *The Royal Hunt of the Sun,* which he had been working on for some years.

I asked him about the critical reception given to the double bill. Generally it was very good, although it was felt that Shaffer had not progressed; that the double bill was, in fact, "smooth, lightweight" commercial theater. "I never know what is meant by progress. Is Bach more progressive than Mozart or something like that? In thirty years' time I can look back at my work and say: Was that me? Then I'll know. It all depends on the sequence of writing. If the critics found no progression in the double bill it is because it was written after *The Royal Hunt of the Sun.* The double bill was relaxation. The Inca play was hell to write. Besides, I've always wanted to write a high comedy."

"How long does it take you to write a play?"

"Four months. Usually. *The Private Ear* was written in four days, probably why I've never been happy with it. It was written over for the American production.

"It's all like those drawings of Picasso," he continued. "I do lots and lots of drafts until they become lighter, less concerned, in the Inca play, with reality, more with essentials. The last version is the most meaningful."

I reminded him of a certain criticism of the double bill. It was implied that he condescended to the working class in *The Private Ear.* Critics felt that Shaffer was more at home among the bourgeois characters of *The Public Eye.*

"They said I identified myself with Ted, who is a working-class snob. If anything, I identify myself with Bob, the other boy. Of course I wasn't happy about it. There was some cheap knock-about comedy in it. But the critics who didn't like the double bill, didn't take it for what it was intended. A *jeu d'esprit.* After all, this is a privilege of writers. Anouilh has his *pièces roses* and *pièces noires.* In many ways it was a breakthrough for me. . . ."

"It has been said that you're the successor to Noel Coward."

"I don't think of myself as successor to anyone. Of course I've had a lot of influences. . . ."

"More precisely, you're not in the avant-garde school?"

"I don't like schools. It doesn't upset me to be thought on the outside of schools."

I wanted to know exactly how he felt about not being part of the movement of writers that includes Osborne, Wesker, Arden, Livings and others. Shaffer stands apart from these, more at home in the West End than in the Royal Court.

"I don't write to a label. One playwright has written to a label and destroyed himself."

"Osborne?"

"I'd like to talk about Osborne. Is that wise?"

"Why not?"

"It is a duty to avoid a label. Not to be destroyed by being hailed as some sort of prophet."

"Like Osborne?"

"Of course Osborne hasn't destroyed himself. It would be terribly stupid of me to say that."

I kept pursuing this: "It's an interesting enough question—has the social commitment of the playwrights following *Look Back In Anger* been merely a lever, a stimulus, to writing plays? Or would these playwrights have emerged anyway, following a deeper and more profound impulse?"

"Anarchy makes art," Shaffer said—he is influenced too by Camus. "*The Rebel* is a terrific book—I think myself infinitely more anarchistic for example. Take, say, an attack on the Church. It is a waste of energy. Not because I'm afraid to attack the Church, just that I think any form of organized religion is so totally ridiculous."

"In other words, a social conscience is not enough to create good theater? Osborne's *Luther* for example—against the old Church—is a rebel rather than an anarchist. He follows the Rebel-as-Hero pattern since 1956." I wanted to know specifically why Shaffer felt himself to be above this: not in a snobbish sense by any means, but as an ordinary writer in the theater.

"Well, they all sell out. Jimmy Porter, the *Chips With Every-thing* idea, *Luther*. They all sell out in the end. It's a lack of a positive belief."

"Then what provokes a play from you?"

"It's very simple really. Take the Inca play. I felt more and more inclined to draw the character Pizarro, who is a Catholic, as an atheist, or at least as a man who explores what and who

he is. When the Church is revealed to him as being wicked
and suspect, and loyalty, friendship, is revealed as being suspect and wicked, he has a feeling of the meaninglessness of life.
It is this: what can one ultimately find to give one strength
and stability?"

"Rather fundamental questions."

"Yes, they are."

"Doesn't this thing of standing on the outside of the school
give you an extra security?"

"I'm something of a chameleon. Invisible. Besides, I haven't
a specific personality. I think I'm an introverted playwright. . . ."

I suggested that most people would think that the double
bill was the work of an extroverted writer.

"Too many people think that self pity and despair are the
signs of an introverted playwright. Behan and Littlewood—in
that she is a creator of theater—they're extroverted writers.
But like the man in *The Public Eye* says, 'Each man has lots
of things in him'. . . ."

On the often-said old-fashioned qualities of *Five Finger
Exercise* and the double bill: "Well," Shaffer said, smiling se-
curely, "as the man said, there are many tunes yet to be written
in C major. And there are many plays yet to be written in a
living room. As far as the form being old-fashioned, I suppose
it is. But *Look Back in Anger* is just as old-fashioned in form.
Anyway, form is dictated by content."

"But other writers are seeking to change forms, find new
forms."

"Keeping up with fashion is a terrible race. Fashion consciousness is superficial. I'm very grateful for the training I've
had with these two plays. I've learned how to tell a story, draw
characters, devise plausible entrances and exits. I've acquired a
technique to stand me in good stead for the greater and less
charted seas of semi- and expressionistic theater. Besides,
The Royal Hunt of the Sun has a large cast, is performed
against black drapes, using a lot of mime, has a narrator, everything—you can't get anything less old-fashioned than that!"

"Is it anti-theater?"

"No. The anti-play is a betrayal of its medium. Look at *Next*

Time I'll Sing to You. It had a genuine and important story to tell—and spent the whole time avoiding it."

"What about the anti-theater of Beckett, Ionesco?"

"Beckett created a genuine myth with *Godot.* Ionesco? No. It's all slight, repetitious. Look at *The Visit* of Dürrenmatt. Someone gets credit waiting for the murder and the rest of the play is spent with everyone getting credit, the point was made and. . . . Anyway my next play is alienated theater. It's based on the Goethe *Faust* legend and is called *Om.* It uses a Brechtian technique—but let's not use that word Brecht. I've seen performances of *No* plays in New York with the Kabuki actors using these same techniques. It's just more practical for compression to announce things, which in naturalistic theater, would take an entire evening to happen. I want to use this technique delicately mixed with naturalistic theater."

"Brecht made no secret of the fact that he was influenced by the techniques of the Kabuki Theater."

We left the theater at that point to talk about films. Shaffer did one of the versions of *Lord of the Flies.* "I was terribly disappointed that I didn't do the final script. I enjoyed working with Peter Brook tremendously—a remarkable man. Eventually he just improvised the script with the children. In films a writer is not his own master. The Americans seem to think it's better to have fifty writers rather than one. The film of *Five Finger Exercise* was a disaster. *The Public Eye* could be a good or bad film, a great Hollywood glossy, or a stylish and original comedy with players of some individuality—like *Jules and Jim.*

And some final comments: "Yes, I work very closely with directors. I over-compensate. Change everything they say. No, I wouldn't try to act. I'd like to of course. I'm too self-conscious. Yes, I'd like to direct. Perhaps I will one day. But when you direct, you have to devise. . . . I've no visual imagination.

"The theater in London? It's always stimulating. A playwright tired of the theater is like a man tired of life. But it's extraordinary how the theater remains so superficial in terms of emotional contact. Two moments in a play, and the rest is bedrock. Even with all the shouting and attitudinizing, plays still squeeze out emotions with an eyedropper."

"Should playwrights be attached to an organization such as the National Theatre, as they are sometimes on the continent?"

"No. Playwrights shouldn't be attached to anything."

On interviews: "I always look at them and think: 'My god, did I say that!' You know the sort of thing, 'Writing this play was *hell*. I had such an *awful* time. It was all *agonizing*.' I mean it *was* all awful and hell and agonizing, but it sounds so camp and pansy in print."

Interviewed by BARRY PREE, 1963

HAROLD PINTER
and CLIVE DONNER

Harold Pinter's play, The Caretaker, *gave him his widest audience. It became his first film. Produced without guarantee of distribution, financed by private subscription, and shot entirely on location at the top of an old house in Hackney, the film involved Pinter and his director, Clive Donner, in an exceptionally close and successful collaboration. Donner, then editor of* Genevieve *and director of several major films, worked with Pinter from the beginning on the script. When they had reached the final stages of editing, I went to visit them to find out their reactions to what had been, for both of them, a new experience.*

INTERVIEWER: What experiences did you have with the film industry before *The Caretaker* film?

PINTER: Well, I'd written an adaptation of a novel. Before I went into *The Caretaker* I'd only done that. I'd never been in a film studio except once as an extra.

INTERVIEWER: How did the idea of making *The Caretaker* start?

PINTER: Donald Pleasance had a great deal to do with it. But we all had it in mind, and then Donald, Bob Shaw and myself discussed it, and finally Donald got on to Clive about it.

DONNER: Yes, Donald asked me whether I thought a film of *The Caretaker* could be made, and how, and what it would cost. I said I thought a film could be made with a very economical budget, shooting on location, with very little adaptation, very little expansion of the play. As far as the budget was concerned, I said we could make it for £40,000. In fact it cost £30,000.

INTERVIEWER: Does that mean that in effect the initiative came from the actors and yourself?
DONNER: Yes, in a sense.

INTERVIEWER: And then what happened?
DONNER: We met Harold for luncheon one day. . . .
PINTER: I paid for the lunch.
DONNER: He paid for the lunch. We said, "We think a film could be made of this."
PINTER: I was very suspicious.
DONNER: He was very suspicious.

INTERVIEWER: Had you been approached to make adaptations of your own work before?
PINTER: Yes, but I'd never agreed to anything.

INTERVIEWER: Why?
PINTER: The circumstances didn't seem right. I thought there were all sorts of things needed for film production which I wasn't prepared to deal with. And I was extremely reluctant to make a film of *The Caretaker* because I thought I couldn't possibly get anything fresh from the subject. I'd been associated with the play, you see, through various productions in London and New York for a couple of years.

INTERVIEWER: What persuaded you this time?
PINTER: It might have been something about . . . I don't know, the general common sense and relaxation of the people I met. I put up a lot of defense mechanisms about it, and said I couldn't possibly even write the draft of a screenplay, couldn't do anything at all, and then someone said, "You don't have to do anything" (though it turned out I did) . . . and I let myself be won over. I was behaving rather like a child about it.
DONNER: I think it's slightly unfair to say that you've been behaving like a child. I think you were expecting a more conventional approach to the adaptation of the work.

INTERVIEWER: How did you get over this feeling of having worked through it?

PINTER: Well, I suppose it was because no one said to me, "This is a film with a capital F." That would have frightened me off, I think. They simply said, "This is the idea, this is the work, these are the characters—how can it all be transposed into a film in keeping with what we have, what must be there." We had long discussions about it and I worked out a kind of draft.

INTERVIEWER: [to Donner] Did you feel you were making the script from the beginning? Do you know what I mean?

DONNER: Not quite, no.

INTERVIEWER: Well, I suppose ideally one thinks of the director as working from the beginning, on the conception, and then through to the final screenplay. Ideally. Agreed?

DONNER: Well yes, but it very rarely happens. It's certainly not happened to me. Yet.

INTERVIEWER: And here you're faced with a script that is settled—not only settled but has been running for a long time. A *fait accompli.*

DONNER: Oh no, I don't think that's quite true.

INTERVIEWER: In what ways wasn't it true?

PINTER: Well, Clive and I did work intensively on the script when I really got excited about the idea. We saw it as a film, and we worked on it as a film. We weren't thinking about something that was set in any kind of pattern. There was an obvious overall pattern to the work, but we had to see it and work on it in terms of movement from one thing to another.

DONNER: And you see there's a sort of compulsion in film makers to "open out" (whatever that means) subjects that they set out to film. I decided from the beginning that this approach was a blind alley. It seemed to me that within the situation, and within the relationships that developed between the characters, there was enough action, enough excitement seen through the eye of a film camera, without imposing conventional film action treatment.

PINTER: It seemed to me that when you have two people standing on the stairs and one asks the other if he would like to be
caretaker in this house, and the other bloke, you know, who
is work-shy, doesn't want in fact to say no, he doesn't want
the job, but at the same time he wants to edge it around. . . .
Now it seems to me there's an enormous amount of internal
conflict within one of the characters and external conflict between them—and it's exciting cinema.

DONNER: The fact that it doesn't cover enormous landscapes
and there aren't hordes of horses galloping in one direction
and hordes of bison in the other has nothing to do with it.
It's a different sort of action, but it's still action. And it's
still capable of being encompassed in the cinema.

PINTER: You can say the play has been "opened out" in the
sense that things I'd yearned to do, without knowing it, in
writing for the stage, crystallized when I came to think about
it as a film. Until then I didn't know that I wanted to do them
because I'd accepted the limitations of the stage. For instance,
there's a scene in the garden of the house, which is very silent;
two silent figures with a third looking on. I think in the film
one has been able to hit the relationship of the brothers more
clearly than in the play.

DONNER: What I think Harold means when he says that the
film has developed on what happened for him in the theater,
with particular reference to the relationship between the
brothers, is that the psychological richness of the original play
was to a certain extent hampered by the need to project out
into a theater.

PINTER: Yes, I think the actors on the stage are under the
delusion that they have to project in a particular way. There's
a scene in the film, also in the play, when the elder brother
asks the other if he'd like to be caretaker in the place. On
film it's played in terms of great intimacy and I think it's
extraordinarily successful. They speak quite normally, it's a
quiet scene, and it works. But on stage it didn't ever work
like that. The actors get a certain kind of comfort, I think, in
the fact that they're so close to the camera.

DONNER: The cinema obviously can deal with that very much
more subtly and specifically. I think that the writing is such

that *The Caretaker* isn't just a piece of theater, but it can go further and further and discover more and more facts to the characters, so that rather than repeating what happened in the theater one can enrich and develop it much more surely.
PINTER: I'm not sure I agree that the cinema will be able to gain in subtlety. I think that when one talks in these terms one thinks of a stage miles away with a vast audience and the characters very small. But I think you can be as subtle on a stage as you can in the film. You just do it in a different way. In this case the director understood what was necessary and what I, the fellow who had written it, meant. Which is a very rare thing. I'd always understood that everything is always bastardized in films, and that film people were a real lot of fakes, phonies, charlatans. The whole relationship between the people concerned was something I hadn't quite met in any medium.

INTERVIEWER: So you had the script. Did you ever consider going through the normal production-distribution channels to make the film?
PINTER: Yes, in fact we not only considered it, we were involved in it. We were right up to our necks in a very affable relationship with an American international distribution organization, but at the last moment they pulled out.
DONNER: We'd also had a great deal of interest from certain sources in England, but in the end they all got slightly cold feet—very cold feet. Then this American distributor pulled out, leaving us committed to crew, house, and various other expenditures.

INTERVIEWER: And that's the point where you collected the money by subscription?
DONNER: Well, we either had to dip into our pockets and pay everybody off, and not make the film, or we had to decide to go on and make the film. Peter Hall, who'd been involved in the financial support of the stage production, had said early on, "If you'd like some support from me on this I'd be happy to give it." When this particular crisis occurred

we took him up on that and realized there was a possibility of raising the rest of the money, in the same way.

INTERVIEWER: Do you find that exhilarating as a way of doing things—or suspenseful—or just hell?

PINTER: My feelings were clear. I hated the whole dealing with the American company from the start. I distrusted it, and I was right to distrust it. They proved eminently untrustworthy, and good luck! I think part of their—excuse me, what am I saying? They *must* be untrustworthy, otherwise they would cease to be respected. . . . So we all sat down in a pub, and we had a marvelous name-dropping session of everyone we were going to write to, all the people who sympathized either with us personally or with the play. We wrote to them, we expressed terms in the letter, and we were oversubscribed. We turned away £60,000. We really thrust through, and what was suddenly clear about it was that each and every one of us wanted to do the film. It was a great moment, that. I had been full of disgust and nausea and spleen and whiskey, and we could so easily have said, "To hell with the whole thing. What's the point?" I could have certainly. It was confirming my darkest suspicion about the film industry. But we didn't. . . .

DONNER: And it wasn't only Harold. It was Mike Birkett, and Donald Pleasance and . . .

PINTER: Not only that. If we're going to indulge in a bit of remembrance—I remember so well that the continuity girl who was down there at the time, engaged by our company, such as it was, a very rocky company, she suddenly, sitting in this pub, offered to put in some money.

INTERVIEWER: How long did it take to collect the total?

PINTER: I think from the time we decided, it was about a fortnight.

INTERVIEWER: So then you were ready to go.

DONNER: Well, during this period we were in fact already rehearsing, and we spent two, three days of our rehearsal time sitting around scratching our heads. So that although we went forward with a certain amount of renewed confidence once we'd decided on the thing, each time that Michael Birkett came upstairs into the room where we were rehearsing with another telephone message, another telegram saying that Noel Coward or somebody or other had come forward, it was very exciting . . . and frequently stimulating.

INTERVIEWER: But you got it all before you started shooting?
PINTER: Yes, we had assured promises of all the money before we started shooting.

INTERVIEWER: Apart from this crisis while you were rehearsing, the thing went more or less as scheduled?
PINTER: Yes, except we lost a few days sitting around eating salt beef sandwiches.
DONNER: If anybody had come forward then, and offered the amount of money that would have made it possible for us to shoot the film in a studio, or in a more lavish way, I wouldn't have taken it.

INTERVIEWER: Did you ever think you might do it in a studio?
DONNER: No, never!
PINTER: I wish the actors were here to ask, but I'm sure that for them it was tremendous—I'm sorry to say this, it sounds rather strange, almost as if I'm asking for realism, which I'm not—but I think it did an awful lot for the actors to go up real stairs, open real doors in a house which existed, with a dirty garden and a back wall.

INTERVIEWER: You were there every minute of the shooting?
PINTER: Not entirely. I arrived late quite often.
DONNER: I think Harold was there most of the time.
PINTER: I don't know whether other script writers are there to the extent I was.

INTERVIEWER: How did you react to it?
PINTER: As a complete layman to the film medium I found that looking around that room where one had to crouch to see what was going on (the whole film was shot in a kneeling or crouching posture)—I found there was a smell to it. Since

then I've been down to a studio, Shepperton, and things are very different. You don't have to crouch, you don't have to kneel, you can absolutely stand up straight, there are lots of lights, the walls open, they float, that's the word, float, and you've got no worries at all. Well, I found the limitations on location, in this house, gave a freshness to the work. I think the actors found that too. They found new answers, answers they hadn't been able to find or at least hadn't within the circumstances been able to find when they were playing it on the stage.

DONNER: And on location, like this house, I find one is dealing in tones of gray. There are no blacks and whites. The sets, the photography, are seen in terms of gray rather than in terms of black. . . .

PINTER: What I'm very pleased about myself is that in the film, as opposed to the play, we see a real house and real snow outside, dirty snow, and the streets. We don't see them very often but they're there, the backs of houses and windows, attics in the distance. There is actually sky as well, a dirty one, and these characters move in the context of a real world —as I believe they do. In the play, when people were confronted with just a set, a room and a door, they often assumed it was all taking place in limbo, in a vacuum, and the world outside hardly existed, or had existed at some point but was only half-remembered. Now one thing which I think is triumphantly expressed in the film is Clive's concentration on the characters when they are outside the room, outside the house. Not that there aren't others. There are others. There are streets, there is traffic, shadows, shapes about, but he is for me concentrating on the characters as they walk, and while we go into the world outside it is almost as if only these characters exist.

INTERVIEWER: What struck me just now was your thoroughness in following the film through the editing stages.

PINTER: Well, this editing stage was for me, of course, completely new. It was the first time, and an absolute eye opener.

INTERVIEWER: I can see you were enjoying it.

PINTER: It's great. It's great that one can move from one thing to another, or duplicate it, or cut it out, the wreck that can be wreaked in editing.

DONNER: Havoc, you mean?

PINTER: The havoc, yes, the havoc is terrifying.

INTERVIEWER: But you must have been involved in television productions, and to that extent you must have had some feeling for what happened and what you could do. You know what pictures roughly you're going to use, in about the same way as you know in a film.

PINTER: But it's very primitive. All that's open to you is just a position of sequences, or possibly cuts, but you haven't got the flexibility that you have in films. For instance in this particular play, there was a moment on stage when the two brothers smiled at each other. That was it. One stood on one side of the stage and the other stood on the other, and they smiled briefly.

INTERVIEWER: That was written into the text?

PINTER: Oh yes. And then one of them exited and that was that. Now, on film, either you're going to hold both things, in other words, the two brothers smiling, then one goes out. But it isn't the same as the stage, you don't get the complex thing which makes it so much of a moment on the stage. The distance, the separation cannot be the same. The balance, the timing, and the rhythm to this, the silent music, as it were, are determined in so many different ways, and I know we both felt, Clive and I, there was something to come there. I said something, I don't know what, and Clive said, "We want to go from one to the other, one to the other. Now the balance of the whole thing is that if you don't go to the other then there's no point made, but if you go from the other back to the first then the point is over-made. The balance, the editing balance, is crucial, as everyone knows, but it needs an eye and a relaxation which the film affords you, and no other medium can. You can sift it, you see, and the sifting is of value. Of course, on the stage, you can say to the girl, "Go out, this won't do, try another one. . . . " And if you make a decision and you're proved wrong, you correct it. But in films you're dealing with something that's going to be finished once you make a decision. You cannot go on changing ad infinitum, and you may make a decision and six months later you say, "That was entirely wrong."

DONNER: This is very interesting about such a moment as the smile. To a certain extent, in the theater, one entrusts the satisfactory presentation of this moment entirely to the actors. You expect that they have either consciously or intuitively sensed the way an audience is going with them and the play at a particular moment, and they can adjust their performance each night, to each audience. Now one of the things that actors feel terribly strongly about in the cinema is that their performances are taken out of their hands. They resent this, and I understand it completely. It seems to me a miserable thing to have to accept, particularly with the sort of actors we have in this film, who are extremely intelligent men, extremely successful, extremely creative. They do it, then they go away to other films, other projects, and leave us with the film to edit in a way that ultimately we have to take a decision alone. Well, as Harold says, you may decide at this moment that one thing is right, and six months later you see it, and you say, "I was wrong"—and actors, alas, have to accept this.

PINTER: Surely with this film, all the actors would subscribe to what is being done. Because we weren't asking them merely to go on there and give their performances as such; we were asking to examine how you should give your performance in relation to producing a finished film.

DONNER: To take creative responsibility, which is the aim of all these ventures, I think.

INTERVIEWER: So now the thing's done. Do you know how, or when, it will come out?

PINTER: Well, not precisely, no. It'll be shown, that's all I know at the moment.

DONNER: There's not much we can say about this, except that I think this piece is not solely an art house film, or need not be.

INTERVIEWER: In other words, you don't want it to be.

DONNER: Well, I don't think it need be, because from my own experience of seeing audiences react to the play, both in London and New York, I know that much wider audiences than would be reached by an art house release, enjoyed the play. But at the same time I think it would be very wrong to put this film out on ordinary general release—for two reasons. One, because I think the piece, by its nature, demands a concentration, a special attention which even unsophisticated audiences coming in coach tours to the Duchess Theatre in London brought with them—by virtue of the fact that they'd made a special journey to be there. Now, I don't think that people going out to their local cinema will make that same special effort, and I think the piece does require an effort for an audience to appreciate, to be able to enjoy it. And I think the other reason why I would not like a general release is because I think it would be very bad if, after all the hoo-ha of a full general release, it failed. Not only for its own sake, but because I think it would then tend to muck up the chances of another film that we or anybody else might make, and which might demand less of its audience than this. I think somewhere between a full general release and limited art house release there is a market for *The Caretaker* which I would like to find.

INTERVIEWER: So what you're trying to do is trace this special audience.

DONNER: Well, I would just like to have it exposed to a wider audience than an art house audience, but not be lumbered with the full heavyweight responsibilities of exploitation costs and print costs which a full circuit release implies.

INTERVIEWER: How do you expect to do this?

DONNER: I think it can be done by cinemas agreeing to show it in certain locations where they know or suspect or are prepared to try and find out that there is an audience prepared to make the effort to come and see this film, and to enjoy it.

INTERVIEWER: [to Pinter] Have you discussed any of this, or doesn't it interest you?

PINTER: Yes, it does interest me. But I think myself the work has been preserved in film, I think it's perfectly true to what I wrote, and I think it's funny. But really I simply feel that whatever happens with it, a lot of people are going to see it, and I can only come down again to the fact that what absolutely amazes me is that there it is. It's been done and as far as I'm concerned it's absolutely on the nail.

INTERVIEWER: So in a sense the kind of classification and squaring off that is done by the press and formers of public opinion no longer matters.

PINTER: Who cares? We all did it for nothing at all, no money, no conveniences, public conveniences, no facilities; the food was bloody awful, the curry was the same as the steak and kidney pudding, and I think it's been worth doing.

Interviewed by KENNETH CAVANDER, 1963

EDWARD ALBEE

This interview took place in Edward Albee's brownstone apartment in New York's Greenwich Village shortly after the much acclaimed opening of Who's Afraid of Virginia Woolf? *It was the first major interview to be granted by Albee, and in many of his remarks there are suggestions of themes from plays which followed. The conversation has been transcribed almost verbatim, in an attempt to remain faithful to the spirit of the discussion.*

INTERVIEWER: What is the most current thing you are doing?

ALBEE: I'm at work on the adaptation of Carson McCullers' novella, *Ballad of the Sad Café,* but at the same time I'm beginning to write a play of my own, called—right now I can't remember what I am going to call it. Yes, *The Substitute Speaker,* which I think is going to be in two acts, and I'm not sure which one I'll finish first.

INTERVIEWER: What can you tell me about *The Substitute Speaker?*

ALBEE: Very little—I don't want to tell you anything about it, except that I think it's going to be in two acts and I suspect it is going to probably have either six or eight characters and I think it's going to be—I hope it will be—just about unbearable.

INTERVIEWER: What is this unbearable theme?

ALBEE: That's something you're going to have to find out when you go see it.

INTERVIEWER: Okay, fine. What about the McCullers novella? Why did you choose to do a task that you yourself have said has not been done well in the past? You have not seen yet an adaptation of a novel for the stage that has been done well. Is that correct?

ALBEE: Exactly for that reason. No. two reasons really, but one of them is that I am interested in finding out what happens when people do adaptations of novels for the stage. Usually there is a tendency to cheapen—to lessen the work that's adapted, but then again, I can't think of very many good playwrights that have ever done adaptations. They're usually second-rate people who do adaptations. I'm not suggesting here that I'm a first-rate person, but I am interested in finding out if it is possible to do an adaptation of somebody else's work—to move it from the pages of the novel to the life of the stage—without cheapening or lessening the work. And then again, ten years ago—Is it ten? yes, probably eleven years now. . . . When I first read *Ballad of the Sad Café*, I said to myself, "If I ever start writing plays I'd like to make this into a play." So you put the two together and maybe you have a fairly decent reason for wanting to do it.

INTERVIEWER: Why this novel from a number of other very good novels?

ALBEE: When I read it, it seemed to me to belong on the stage.

INTERVIEWER: Just a dramatic event?

ALBEE: Exactly.

INTERVIEWER: You have been saying some very interesting things about the difference between compassion and pity. *Time* magazine in particular criticized *Who's Afraid of Virginia Woolf?* for being written by a man who has no compassion for his characters. I understand that you feel exactly opposite.

ALBEE: Yes, indeed. Pity is the sentimentalizing of compassion . . . in a way. Pity is a demeaning emotion for the person being pitied. Compassion is not demeaning. I'm not concerned with pity—I'm concerned with compassion.

INTERVIEWER: Do you feel your audience should be too?

ALBEE: Indeed yes. One of the troubles with audiences is that they concern themselves with the residue of things. They concern themselves, for example, with pity rather than compassion —they concern themselves with sentimentality rather than with sentiment. Pity is smug—pity is a smug emotion. Compassion is a sharing emotion. Sentimentality is a facile substitute for sentiment.

INTERVIEWER: The real way to empathy with a play is compassion?
ALBEE: Define empathy.

INTERVIEWER: A feeling of togetherness with—a projection of yourself into what is happening on the stage.
ALBEE: At the same time, I am not so sure that I like what audiences want as empathy. They don't really want something healthy, they prefer to have a kind of vicarious experience rather than real experience. They don't want to be affected for themselves. They want to have the illusion of being affected by something. They don't want the real thing.

INTERVIEWER: Well, you said that you write to arouse audiences. You want them to be aroused in this way—affected by the real thing?
ALBEE: That's not the reason I write. I imagine that somewhere along the line I was trapped into saying that I wrote to arouse people. I write for me. For the audience of me. If other people come along for the ride then it's great. After I've written a play and people have talked about it, then I start looking at it as if it were written by somebody else and I start making up answers for "the intention." And a lot of people are aroused, Off-Broadway at least—Broadway audiences are such placid cows. At almost every performance of *The Zoo Story* and *The American Dream* people used to get up and walk out and yell at the actors saying, "God damn you, how dare you talk this way, how dare you do this, how dare you offend me?" I suppose that's affecting, getting at, an audience—I'd prefer the people stay rather than walk out, only because the people who walk out disturb the people who are staying. But

you have two alternatives; you either affect people or you leave them indifferent. And I would loathe to leave an audience indifferent. I don't care whether they like or hate, so long as they're not indifferent.

INTERVIEWER: You've said that you have material in your mind now for something like two years in advance of what you're writing. How do you construct this in your mind? How does it come to you?

ALBEE: I've material for two years in advance because I'm very lazy; I usually write only one play a year. How does the material come? I don't know. All of a sudden I discover that I have been thinking about a play. This is usually between six months and a year before I actually sit down and start typing it out. The characters are sort of cloudy but clear at the same time; the nature of the play is quite clear but unspecific; what is going to happen is sort of definite but terribly imprecise. And so I think about it on and off for between six months and a year. I may not think about it for two or three weeks but all of a sudden I'll be walking down the street looking in a window or doing whatever I do when I walk down the street and all of a sudden, the idea of the play or something about the play that I discover that I have already started thinking about—something about the play will pop into my mind. It may be something that I have never thought about before, which would suggest—and make me very happy to think about it this way since I'm such a lazy person—that a great deal of the work that I do, I do unconsciously, that a great deal of the play is formed when I am thinking without using the most limited part of my mind which is the conscious part.

INTERVIEWER: When you speak about the form of a play, you have said that the best advice you could give to a young playwright was to study musical composition, and it seems to me that the studied structure of a musical composition is something very different from the workings of the unconscious mind.

ALBEE: I don't think so at all. The only thing that the un-

conscious mind can do is make use of the things that the
conscious mind has assimilated. Musical composition should be
studied by playwrights, I think, because I find play construction and musical composition enormously similar.

INTERVIEWER: Can you give me an example of its use in one
of your plays?
ALBEE: No, but I can carry on an analogy between musical form
and play structure all night if you'd like me to. For example,
musical notation and play notation can be and should be quite
similar. A composer can notate, can take a note and equate that
to a word. He can take a note and he can put a dot at the end
of it which suggests if it's above the line that it's to be extended more than it should be if it's below the line—it should
also be extended more than its value except less or one or the
other, above or below—depending upon the number of brush
marks he puts on the note. This also suggests how long it
should be spoken. He has tempo markings he can put down—
for a violinist he has bowing markings—a musician can be
terribly precise just by little marks that he puts on a page
of music. And a playwright can be exactly that precise since
it's an imprecise craft at best, since one must deal with actors
and a director, who also pretend to be human beings. So a
playwright can notate enormously precisely—Shakespeare for
example, never had stage directions; he didn't need them because he was a pretty good playwright. The only good playwright that I know of who has enormously precise stage
directions (which is not the same thing as notation)—is Eugene O'Neill. He was a good playwright in spite of those
stage directions. The playwright should be able to write a
line and notate it in such a way that it's impossible for an
actor to say the line incorrectly. It can be just as precise as
musical notation. Look at Samuel Beckett, for example.

INTERVIEWER: But this notation is not in the stage direction?
ALBEE: No. Beginning playwrights always make the mistake of
putting their entire play in stage directions and not bothering
to write it in. O'Neill's one act play, *Hughie,* which hasn't been
done in this country, exists in its stage directions. So much so

that when anybody does the play they're going to have to find some way to act the stage directions.

INTERVIEWER: I know you have done a lot of traveling in Europe and South America and so forth; what are the currents over there? Do you think that this is where the real leaders in drama are coming from?

ALBEE: Well, I suppose that Paris is the center at the moment of twentieth-century theater—it's moved away from Germany. Brecht is dead and he's being misplayed all over New York right now, but he was a unique phenomenon. But I would imagine that the nature of what is going on in the theater is stated pretty much by French playwrights. An Irishman like Beckett, a Rumanian like Ionesco and a Frenchman like Genêt. Ionesco is sort of a sleight of hand artist. He's nowhere as important or interesting as Beckett and Genêt and Brecht.

INTERVIEWER: What about some of your American contemporaries?

ALBEE: By contemporaries do you mean people who are writing for the theater at the same time that I am writing for the theater?

INTERVIEWER: Like Gelber, Richardson.

ALBEE: In other words you are talking about Jack Gelber, Jack Richardson, Arthur Kopit and not people like Arthur Miller and Thornton Wilder and Tennessee Williams?

INTERVIEWER: That's right. How do you place their contribution?

ALBEE: They're alive and they're writing and they're writing things that are alive and the fact that we have people like Jack Gelber, Jack Richardson, Arthur Kopit, who are writing for the theater now in this country and are writing with their own voice—well, more or less—is an exciting phenomenon. I hope that you're not asking me to tell you what I think about Jack Gelber or Jack Richardson or Arthur Kopit?

INTERVIEWER: No, I am trying to get an idea about your feeling about where the real life of the theater is at this time. What are the currents—what are the cross-currents between Europe and America and so on and so forth.

ALBEE: This is always in a state of flux. I think we're moving away from a naturalistic base and we're moving away from Ibsen and Chekhov— No, I won't put it that way because they are always good men to learn from—Ibsen and Chekhov—but I think we are moving away from the facile use of their technique which has become a naturalistic theater. There has been a misuse, a misunderstanding, a facile misunderstanding, of the naturalistic tradition of theater. Reality isn't as simple as it used to be and I suspect that the theater, the adventurous, the new, if you will, the new theater in the United States, is going to concern itself with the re-evaluation of the nature of reality and therefore, it's going to move away from the naturalistic tradition.

INTERVIEWER: Your view of reality has been rather harsh. You said that contemporary society represents the substitution of artificial values for real. What do you think caused all this? Where did this come from?

ALBEE: It came because it's easier.

INTERVIEWER: Sheer laziness?

ALBEE: Yeah. Moral, intellectual, and emotional laziness. People would rather sleep their way through life than stay awake for it.

INTERVIEWER: Well, you seem to be interested in awakening them. In other ways than your own plays. . . .

ALBEE: What do you mean by that?

INTERVIEWER: Well, I mean some of the things that you have participated in. . . . You've been going to several colleges; you've been helping out in judging writers' contests; you've been teaching in writing schools, theater schools.

ALBEE: No, that is slightly inaccurate—I don't teach at writing schools. I do like to go to speak at colleges because that is where the new audiences are coming from and I think that people should be corrupted young. I like to participate in judging playwriting contests also so that I can corrupt and make sure that something new and alive will win the contest rather than something that is the imitation of the familiar. I referee a playwriting workshop at The Circle in the Square which is not the same thing as teaching playwriting and anybody that says that he can teach playwriting is either a charlatan, a liar, or a fool. I referee a playwriting workshop in which people come and have a play of theirs performed on a stage for them by acting and directing students at The Circle in the Square and then they're asked to examine the relationship between their intention and what occurred on the stage. They're asked to talk about their dealings with actors and directors. People ask me a lot, "How do you do this?"—"What are the rules, how do you make a play good, how do you do this and how do you do that?" There is only one rule, which is: you can do anything in the world that you like as long as you make it work. There is only one length for a play for example and that is the play's proper length. There are no rules except for the rule of a successful work of art, as it is in all things. And for some obscure reason, people think that playwriting can be taught. Playwriting can't be taught, musical composition can't be taught. The *elements* of musical composition can be taught—harmony, theory, counterpoint—but that's because musical craft is more precise than the theatrical craft. I never dream of teaching playwriting but I like to indulge in a discussion of why and where a thing was successful, where it wasn't and why. And I suppose in the long run, the greatest value of a theater workshop, of the sort that I referee, is to let people find out whether or not they have the playwright's mentality and whether or not they should continue writing for the theater.

INTERVIEWER: You're also interested in a Pan American project—is that right? Encouraging better cultural relations between South American and American writers and musicians and so forth.

ALBEE: There was a conference in the Bahamas last fall of

fifteen United States and fifteen South American writers, composers, poets, anarchists and all the rest, in which views were exchanged and during which it was discovered that the South American members feel that there should be an enormous kinship with United States writers, composers, painters and anarchists. I'm not convinced that there should be since South American writers, etc., are still a good deal more alive to the European tradition than people in the United States are. They are (not intellectually, but in the sense of how they have been able to form any sort of national statement—or national voice) about fifty to seventy-five years behind the United States. However, the assumption on the part of the South Americans is that there is or that there should be an enormous relationship between North and South American writers. Well, naturally we are interested in finding out what's being written by Latin Americans. In the theater for example, Gore Vidal and Paddy Chayefsky and Harold Clurman and I are concerned with reading plays by Latin American playwrights in rough translation. The only time we have at the moment is to read them in rough translation, decide which are the good ones or the better ones, and assign them, either to ourselves or to other people for accurate translation (not adaptation, I dislike the word adaptation). Between the four of us we know the majority of the people involved in the theater (producers, directors and actors) and know about finding outlets for the plays. Some may be done Off-Broadway—those will be the best plays, since the best plays are done Off-Broadway, the second-best on Broadway and the others farmed out to college theaters. I don't know what will come of it—I don't know very much about Latin American writing. But we are interested—this is one of the outgrowths of the conference we had in the Bahamas.

INTERVIEWER: You seem to take very seriously your somewhat new role as a cultural hero or leader in the arts and are doing a lot to encourage this sort of thing. How has this changed your way of life? How has this affected your writing?

ALBEE: One of the few values that the idiotic "success bit" brings to a man is that he is placed in a better position to try to change the situation that brought him his idiotic recognition in the first place. When you put a play on, there are two alternatives: it is either going to be successful or it is going to be unsuccessful. Ideally, it would be successful with honor. Now any playwright who has any respect for his work and is successful assumes that he has been successful with honor. And since he assumes this, he assumes that he can now corrupt, he can try to move the theater into the image of himself or the people whom he admires. (And the playwright always admires himself beyond all other playwrights. He knows that there are better playwrights than he is but he admires himself.) One of the really good things that happens from being caught up in the talons of the Bitch Goddess is that you can say a sentence and it's going to be believed by people you know, whether it's a stupid sentence or not. And so a playwright can, indeed, corrupt the audience in the direction of the good or at least what he thinks is the good. Ideally, the theater should be made up of only good playwrights. And in spite of the fact that playwrights are a suspicious, envious, anti-social bunch much as all writers are, I can't imagine any playwright as good as he thinks he is. So success is useful not only because a playwright is able to have the security to do what he wants without feeling that he is going to lose anything by it but also he is in a position to influence. Now if you had a theater of successful playwrights, all of whom were insane—and only half of us are—then you would probably have an audience that would eventually be corrupted the wrong way. But I think that playwrights are saner than most people and I think the theater can be corrupted in the right way. The audience can be corrupted in the direction of the truth as the playwright sees it. And if that can't happen, there is no point in having a theater at all.

INTERVIEWER: How about the corruption of the playwright as he reaches success? Did you find that you had to make a great number of compromises when you came on to Broadway with *Virginia Woolf*? Did you feel for instance that you underwent the same experiences that William Gibson relates in the *See-Saw Log*?

ALBEE: *Who's Afraid of Virginia Woolf?* was produced by the same two men that I worked with as producers all the way along the line Off-Broadway, Richard Barr and Clinton Wilder. These were two men who had both produced on Broadway and they didn't like Broadway very much—they didn't like the compromise and the corruption of Broadway. And so they both decided more or less simultaneously to produce Off-Broadway where plays are allowed to exist on their own terms. So we all got together by great fortune and we started working Off-Broadway and it was their intention to bring the Off-Broadway standards to Broadway. And for some reason which can be explained only by them, the first play they decided to do on Broadway was one of mine—*Who's Afraid of Virginia Woolf?* But what we did—I say we because I was made one of the producers on the assumption, on Barr and Wilder's part, that a playwright should have some say in the matter—was to decide just to do a play exactly as we would have done it Off-Broadway, which means that we got the best actors for it and we got the best director for the play. The result was that the playwright was allowed to make his own mistakes—I was allowed to make my own mistakes, rather than have to suffer the mistakes of other people. These men should be given medals hammered out of solid gold because they don't know what the term Broadway means (except in the business sense; they are the shrewdest producers I have ever met). When Richard Barr worked on Broadway before—before he went Off-Broadway— he produced *Richard III* in about 1948 on Broadway for $12,000. (I have to bring money into it because this is the only thing that people who are concerned with the Broadway theater will understand and I assume that maybe somebody will read this interview to the people who produce on Broadway.) Of course prices have gone up since then. But it was unheard of to produce a play on Broadway in 1948 for $12,000. Barr and Wilder produced my play, *Who's Afraid of Virginia Woolf?* for $42,000 which was unheard of, because most Broadway productions today cost upward of $100,000. The money bit is important because theater costs have been priced out of sense and intelligence, and this attrition leads to high ticket prices; it leads to the theory that a play must please all of the critics or close because it is so expensive. There was a time, not before the time I started going to the theater, because I started going to the theater when I was five years old and the first play that I ever saw was *Jumbo* at the Hippodrome and that was around 1935. (I wasn't five, I was seven, because I'm thirty-four, aren't I?) There was a time when good plays—plays that were not constructed for the mass market only but plays that were honest with themselves and also honest to the historical continuum of the theater—there was a time when those plays could run on Broadway, if they didn't get the palsied nod of the Seven Men. That's no longer true. As an example, the play that won the Pulitzer Prize last year or the year before—the Pulitzer Prize is being given to adaptations and musicals these days—was the adaptation of James Agee's novel *A Death in the Family*. The title was changed to *All the Way Home* because the producers thought they couldn't have "death" in the title and have a successful play, forgetting *Death of a Salesman*. It got mediocre reviews, but Fred Coe and Arthur Cantor kept it going for a whole season and they ended up getting the Pulitzer Prize for it. A play just as good by Hugh Wheeler got the same kind of notices and closed after four performances. The panic set in, in other words. These aren't very good examples because I have to qualify each one. *All the Way Home* was not a good adaptation and it was kept running (which is a good thing because it was interesting and it was better than the run of the mill) for the right reason for the wrong play. And the Hugh Wheeler play was just as interesting but it was closed for the wrong reason.

INTERVIEWER: Let's talk about *Virginia Woolf*.
ALBEE: I think she's a very nice writer.

INTERVIEWER: No, I mean your play. Why did you move from the sort of surrealism of *The Sandbox* and *The Zoo Story* and *The American Dream*? . . .
ALBEE: There is no surrealism in *The Zoo Story*.

INTERVIEWER: It's all realism?
ALBEE: Uh huh.

INTERVIEWER: Okay—of *The American Dream* for example . . .
ALBEE: You're talking about stylization.

INTERVIEWER: . . . into the surrealism of *Who's Afraid of Virginia Woolf?*
ALBEE: Is *Who's Afraid of Virginia Woolf?* a surrealist play?

INTERVIEWER: Well, do you have that impression?
ALBEE: No.

INTERVIEWER: All right, why did you write *Who's Afraid of Virginia Woolf?* in a fashion different from the Theater of the Absurd as we know it? *Who's Afraid of Virginia Woolf?* is not really related to that stream.
ALBEE: I've written five plays; each of them is in a different style. I consider myself in a way the most eclectic playwright who ever wrote. As a matter of fact, I made a list about a year and a half ago, of the number of playwrights, according to the critics, that I had been influenced by and it got to be a drag after I had listed twenty-six. And this list of twenty-six included three playwrights whom I had not read or seen. So I made a point of reading these playwrights and I found that I had indeed been influenced by them. Every play, I think, is written like this: form and content, matter and manner, substance and style must occur at the same time. They determine each other. A man's style as a writer is his voice, the sound he makes—a playwright's voice is the sound that he makes and the style that he works in doesn't determine that at all. It is something that one catches by the ear. Take Tennessee Williams for example, who has written in a number of styles, but all of his plays sound like Tennessee Williams—thank heavens. That is the Tennessee Williams style. Something that gets you by the ear. . . . Something you can hear and say, "Yes, this is Tennessee Williams" or "Yes, this is Beckett." The manner and matter determine each other and have nothing to do with the style of a playwright. In other words what most people think of as the style has nothing to do with style at all.

INTERVIEWER: Do you think the critics and the drama theorists have much to offer in the way of helping a playwright or helping the theater today?

ALBEE: Inevitably *no,* since everything they say is after the fact. They'd be a great deal more use if they would advise the playwright before he made his mistakes. But, the pride that some critics take in coming upon The Error and pinpointing, that is fairly useless. Ideally, a critic should be able to contribute to a playwright, but damn few of them do. A man like Harold Clurman does; Walter Kerr, once you get to know his vaulting prejudices, does; Kenneth Tynan, once you get to know his insupportable prejudices, does. Very few critics are the teachers that they should be. After all, most of them consider their job to be only that of a reporter and most of them write like reporters. And most of them write like bad reporters.

INTERVIEWER: A sad commentary on the state of criticism.
ALBEE: As I think Bernard Shaw said when he was a critic—A critic should be an enormously prejudiced man. Indeed he should. A critic should know something about the craft he is commenting on. Ideally, I think he should be a prejudiced practitioner of the craft he is commenting on. But the majority of critics assume that their responsibility is to reflect the taste of the people who buy the paper they work for, and therefore their opinion is of no more value than any lay audience's opinion—which is of no value.

INTERVIEWER: Well, I suppose that's true. To shift very radically, getting back to the so-called influences on your writing, do you feel that the background of the Albee family, the whole theater tradition behind them, had much influence on your writing? Do you think you got a lot out of what happened in your youth?
ALBEE: Do you mean the fact that my grandfather, who died when I was two years old, owned a bunch of vaudeville theaters?

INTERVIEWER: Well, yes.
ALBEE: I have no way of knowing. It may have been a theater family ending with my grandfather, but I had no connection with the theater at all. But I was exposed to theater young. You know, when other kids would go to movies on Saturday after-

noon, I was shipped off to live theater. It may or may not have had an influence, I don't know—I have no way of judging. I wouldn't say that it was a theater family at all. My mother was not a chorine nor was she an actress either. I don't know, I have no way of telling.

INTERVIEWER: You've been quoted as saying that the theater is a collaborative effort at best. What do you mean exactly by this?

ALBEE: What I meant by it, very simply, is the fact that getting a play from the author's intention onto the stage and back to the audience is crowded with imponderables and difficulties. It is imprecise. Ideally a playwright can get his play from a page onto the stage and back to the audience, rather like playing tennis against a backboard. But this very seldom happens, because you have to deal with human beings. You have to deal with actors and the director. No performance of a play that is halfway decent is ever as good as the performance the author saw when he wrote it. You must accept this as fact. The worse the play, the better the performance, in that sense, because the actors and the director compensate for what the author did not do. The best play in the world will never get its best performance, because the best play in the world has its best performance in the ear and eye of the man who wrote it. But the most disturbing thing is the encouragement that has been given to directors and actors—mostly directors, I suspect —in the United States in the past fifteen years, to consider themselves coauthors of a work. The corruption—you notice I use that word a lot, I must be obsessed with corruption—has gone so far that many playwrights compose their plays on the assumption that the director and the actor will do their work for them. And indeed some directors in the United States want plays to come to them that are not thorough so that they can impose their personality on the work. The playwriting craft is enormously imprecise since it has to be filtered through other people. It seems to me that it is the playwright's responsibility to come as close as he can to the ideal—the ideal is that everything that has gone before, the nature of the characters, the style that the play is written in, the author's inten-

tion, is so precise that any sentence that comes in the middle
of a play can be spoken only in one way and understood only
in one way. This relates back to what I was saying before about
music. We've been breeding playwrights in this country for
a while against this theory. We have been breeding playwrights
who think of themselves only as craftsmen rather than artists,
and bad craftsmen at that, who consider themselves small cogs
in the wheel. I think they'd do better to remember the fact
that damn few actors and damn few directors have their names
survive their time, and playwrights do. The craft is not imprecise, the relationship between playwright and audience has
become enormously imprecise, and basically because the playwrights have been abdicating their responsibility to their craft.

INTERVIEWER: What happens when there is another voice
beyond that of the playwright (and the producer, director and
actors) thrown in? For instance, when you are adapting another
person's novel and I am speaking specifically, of course, of
Ballad of the Sad Café.
ALBEE: My responsibility, of course, in putting Carson McCullers' novel on the stage is to make it seem as if Carson
McCullers had written it for the stage. So I must indeed become Carson McCullers. I must think like Carson McCullers.
The novella *Ballad of the Sad Café* has two lines of dialogue. That's all in the entire 110 page book. A play must
be mostly dialogue. It's my intention (and I hope I succeed
in it) to turn all of that narration into dialogue which sounds
as though it were written by Carson McCullers. That's my
particular function in that particular item. It's involving to do
that but it's involving in a different way. I know that any
play that I am working on is going right if I become involved
in it, and if I am not involved in it, I think it is going badly.
If I am moved, then it is moving. If I laugh, then it is funny.
If I am indifferent, then it is indifferent. But in doing an
adaptation, I have discovered, I must think that things are
moving, involving, funny or whatever in Carson McCullers'
terms. It is rather an eerie experience. I think that "eerie" is
the word that Carson would use.

INTERVIEWER: You think that you're attempting to speak in her voice?

ALBEE: I am using my judgment and whatever craft I have (and naturally I must be speaking of my own voice). I am using whatever craft I have to make the piece completely Carson McCullers.

INTERVIEWER: You remarked last week after a rather hectic series of sessions with students from a New Jersey college— that if Shakespeare had been alive today he might have killed himself from having been asked so many questions. What did you mean by this?

ALBEE: I didn't say that he might have killed himself. I said that he would have killed himself. People tend to be in this country more interested in the person who does the stuff, than in the stuff itself. And we are interested in persons and personalities rather than the work that they do. This has destroyed or helped to damage a lot of first-rate writers in this country. Thank heaven, for example, that Melville wasn't exposed to it. It's a shame that Whitman was. Ernest Hemingway, for example, started to think that he was Ernest Hemingway, in caps, which was a bad thing. What I meant was that if Shakespeare had been exposed to the glaring klieg-lights questioning of how he wrote, and why he wrote, he might very well have killed himself. Either that or moved to the country. The only depressing thing about facing any sort of audience for questions and answers is that most people ask questions like, "Why do you write?" and your only answer is, "I write because I am a writer," and that doesn't satisfy people. They not only ask "Why do you write?" but "Tell us how you write," and the only answer is when I am writing I get up at seven in the morning and go for a swim, come back to the house and have breakfast, smoke a cigarette and go to the bathroom and come out and sit down at the typewriter and write for four or five hours until I get a headache. That is *how* a man writes. The invasion of it, it isn't even privacy, it's the invasion of the nature of the man who is a writer, is one of the most puzzling and unfathomable things to me. Writing is a job in the sense that it is what one does but you can talk until you are blue in the face and say to people over and over again, "I write because I am a writer and I do not wish to examine the reasons why or how because that would lead to an enormous amount of self-consciousness." And people will frown and they will mutter because they are disappointed. They seem to want—a very strange thing—do you have any idea what it is they want?

INTERVIEWER: I think they want to know what makes a creative person.

ALBEE: The thing that makes a creative person is to be creative and that is all that there is to it. And they must not concern themselves with how or why. I know for example of two playwrights who had never thought about why they wrote and a number of their well-wishing friends said, for a variety of reasons, that they should go into analysis. Well, they went into analysis and they found out why they wrote and in both cases it took them two years before they could get back to writing. They became terribly well-adjusted people but they weren't writers any more. I am suggesting that people write only through social maladjustment. They are not adjusted to society as it is. That is the only reason that people write—the predominant reason that people write. And if you ask them why or how, you are going to tamper with something very rare and very private, you're going to start these writers asking the questions of themselves and when they start asking the questions of themselves they will start thinking of themselves in the third person and they will eventually go quietly and finally insane.

INTERVIEWER: You've criticized the writers of the thirties for being somewhat dated in their sort of "social message" outcry, and you and most of the other contemporary writers don't seem to offer a way out of our contemporary dilemma.

ALBEE: I never criticized the American playwrights of the thirties for being dated. I don't like most of them, which includes the thirties work of Clifford Odets and all the people who were called Clifford Odets during the thirties, because they were aggressively socially conscious and propaganda took over from art. It may be as simple as this: that in the thirties, with all the crypto-Communists we had in this country, the intellectual Left, the innocent Left is probably the best way to describe it, was enormously popular. The majority of the innocent Left came to its senses after the purge trials of 1935 and 1936 but during that period the whole Popular Front movement of art in the United States substituted propaganda for art. That's why naturally the works by basic political in-nocents, if nothing else, were bound to date, once political sophistication occurred. But there are larger things involved here, I think. Maybe there were easier answers in the thirties than there are now in the sixties, even indeed than there were in the fifties. I suspect that there were easier answers. We were gullible, naive, and we also did not have at that point, potential for destroying ourselves quite so efficiently as we have now. The existentialist and post-existentialist revaluation of the nature of reality and what everything is about in man's position to it came shortly after the Second World War. I don't think that it is an accident that it gained the importance in writers' minds that it has now as a result of the bomb at Hiroshima. We developed the possibility of destroying ourselves totally and completely in a second. The ideals, the totems, the panaceas don't work much anymore and the whole concept of absurdity is a great deal less absurd now than it was before about 1945, for example.

INTERVIEWER: What I meant is that you and other people are writing about the absurdity of modern contemporary life and about the somewhat meaningless so-called dilemmas of our present society and about the artificial values that we have accepted and yet you don't show us any utopian way out. What is the way out?
ALBEE: I have absolutely no idea if there is a way out or not.

INTERVIEWER: Have you found a way out?
ALBEE: Me, personally? For me?

INTERVIEWER: Yes.
ALBEE: I'm getting through it in a way that makes sense for

me. I'm not sure that it's the responsibility of a writer to give answers, especially to questions that have no answers. The responsibility of the writer is to be a sort of demonic social critic—to present the world and people in it as he sees it and say, "Do you like it? If you don't like it change it." Too many people go to the theater wanting to be taken out of themselves, to be given an unreal experience. The theater must always be entertaining, but I think that *Oedipus* is entertaining. I don't think that it is the responsibility of the playwright to present a dilemma and then give its solution, because if he does that, and he is at all concerned with how things are and how people are now, almost inevitably he is going to present a slightly less puissant dilemma. Because you have to do that to be able to give an answer to it.

Interviewed by DIGBY DIEHL, 1963

ANN JELLICOE
and DONALD McWHINNIE

Two more dissimilar people than Ann Jellicoe and Donald McWhinnie couldn't be paired in an article such as this. Mc-Whinnie is a rather shy, quiet man who could easily pass for a provincial schoolmaster. He is a skilled and subtle director and he has done some of the most difficult and sophisticated plays to appear in London, including Pinter's The Caretaker *and* Everything in the Garden *by Giles Cooper. With a scrupulous emphasis on the shadings and nuances of the spoken word, his work has a wry, ironic quality combined with considerable dexterity and comic invention.*

Miss Jellicoe could never for a moment pass as a provincial schoolteacher. She is exotic, flamboyant and tends to wear leather jackets with strange Siamese-looking jewelry. Being basically a director, her plays are unusually visual, superbly theatrical and solidly constructed. But a great deal is left open for the director himself to handle. In fact, they are really brilliantly worked-out rough sketches for a director to develop. The director who is intended is usually herself. Although the plays seem superficially obsessed with sexual complexities of every variety, their themes are really the basic hostilities between people (male vs. female, male vs. male, etc.) and how these hostilities explode into fear, hatred, violence and even Fascism. Although her work has been called experimental and improvisational, not many have pointed out that it's enjoyable. The Knack, *for all its seriousness, is a very funny play. There is nothing decadent about it, in spite of the two sexually-maladjusted characters, because Miss Jellicoe advocates a genuinely guiltless sexual attitude. The play is a kind of romp in*

*which the fears and the rape fantasies—the lot—all become
somehow very funny.*

ANN JELLICOE

INTERVIEWER: Could you tell me something about how you
began in the theater? Did you always want to be a playwright?
JELLICOE: No, when I was a child I wanted to be an actress.
But unfortunately I went through adolescence feeling that I
was like the back of a bus. I had no confidence in my appearance, no confidence in myself at all. I probably had talent,
but I couldn't sell myself as an actress. Sometimes I'm sorry
that I didn't pursue acting, because I think it can work as a
compensatory thing for some lack in one's childhood.

INTERVIEWER: So, you compensated by becoming a director?
JELLICOE: Yes, at drama school I discovered myself as a director. I had found that as a director I was able to create something outside of myself, something quite independent of myself which I could sell. It was a way of being involved in the
theater without subjecting myself to the ego-crushing business
of trying to be an actress.

INTERVIEWER: How did your experience as a director help
you later as a playwright?
JELLICOE: As a director I learned the importance of leaving
a great deal open for actors to interpret for themselves. And
this originally came from my experience in acting; the ability
to be able to sense if a thing is right or wrong. I am convinced
that the best way to teach anybody is to make them discover
for themselves. So when I wrote *The Sport of My Mad Mother*
I put in hardly any stage directions. Everything that is relevant
and necessary to that play is in the text. It must be discovered
by the actors and the director through a kind of natural evolvement that can only happen when everyone is totally involved
in the play. But when I wrote *The Knack* I decided to put in a
bit more stage direction. What I didn't actually write in, I
knew instinctively.

INTERVIEWER: In other words you more or less write your plays with the intention of directing them yourself?

JELLICOE: No, that isn't quite true. Anyone else can direct them if they are prepared to take the trouble to study them. It is all there, it is inevitable, if you study the play correctly. The Bristol Old Vic Theatre School did a splendid production of *The Sport of My Mad Mother*. I think other people can direct my plays if they can manage to get the truth of the characters and bring them to life. But frankly I prefer to direct my plays myself because I feel that the writing and the directing of the play for me are inextricable. I find that my personal involvement in the play doesn't stop until the final curtain comes down at the end of the run. In other words, the writing, the casting, and the directing of the play are all part of the same creative expression. When I don't direct one of my plays myself, I feel creatively starved. I feel I'm being cut off from it just when it starts coming alive.

INTERVIEWER: Were some people stunned by the way the subject of sex was handled in *The Knack*?

JELLICOE: Yes, I think there were some who were shocked by the fact that sex was funny in *The Knack*. It's unusual for a lot of people to see sex treated as comedy and tragedy at the same time. They are used to having the subject shrouded in romantic double talk or thrown at them in crude escapist displays of bare legs, leather jackets and girls in boots.

INTERVIEWER: Then how did your approach to sex in *The Knack* differ from the usual romantic or fetishist handling of it?

JELLICOE: First of all, the play is against this leather fetish sort of thing and against the sadism that it implies. One of the characters, Tolen, is meant to be an extreme example of a case where sex is used as a power compensation. So *The Knack* is really a lecture on sexual attitudes. I feel that sex is one of our chief contemporary problems and that once we get our sexual attitudes, not habits, but attitudes right, a lot of other things will fall into place. The character of Tom is the only one with the right attitude. His feelings are: have it, be relaxed

about it, be honest and straightforward about it. Just as his
sexual attitudes are unwarped and healthy, his relationships
(non-sexual) with people are honest and healthy. I think
it's interesting that one critic misinterpreted Tom as being
homosexual. This must indicate something when a supposedly
intelligent and perceptive man mistakes a character like that,
the only character in the play who is nearly sexually adjusted,
as being homosexual.

INTERVIEWER: In other words, in *The Knack* you were using
sex, bringing it to the surface, to explore other aspects of human
relations?

JELLICOE: Exactly. It is not a play about sex. It is a play about
how you should treat people. It is only about sex insofar as sex
is the key to how we really treat people. You should not treat
them as a means to power as Tolen does, and you must treat
yourself with self respect as Colin is unable to do.

INTERVIEWER: Then you have done the reverse of what most
playwrights do. While in most plays sex is in the background
with a lot of talk going around the subject, you have reversed
the procedure.

JELLICOE: Yes, I did this partly because I feel that an awful lot
of plays dishonestly use sex as a sort of power medium without
ever bringing it up. This is just another indication of how
wrong our sexual attitudes are. And the other way of using
sexual stimulation on the stage is just as bad. It is done for all
the wrong reasons, to titillate or to excite without any real
purpose. I find that approach degrading.

INTERVIEWER: At one point in *The Knack* Tom says, "I think
that we are all of us more or less total sexual failures." Does
that express your own feelings?

JELLICOE: Yes, it does. I think most people are more or less
sexual failures and it's understandable in a breaking-up society
that has hovering over it the threat of atomic bombs and hydro-
gen bombs. It is understandable that people's sexual lives should
be in a state of flux when the world is in a terrifying state of
flux. A hundred years ago people had social safeguards that no

longer exist in the same way now. Society was a fixed thing with fixed values that made it easier to live in. They had built-in outlets such as hunting and shooting and even going to war. But the social structure has changed so radically since then that with the increasing sexual freedom people are becoming inhibited, unbalanced and more guiltridden than ever.

INTERVIEWER: Are you writing a play at the moment?

JELLICOE: No, I'm translating Chekhov's *The Seagull* which is going to be done at the Royal Court.

INTERVIEWER: Do you speak Russian?

JELLICOE: No, I'm doing it with the help of a Russian woman who translates it for me word by word, giving me the exact literal translation.

INTERVIEWER: Do you find it difficult?

JELLICOE: No, once you get used to the technique, it all becomes very clear. It's as though I were learning the language as we progress from line to line. I enjoy it enormously, partly because I respond to Chekhov more than to any other playwright. I find that in his plays the essential structure is not literally what is said but what is thought and felt. The words form a pattern, an almost formal lyrical pattern over the thought. The play progresses on the level of feeling, developing the relationships of character to character and showing what people want and cannot have. The words either hide these feelings or reveal them, but they don't directly state them. They form a web, a sensuous pattern of sound which is at once delicate and powerful.

INTERVIEWER: Do you feel that most of the translations catch these qualities in Chekhov?

JELLICOE: No, I don't. I think that most of the translations seem to impose a dead rhythm on Chekhov. They are heavy and static, and they force a particular inflection on the actors that is all wrong. The mood of these productions is usually one of tearful nostalgia which is not what Chekhov intended at all. He said himself in a letter to someone that it was Stanislavski

who imposed this sort of weepy-weepy business on the plays.
What he himself wanted to do was to show people how dreary
and ordinary their lives were in hopes that once they realized
this they would have to do something about it. I'm not saying
that he was a social realist but he was more than simply a
poetic dramatist.

INTERVIEWER: In trying to avoid this dead rhythm that you find
in the other translations, how does this Russian woman help
you? Does she give you several alternative translations when
there's a doubtful word or phrase?
JELLICOE: Yes she does. And she is translating it for me in the
Russian word order which is very different from English. I
hear every word in Russian, often several times over, so that
I learn the sounds before I begin putting the words down in
English. I think it's incredible that so many of the translations
of the plays by people who supposedly speak Russian tend to
vulgarize the dialogue. There is a fake jollity about them with
a constant adding of small words which soften the tone. The
sentences are constructed in such a way to give a dying fall to
the voice. The actor is forced to speak in a sort of sing-song
one-two-three, one-two-three rhythm. All this adds to the weepy
over-nostalgic mood of so many Chekhov productions.

INTERVIEWER: Have you ever directed a Chekhov play?
JELLICOE: No, I've never directed or acted in one. I never really
understood him until the Moscow Arts came to London. I saw
that these plays weren't sad or nostalgic. His hope was in the
future. He saw that he was living in the middle of a dying
society and he was trying to look forward to something better.
I'm not saying that he was looking forward to Communism,
but he was certainly looking to a better society and not
hankering after the past. He wanted to show people how dull
their lives were so that they would do something about it. In
The Seagull Nina has a speech recalling the happy days of
two years earlier when she was still in love and innocent and
gay. She describes how beautiful it was, but it is not a speech
hankering after the past as such, it is hankering back to youth
because her life has gone bad through the circumstances in

which she has lived. Chekhov himself is not yearning for the past. He is showing lives which are led with false values. I think he is a very modern writer; he has the same quality of some of our best writers today. It is a quality which involves a search within oneself for absolute strength. At the same time there is this sense of guardedness toward the world because he has learned that the world is ready to cheat him or invade his inner standards of goodness and strength. I got this same feeling when I talked to Beckett, that here was a man with a tremendously strong personality, full of goodness and searching for some absolute truth. Chekhov gives one this feeling in his writing and he wants you to discover for yourself what he has left there. He drops hints rather than make statements. So when he describes his plays as "tragic comedies," the statement should be taken in relationship to the circumstances in which it was said and to whom it was said. He was not a man who would say, "It must be done like this." When Stanislavski interpreted Trigorin as being a rather chic literary man, Chekhov said, "Oh, no, but his boots have holes in them, and he wears an old jacket." And then he added: "But he smokes a good cigar; well, anyway it has a bit of silver paper around it." He is always aware of the contradictory elements in human beings. This was part of his conflict with Stanislavski who saw the plays as tragic. Chekhov saw them as tragic and comic and hopeful. He would never plunge in and make a direct statement about his work. This is what I find modern about him, this striving to find some absolute values in a world in which he knows it is impossible to state absolute values.

DONALD McWHINNIE

We began our conversation with a standard opening question: "How did you begin in the theater?" McWhinnie explained that he began acting in school plays, then at Cambridge he joined the amateur dramatic club where he acted, directed and wrote music for revues. All this seemed a familiar beginning for a stage director until he began talking of his experience during World War II. He said:

"In the R.A.F. I did a number of troop shows, concerts and plays. When the war ended I stayed in Germany for about eighteen months with a unit which was producing plays and sending them around to tour the army centers in Germany and France. After that in England I joined the BBC radio and spent a few years scriptwriting and directing documentaries and plays. When television appeared, I combined that with radio; then in about 1958 I moved back to the theater."

This struck me as an interesting background—Army troop shows, radio scriptwriting, etc.—for a director who was later to produce plays by Pinter and Muriel Spark. I immediately asked him how he felt about the connection between radio and theater and how he personally found the transition from the theater to radio then back to the theater. He said simply that they are both aspects of the same thing and that although the technique is completely different, the essential core of both radio and theater is the test which must be interpreted by actors.

"The great value of radio to me," McWhinnie explained, "was that it made me much more aware of the text. I was forced to devote much more attention to the text than I ever had before. Since I was dealing entirely with words, it was strongly borne in on me that one had really to dig underneath the words and get everything out of them."

Explaining his radio experience as a sort of lesson in the importance of the text, I began to see that his later productions of Pinter tied in with his earlier experience. I asked him about directing the Pinter plays in which the nuances and the cadences in the text are so important. I asked him if his radio experience did, in fact, help him in this way.

"Yes, I'm quite sure it did. In fact I had first worked with Pinter on radio. After the disaster of *The Birthday Party*, which was a tremendous flop, he was very depressed and we at the BBC, thinking him a writer of great talent, encouraged him to write for radio, which he did. The first thing he wrote for us was *A Slight Ache*, which we later transferred to the stage. But I found it difficult making the transition."

"How was it difficult? Did you find that adding the visual element to the play distracted one from the text and made it less pure perhaps?"

"I think it did make it less pure. I think a play like that which is properly written for radio won't really translate to the stage without being coarsened. Dealing with the words only, the writer is able to get a very pure expression almost like poetry, which in the theater has to be broadened and made more obvious in many ways."

"What about *The Caretaker*? That was written for the stage, wasn't it?"

"Yes, it was. But it has a highly organized, more precise, and more orchestrated script than one normally has to deal with. Most other plays are looser, more changeable and modifiable. We found in rehearsing *The Caretaker* that we really didn't want to change a word."

"Then as a director what special demands does this put on you in interpreting a play like this? If most of the emphasis is on the words, do you specifically tone down the action in the play?"

"Well, one has to. Because while in most plays the writer is concerned essentially with situations and the clashes of conflicts, Pinter is mainly interested in the strangeness of what people say to each other and the vibrations that they set off. Obviously one has to get the truth of the characters and their relationships. But at the same time one has to concentrate on the peculiar rhythms of the text. So it's a question of a synthesis between these two things. It's a fascinating exercise."

"What about the actors? Are there any special requirements needed for acting in one of Pinter's plays?"

"They must be very skilled. They need a good ear and a flexible voice in order to catch the undercurrents going on in Pinter's plays. I feel very strongly about his work. I don't think I consider it as despairing or pessimistic as some people think. But it seems to me that his particular way of seeing personal relationships and people in relation to society and the forces which are pulling them this way and that—is very much of the moment. (I feel this about Beckett too.) Pinter's plays are part of a current which is running through this decade."

About a month before this interview McWhinnie directed a play called *Rattle of a Simple Man,* which received mostly favorable reviews but one or two rather heated attacks. One critic said that it was a philistine play which was anti-sex. The play is almost a duologue between a forty-year-old male virgin in London for the weekend to see a football match and a lonely young prostitute with a strong fantasy life. The central problem of the play is will he or won't he and the prostitute tries everything to coax him. The author (John Dyer) does not commit himself in the end and leaves the audience wondering if the affair will be consummated. I asked McWhinnie what his reactions to some of the criticisms were.

"I was rather taken aback. I thought one review in particular was very silly. The fact is, *Rattle* is not a great play. None of us ever thought it was. It's rather a simple old-fashioned piece by a very good craftsman. It has a lot of humanity and a lot of humor. I was surprised that the critics took it so seriously or rather judged it as something which it never set out to be. Basically it sets out to be an entertainment about a couple of real people. We did *Rattle* because we liked it. It entertained us; we liked the characters and it was an interesting piece to do. We never said we were presenting something new and profound and different."

"Do you think one of the things about the play that annoyed some of the critics was that at the very end you're not sure whether he does sleep with her? In fact there's more of a suggestion that he won't quite make it."

"Yes, the ending is a slight cheat, I suppose. But I think there is a very warm atmosphere at the end, even though he says, 'I don't know whether I'm going to or not.' One feels that he will sleep with her eventually and that they will go and have that holiday together."

"There was a curious situation between the girl and her brother who comes in briefly. I thought that at any moment it was going to develop into an incestuous relationship, but it didn't quite. Now was this up to you to interpret it that way or was that how the play was written?"

"No, the incest is there in the original script. We chose to play it down because I felt that relationship belonged to another play. It went off into another area that simply was not followed up in the last act. We had a lot of talk with the author about this and we all agreed that the play actually seemed to lose unity through it. I think the audience would have been foxed and would not have known whether it was funny or tragic. Besides, the brother appears rather as a theatrical device in order to get the other chap off the stage for a while. I think the brother is bound to be an unsatisfactory character because he introduces an unexpected and really unpleasant theme, emphasizing the fact that his sister is a prostitute and developing the possible incestuous relationship between them. If the author had developed this theme properly, he would have ended up with a very different play; a much more serious and disturbing one. But I don't see that one could bring the audience back in the last act to all being charm and sweetness after this kind of diversion. That's why we played down the situation with the brother, to keep a unity going through the evening as a whole. Yes, I was very surprised by the press reaction to *Rattle* because it seemed to take the play much more seriously than we'd expected it to be taken. And in contrast to this, the reaction to Muriel Spark's play, *Doctors of Philosophy,* on the whole tended to brush the play aside, implying that the author did not really know what she was doing. This may have been because Muriel's play was done at the Arts which puts an experimental label onto it and may have led people to expect something which in fact they didn't get. It was certainly unconventional; no strong curtains and it was episodic. But it was elegant, witty, stylish and very civilized, and perhaps this kind of play is out of fashion at the moment. It is a witty play on a lot of serious subjects and not many of the critics pointed that out."

From this point on the conversation skipped lightly over to New York and the plays McWhinnie had directed there (*The Caretaker* and *A Passage to India*) and then to *Under Plain Cover,* Osborne's recent double bill at the Royal Court. "I like them less than any of his plays," McWhinnie said. "I felt they were over-inflated, that he went on writing them long after his subject matter had stopped and was trying too consciously to get the message across. I found only parts of them amusing, the rest not very funny."

When I asked him if he'd seen Ann Jellicoe's plays, he said: "I don't like *The Knack* at all. Perhaps I'm on the wrong wavelength, but I found it tricksy and pretentious and it meant nothing to me."

"Is it the visual extemporaneous quality of it that doesn't interest you?"

"It is in fact the kind of thing that does interest me but I think it's got a very limited application. I'm on the side that says that words are most important in the theater, more important than anything. Which doesn't mean that I'm against visual excitement and interest in ingenuity, but I think without words your theatrical experience is bound to be limited, because it's over-simplified. When I watch this kind of play I begin to wonder, why bother with words at all, do it balletically."

Turning from the subject of Ann Jellicoe's plays and the Royal Court, I asked McWhinnie how he felt about the new-style British actors.

"I think what they bring to the theater is a sort of regional personality—appearance, physique, voice—but most of them as far as I know have orthodox training and they know their craft; they've all learned the technique. They work in perfectly conventional terms. The only difference is that they look different, sound different, but technically I don't think they approach acting any differently than actors did, say, twenty years ago. The more successful actors now are those who learn their craft from the drama schools and avoid picking up the "drama school voice." They tend to hold onto their regional identity and even cultivate it because the plays that have been written lately seem to offer more parts for this kind of working-class hero than ever before. It all comes from a new kind of hero figure in the last ten years, don't you think?"

"How would you define this new type of hero figure?"

"I suppose he's working-class, he's independent, he's tough, he's sort of a rebel. I think it comes directly out of the war: out of the thing which brought that tremendous political support for the Labour Government at the end of the war. An enormous number of boys from the provinces became independent, found their own feet away from their own town for the first time ever; they were on their own and liking it and doing very well. This must have influenced a lot of the writers who were young men at that time. I remember very well this feeling in the air: 'This is new, this is different, we are not pushed away in a corner any more, we're going to be in there.' "

"Then suddenly they were heroes?"

"Yes. Before the war in the provinces their outlook was very limited. All one's chums were quite happy to be in the provinces, in a backwater. In those days the heroes were Ronald Colman and the young Olivier, well-bred, upper-class. The boys from the provinces were nobody's subject matter. Now they've become our national heroes. I think it's a wonderful thing."

Interviewed by ROBERT RUBENS, 1963

JOSÉ QUINTERO

José Benjamin Quintero was born in Panama City, Panama, in 1924. He studied at the University of California, first directed at Woodstock, New York, and came to New York City as one of the founders of the Circle in the Square Theater. At the Circle in the Square, and on and Off-Broadway, Mr. Quintero has, to great acclaim, directed plays of Tennessee Williams, Thornton Wilder, Jean Genêt, Brendan Behan, and Eugene O'Neill, also the film version of Williams' The Roman Spring of Mrs. Stone.

Mr. Quintero lives in a penthouse apartment on lower Fifth Avenue, in Greenwich Village. His posture is continually relaxed, he speaks with a slight Spanish accent, and punctuates his words with gestures and smiles.

INTERVIEWER: Mr. Quintero, would you tell us what the primary function of the director is in bringing the play from the script to the stage? Is it to edit, to inspire, or to dictate?

QUINTERO: Well, I've always thought that the main function of the director is to translate something from the literary form into an active dramatic life—to translate rather than to dictate or to inspire. Of course, you have to inspire your actors as the script inspires you. But I think it is mainly a question of translating.

INTERVIEWER: In the give and take with the actors are you the final judge?

QUINTERO: Yes, I suppose you are. But you are restrained by the framework that the play imposes upon you. You are working within the horizons that the play has already established.

INTERVIEWER: The New York theater is seriously influenced by what is, perhaps significantly, called the Actors' Studio. Do you think that in America the director is the primary figure?

QUINTERO: I have always thought that the writer was the primary figure.

INTERVIEWER: Doesn't the director in France and England figure more than the director does here?

QUINTERO: Do you think so? I think that the theater in America is probably more of a director's theater than any other theater in the world. Why, you have such figures as Kazan and Logan who are, you know, sometimes the main features for attracting the public.

INTERVIEWER: Greater attractions than the actor?

QUINTERO: Of course, in every country your stars are the ones that have the greatest pull for a public. But I also think that here in America, unlike countries in Europe where I have been, the director has become far more important—more important than, let's say, any director in England for a given play.

INTERVIEWER: More important than Barrault in France?

QUINTERO: Well, Barrault is an actor too. He has a company of his own, but he's also an actor. There are very very few directors' names that have the potency of, let's say, Kazan's name here in the United States.

INTERVIEWER: Is this as it should be, do you think?

QUINTERO: I really think the play should be the most important thing, then the actors, and then the director.

INTERVIEWER: Are you associated with the Actors' Studio, incidentally?

QUINTERO: No! I have only been there twice.

INTERVIEWER: If you had your choice, and everything else were equal, would you prefer to work with an actor trained at

the Actors' Studio, trained more classically, or not trained at all?
QUINTERO: That is a very difficult question: My preference is
to work with an actor who is very talented.

INTERVIEWER: So that the training doesn't matter?
QUINTERO: Not to me, no. It matters if the actor is restricted by
the technique he has learned. I don't like that; I don't want
that. His technique is his own private affair, but I want certain
results. How the results are achieved by him, that's his own
business.

INTERVIEWER: Is there a particular technique being taught at
the Circle in the Square School?
QUINTERO: I think that you could say it's pretty much our understanding of the Stanislavski method.

INTERVIEWER: And that's by your own particular choice?
QUINTERO: It is. But different plays demand entirely different
techniques from an actor. I think that, for instance, the Studio
has specialized in a particular technique to satisfy a particular
kind of realistic drama, but that now there is a struggle in
American schools, as in our school, not only to satisfy the needs
of realistic dramas, but to equip the actors as well for the demands of Shakespeare and the demands of Sheridan.

INTERVIEWER: Europe has its great schools and theaters—Barrault's, Reinhardt's, the Old Vic—that represent and encourage
a whole theatrical direction. The Circle in the Square seems a
most likely place to bring this tradition to America. You have
a producing theater, a dominant director, a school, and actors
who are personally faithful to the Circle and to you. Have
you any plans in this direction?
QUINTERO: Well, I think the Circle is the product of the
original plan, which was to do something like that, to form
an organization that would draw from its own people that it
had developed, and to find its own way of expressing the need
of the theater in America. But it's very difficult, as the economic conditions in America are different, or I should say
very different from the economic conditions that prevail today

in France (in France, from which the great Comédie Française sprang) or the conditions in England with the Old Vic. Our economic pressures are entirely different. Now, for instance, the Circle has 210 seats. The original plan was to run a play for no more than eight weeks. But even if we sold out completely every night for those eight weeks we could not pay for the cost of the production. We are not subsidized by anybody.

INTERVIEWER: Would you be subsidized by the state if you could be?
QUINTERO: We have applied. It becomes very difficult to do a play every eight weeks. You have to depend on running a successful play as long as you can so as to maintain the plays that are not successful.

INTERVIEWER: Do you have any dominant philosophy for the Circle?
QUINTERO: The dominant philosophy of the Circle is that everyone—actors, directors—has absolutely to subject himself to the demands of a particular play. That's why we have no stars. Nobody is really featured.

INTERVIEWER: So the playwright . . .
QUINTERO: The play's the thing.

INTERVIEWER: You yourself, I understand, just jumped into the field of directing. What would you tell a young man today, who doesn't have the same opportunity, to do? Should he stage manage or act or study?
QUINTERO: I did jump in. But I made my own pool to jump into, and that would be my advice to a young director. He should find a group, or form a group if necessary. There are a great many young directors walking in the streets of New York, making rounds, but I don't think a producer is going to entrust one of them with a production that will cost him $150,000. And not only because of the money, but a producer has to have stars, and stars will not trust their reputations to somebody they don't know. You could be a stage manager all your life, and not be able to make the transition. I think if you are a director you have to figure out some way that you can direct.

INTERVIEWER: Not stage manage?

QUINTERO: No, you could stage manage. . . . I have never stage managed a play. Never. I started directing. Now that was with a very tiny group: it was in a loft, but I started directing. That's what I wanted to do and that's what I did. I think if you want to sing, and if you don't sing but you just go up to the Met all the time you may become a great aficionado and know all about the operas, but you are not singing.

INTERVIEWER: You have just finished directing a film based on a novel of Tennessee Williams. Previously you directed his *Summer and Smoke* and *Camino Real* Off-Broadway. Can you tell us something of your feeling about Williams' writing?

QUINTERO: I think he's a great playwright. I think he's one of the few poets we have in the theater. I think he brought poetry back to the theater. What else can I tell you? Do you want me to say whether I think he is positive, whether he illuminates some part of the human mind?

INTERVIEWER: It is sometimes said of Williams that he illuminates too small a part of the mind, a neurotic part. Do you go along with that?

QUINTERO: No, I do not. I don't think that. I'm very grateful if any playwright will illuminate part of the jungle that is within me or the outside world. Now, I don't measure it in terms of how big it is, but how deep it is. And it may be a pinpoint, but it goes right to the center of you.

INTERVIEWER: You are probably the single person most responsible for the O'Neill revival in this country. Do you think we have any other playwrights of that stature?

QUINTERO: No, I don't think so. I think the greatest play by an American that I have read is *Long Day's Journey into Night*. I have never come across a play of that magnitude. If I had, I would have done everything to put it on.

INTERVIEWER: While we're on plays, have you seen any of the plays of Edward Albee? Do you like his work?

QUINTERO: I have seen only one play of Edward Albee, that was the first one—*The Zoo Story*. I found it the work of a very

very talented young man. It was a one act play and I think that is the extent of my feeling.

INTERVIEWER: Do you feel a one act play is inferior to a longer one?
QUINTERO: No, but I think it's not as difficult as a three act play.

INTERVIEWER: Did you see *The Caretaker*?
QUINTERO: Yes I did, in London.

INTERVIEWER: Did you like it?
QUINTERO: I enjoyed it very much. It tantalized me, it stayed with me, it hit not only my conscious mind but it went much further. It lodged itself somewhere in my subconscious and affected me enormously.

INTERVIEWER: The announcement by Thornton Wilder of his forthcoming one act plays, to be directed by you at the Circle, appeared on the first page of *The New York Times*. Do these plays make a particular social or political commentary? Do you think plays should attempt to do this?
QUINTERO: Oh, I think the plays that make a commentary about something that is more lasting than a political or social phase are greater plays. I think that Thornton Wilder makes a human statement in his plays that transcends any momentary political evolution. For instance, and I may be misquoting him, I think he said, "It is better to burn mature than immature."

INTERVIEWER: In England good new plays can be seen at the Royal Court. You just opened a new play on Broadway, *Look, We've Come Through,* but at the Circle where presumably more daring plays could be done, there's been nothing completely new and American by a new playwright in a long time. Why is that?
QUINTERO: I haven't found any.

INTERVIEWER: There are none about?
QUINTERO: Not that I've read. We've done new plays—*The Balcony*, for instance. And I'll tell you one thing, I really don't

recognize, in art, national boundaries. I would like to do a new play, whether it were written by a Frenchman, Spaniard or American, as long as it were a good play.

INTERVIEWER: I was about to ask you if you thought it important that people should speak of a specifically American theater.
QUINTERO: No, because I think that the world has become a very, very small place. And the boundaries that there are I think of as restricting rather than positive.

INTERVIEWER: Have you directed outside America?
QUINTERO: Yes.

INTERVIEWER: Where is that?
QUINTERO: I have directed in England and I have directed in Italy.

INTERVIEWER: Have you thought of directing in South America?
QUINTERO: I would like to, but I have economic reasons preventing it.

INTERVIEWER: Has the Circle ever thought of an international touring company, or an exchange of some kind with another country?
QUINTERO: Yes, we have. As a matter of fact we had an elaborate plan for touring Circle productions in schools and universities, but it turned out to be economically unfeasible.

INTERVIEWER: I have read that you yourself thought of the priesthood, and your family of medicine, as a career before you finally opted for the theater. There is something devotional about the priesthood and medicine. Is there also something devotional about your attitude toward the theater?
QUINTERO: I suppose so. The theater is a task you don't leave. It's something that takes twenty-four hours. You come home and you don't leave it. Sometimes I dream about scenes. So

I mean my mind, my whole being, is completely dedicated to it.
INTERVIEWER: Do you think of it as a kind of ministering to
people?
QUINTERO: No, I don't have that kind of lofty attitude about
my work. It's the only thing that I can do, that seems to me
worthwhile dedicating my life to.

INTERVIEWER: Do you believe that in today's world a single
play can make an effective difference in a man's life?
QUINTERO: Oh, my God, yes!

INTERVIEWER: A single play?
QUINTERO: I was not an observer—I was a director—but my
working on *Long Day's Journey into Night* changed my whole
attitude toward my parents.

INTERVIEWER: Is there any play that you've seen, rather than
worked on, that you feel has basically changed your life?
QUINTERO: I think that every play that I've seen, with the exception of a few that I have walked out on in the first act because
I didn't think they were going to have any kind of contribution
to make in my life, I think that every play that I've seen in
some way changed my attitude toward myself.

INTERVIEWER: And you think that's true of most people?
QUINTERO: I like to think that. Yes!

INTERVIEWER: You have here in your apartment some contemporary paintings. Is there any correlation, do you think,
between the current theater and other arts?
QUINTERO: I think so. I think the theater is a little behind the
other arts in terms of expressing a reality. It often uses terms
which are outmoded and sentimental. But I think Genêt, and
Mr. Pinter, throughout *The Caretaker,* use forms in writing
for the theater which begin to match the advances that have
been made in music and painting. I think the important
theater is oriented that way.

INTERVIEWER: Have you seen any of the avant-garde productions at The Living Theater?

QUINTERO: No, I haven't seen anything at The Living Theater. I think there's a very frightening thing happening in the New York theater today. Probably, the way it's going, Broadway will soon have only musicals.

INTERVIEWER: *The Caretaker* was on Broadway.

QUINTERO: It's the one thing out of the whole panorama. And it had its great success in London to back it.

INTERVIEWER: You directed a revival of *Lost in the Stars* at the City Center. Do you think the American musical comedy is a valid form? And can it go further than it has gone?

QUINTERO: Well, I haven't seen it go further.

INTERVIEWER: What about *West Side Story?*

QUINTERO: Well, yes, I think that *West Side Story* made a step forward. But that's one musical. Most of the musicals coming in are all of the same pattern, and have almost taken a step backward . . . you know, like *Kean* and *The Gay Life*. They go back, way back before *South Pacific* or *Oklahoma!* I think they are almost like operettas.

INTERVIEWER: But if you found one that was new enough and advanced in form somewhat would you do it at the Circle?

QUINTERO: I would do it at the Circle. I would do a musical on Broadway if it were something that I liked. I'm not quarreling about the form, but I don't think the theater is small enough to be restricted, or should be restricted, to just one particular form.

INTERVIEWER: Did you specifically choose the arena shape of the first Circle in the Square theater? Or was it simply the area available?

QUINTERO: It was an accident.

INTERVIEWER: But now, in the new Circle, you have the same shape. Was that also an accident?

QUINTERO: Oh, no. Well, you see, I say an accident—I laugh, because I don't really believe in accidents. It was an accident and I was unaware of all the potentials of the form, but when I began working in it I rediscovered them. It's not a new form. You know the Greeks used it, and Chekhov for certain used it, but I wasn't aware of it myself. When I say I don't believe in accidents, it is because I think you come to a thing and accept it because there is something in you that is ready to accept it, and therefore it is no longer an accident. It so happened that we were here in New York and there was no space available. My partner, Ted Mann, said, "There's a night club. Let's go and see it." We went to see it and I said, "Yes, it seems fine, let's do it." But we didn't set out to look for that.

INTERVIEWER: But now you prefer it to the proscenium and other types of stages?
QUINTERO: I don't prefer it. I love its virtues as I love the virtues of the proscenium. I think the physical structure of the theater is the only thing that's inflexible in the production of a play, and it shouldn't be. I am waiting eagerly for Lincoln Center because they tell me that they have stages there that will absolutely change according to the demands of the play. So we'll see.

INTERVIEWER: Did you find directing in the Circle—or is it in the Square? . . .
QUINTERO: No, it's the Circle—it's really not a circle: it's an oval.

INTERVIEWER: Did you find that more demanding than previous directing you'd done?
QUINTERO: No, because I began directing there. There was Woodstock first, but then it was the Circle. I really have never found it difficult. I didn't decide to do it that way—it just happened.

INTERVIEWER: And you didn't find it hard on the other hand when you came back to the proscenium?

QUINTERO: I did. And I tell you, working in the Circle helped me a lot about breaking some of the set rules of the proscenium. I don't care about the backs of actors being shown for a long period of time.

INTERVIEWER: You didn't go out of your way to make sure that each part of the audience saw?
QUINTERO: No, because I learned that the back of an actor can be actually terribly exciting to an audience. I broke that taboo.

INTERVIEWER: You directed *Pagliacci* and *Cavalleria Rusticana* for the Metropolitan Opera. Do you think opera, because of the added musical element, is a more complete art form than theater?
QUINTERO: Oh no. One form is not more complete than another. I think it's a form unto itself. I'm going to quote Mr. Wilder about opera. He said to me (he had just written an opera), he said: "You know, I like opera. I don't believe in opera . . . I like opera but I don't believe in it." Well, that in a way is how I felt about opera. I don't really believe in it. You know, how can people sing away their troubles? How can they all make love to each other singing? I can't quite believe it, but I like it and can appreciate the music. As a form, it's complete unto itself.

INTERVIEWER: Did opera direction present very special problems?
QUINTERO: Yes, because a great many opera singers have never thought or looked at opera as musical theater. It was a struggle of theater-with-music or music-with-theater.

INTERVIEWER: Was your function there a lesser one than in straight theater?
QUINTERO: Well, I'll tell you, I worked harder on those operas than I ever worked in my life. And, it's funny, I did lose my voice, from screaming and yelling.

INTERVIEWER: It's a big stage.

QUINTERO: Enormous stage. They have a chorus of . . . I don't know . . . about 125, and all of them have to be able to look at the conductor, and the tenors have to stay together, and the baritones have to stay together. *Cavalleria* opens with a festival in a village. Pretty soon, trying to please the demands of the singers, I found that all the women were on one side, and all the men were on the other, and I said, "What kind of a village is this? You know we've got to mix them." I was in an enormous fight because the sopranos had to stay together.

INTERVIEWER: Did you enjoy it enough to do another opera?
QUINTERO: I did another opera at City Center. I don't think I'm an opera director. I did the operas because I wanted to learn something about the position of movement and voice, and how much a singer can do physically on the stage without blocking the voice. I found that they can kneel down or do anything, anything. They are marvelously trained, you know, and as long as they are aware of the line between wherever the voice stems from and the mouth, they can be in any position and it doesn't matter.

INTERVIEWER: You have been quoted as saying: "Ideally I'd like to devote the Spring and Summer to making films, and the Fall and Winter to plays." Would you, like Ingmar Bergman, like to use the same actors for the stage as for the film?
QUINTERO: I would like to use good actors. I like to use stage actors and I like to use movie actors when they are good.

INTERVIEWER: Is it the same talent that's required from the actor for both film and stage?
QUINTERO: Talent, yes. Technique, no.

INTERVIEWER: It's a different technique?
QUINTERO: I think so. A movie actress . . . for instance, I worked with Vivien Leigh who has worked on the stage, and if a stage actress becomes a movie actress, well it was a marvel for me to watch her redo and redo scenes every day for the camera. She let the camera do the projecting, whereas she would have done it herself on the stage. The stage is very,

very far away from the audience. The camera is not. The difference, I think, between the movie and the stage, is the mural you are doing. In the movie you make it out of tiny, tiny little pieces of mosaic. On the stage you use large blocks, the blocks are bigger because they have to project much further. In the film the camera does the magnifying. A flicker of the eye becomes enormous in the camera, and on the stage you would never see it. Therefore you have to use another vocabulary.

INTERVIEWER: In a film do you feel that your direction of things—their placement, their textures, their shape, the duration of a shot, and so on—is as important as your direction of people?

QUINTERO: Well, the actor in the film is not as important as the actor on the stage, no. But that's all sort of relative because you couldn't do a film without actors. Your eye has to be sharper for detail, of course, but you spend as much time with an actor in a film as you do with an actor on a stage. Without actors you might make a film about scenery, but that's a travelogue.

INTERVIEWER: Were you occasionally surprised at the results in the rushes of *The Roman Spring of Mrs. Stone*? Did you see things you didn't expect?

QUINTERO: Was I surprised? The number one thing I didn't expect was that I could make a movie at all. So it was a great surprise, and the rushes were a constant source of amazement because I had never made any movies before.

INTERVIEWER: Did you prepare for this one in any special way?

QUINTERO: Not in any special way, no. I had prepared a few things in my mind, but my first day of shooting was the first time I had been around a movie camera so I couldn't prepare very much.

INTERVIEWER: Would you now do the film differently?

QUINTERO: Well, I suppose I would do it differently because after the experience you are a different person.

INTERVIEWER: Your vision changes?

QUINTERO: Yes. You change in that way, consciously. The film is something I've done, and the experience is over. But, of course, like the first time you walk, if you ever crawl again . . .

INTERVIEWER: What are a few of what you would consider great films?

QUINTERO: So many and so varied. I would say the first *St. Joan,* a great film. It ranges from there to, oh, *King's Row,* which I also loved.

INTERVIEWER: Do you agree that television is a hybrid form with the disadvantages of both the theater and the movies?

QUINTERO: I do, yes. You haven't got any of the advantages but you have all the disadvantages of both mediums.

INTERVIEWER: Have you directed for television?

QUINTERO: Yes, *Our Town* and *Medea.* But it's not a complete art form. I think television is the greatest reporting medium ever, and it should be used as that, but it's not a dramatic medium.

INTERVIEWER: Are there any types of plays or films, or any particular book that one could be made from, that you would like to see done?

QUINTERO: *The Heart Is a Lonely Hunter,* which I hope to make into a movie.

INTERVIEWER: Anything else?

QUINTERO: Good ones, yes.

INTERVIEWER: I have one more question, if you don't mind. Do you ever direct anything you don't like?

QUINTERO: I have found occasionally when I was in the middle of directing something that whatever I had thought was there wasn't, but I don't think I have ever taken on anything I have not liked.

Interviewed by JEAN-CLAUDE VAN ITALLIE, 1962

MARCEL MARCEAU

*Marcel Marceau is recognized as the foremost exponent of
the art of mime. His work can be seen as the culmination of
a movement begun in France by Charles Dullin (at the insti-
gation of Jacques Copeau), Etienne Decroux, and Jean-Louis
Barrault. But his pedigree goes back much further than that,
to the very roots of drama: to the Greek and Roman mimes,
to the mountebanks of the medieval fairgrounds, the commedia dell'arte, the forains, and, most important of all, to
Deburau, whose Pierrot became the apotheosis of the Romantic
movement. The tradition of Deburau, transmitted through
his successors, could still be seen in Marseilles in the first
decade of this century. Parallel to this development, the English offshoot of the commedia dell'arte brought the glories of
the Victorian Music Hall, which in turn led to Chaplin,
Keaton, Laurel and Hardy, and the classic comedies of the
silent screen. Both these traditions, personified by Deburau
and Chaplin, stand godfather to the art of Marceau. Having
rescued mime from obscurity, Marceau faced at the time of this
interview a critical junction in his career: where to go in the
future?*

INTERVIEWER: It seems to me that the program presented by
you in London marks the beginning of a new phase of your
career, or, more correctly, a development which began with
the creation of *The Mask Maker*. Would you agree?
MARCEAU: Yes, because *The Mask Maker* was the first mime
in which I showed a split personality. Until then, I always presented my shows—I'm speaking now about my one-man shows
—in two distinct parts. The first part, the Style Exercises,

showed man struggling with, or identifying himself with the elements, like *Walking Against the Wind*. Or else there were symbolic statements like *Youth, Maturity, Old Age and Death*. The second part was always devoted to the character of Bip. He was involved in a struggle with his job or with people, with society, with concrete down-to-earth problems. *The Mask Maker* was the first mime in which I showed a man with a certain destiny and, through the use of his many faces, the problem of illusion and reality. Hence the Pirandellian effect.

INTERVIEWER: Have you now reached the point where, having perfected your technique, you are becoming increasingly concerned with the content of your work?

MARCEAU: That's right. You see, it took me many years to show the public what mime is. But merely to show what mime is has nothing to do with art. It is necessary to stimulate the imagination of the audience. In France, we love what we call "The Theater of the Marvelous": we want to see men fly like angels. I want to use the theater with the freedom of the painter or the film maker. A theater that cannot make people wonder is no theater for me. We have to try to do things nobody else can do. I want to be a god on the stage. As Charles Dullin used to say: "We don't need the machinery of gods, we need the gods themselves." That's why people go to the theater. It's not just to see a man struggling against the wind; what makes it interesting is that there is no wind, but still the audience can see it. The unseen becomes visible, and mystery becomes real. And then, once the public has become accustomed to your form of art, you can use the various techniques you have acquired to give your work greater depth. You can play things like *The Cage* or *Contrasts*.

INTERVIEWER: Was this new emphasis on meaning a conscious decision on your part?

MARCEAU: Yes, it was. You see, five or ten years ago it would have been too early. People would have said "Balanchine" or "abstract ballet" or something like that. Now that they really understand what mime is there is no such difficulty. Take *The Cage*: a man finds himself imprisoned in a cage. The

cage contracts, getting smaller and smaller. Terrified, the man
bends the bars and escapes—only to find himself in a bigger
cage, which likewise contracts. The meaning here is obvious.

INTERVIEWER: I think *The Cage,* because of its visual intensity, makes a profound impact. It puts one in mind of
Kafka, or of the paintings of Francis Bacon. From now on, are
you going to make more philosophical statements of this kind?
Are you going to demonstrate your view of life, rather than
entertain?

MARCEAU: Well, I think I should do both. But it is quite true
that the present show is not as funny as my last. There is more
cruelty in it: in *The Tribunal,* for instance, and in *Contrasts,*
too.

INTERVIEWER: Let us talk about *Contrasts,* because here it
seems to me that you have departed, not only in content, but
also in form. For the first time you use an impressionistic technique, a sort of shorthand, reminiscent of the crosscutting in
films.

MARCEAU: That's absolutely right.

INTERVIEWER: This presupposes that the audience is familiar
enough with the grammar of mime to understand immediately
what you are saying.

MARCEAU: Those who are not familiar—it is very interesting
—those who never saw me don't understand *Contrasts.* And
all those who have seen me understand it perfectly and are
very happy. But if *Contrasts* is related to movie technique, I
would say that movie technique derives from mime technique.
What is a movie? A succession of images, arranged by cutting.
And what is mime? A succession of images—only with me
playing the camera and the editor at the same time. We do
the cutting ourselves. You see? Our eye is like a camera eye:
we use close-up, flashback, exactly as in the movies. But,
whereas movies are concerned with reality, we rely on the
imagination of the audience. It's quite possible, however, that
if movies hadn't existed, the public would have greater difficulty in understanding mime.

INTERVIEWER: There are two recurring images in *Contrasts* which one immediately remembers: the cripple and the man shot by a firing squad. They form a kind of *leitmotif*. Are these figures with which you identify yourself, or just symbols for the predicament of man?

MARCEAU: Not myself, no. I am trying to show that when we drifted to war in 1939, people were not really aware of what was happening. Alongside the fairgrounds, the traffic, the marriages, the office routine, the cocktail parties, men were shot in concentration camps because of their ideas, or their race. People could not imagine that military parades can lead to war. People were shot and people died, and life continued as usual. And suddenly—wham!—war was at our door, and we were all guilty. In *Contrasts* I want people to remember that what happened must not happen again. A war which will destroy humanity has no sense; war really has no sense. The great parade led to war, to destruction—and then it begins again.

INTERVIEWER: Now that is a definite message, isn't it?

MARCEAU: Yes, the message is that it must not begin again. Did you notice, in *Contrasts*, after the war, the fair music comes back again, the man comes back from the war, and suddenly he remembers that once he was in the fair, once he enjoyed life. Maybe he'll begin to live again—but he cannot forget. Of course, *Contrasts* is what its name implies: contrasts in rhythm, contrasts in image. The military march, the cripple; people who eat—people who are starving; the man is killed—he marries—he's killed again. There is no continuity of time. Past, present, and future intermingle. You see? That means that life is like a puzzle. You can show a man at different periods of his life, first old, then young, and then young and then old again. It doesn't matter—you make a big puzzle of it. Because once life is accomplished, you can pick out any part of it: it still makes sense—in retrospect. The tragedy is that you only discover your mistakes when it is too late. It's like the problem of *Faust*. When he is old and has to die, he feels he has done nothing. He has not discovered the great mystery of life. He has wasted his time—in spite of all his knowledge.

INTERVIEWER: Am I right in thinking that you want to use the *Faust* theme for a *mimodrame?*

MARCEAU: That's right. I see it as the great tragedy of man. When he gets wise, he gets older. And when he is young and potent, he is not wise.

INTERVIEWER: One or two critics have accused you of pessimism.

MARCEAU: Oh, no, I am very optimistic. As long as we are aware of what is happening we can find a solution.

INTERVIEWER: But what about *The Cage?* The message of *The Cage* seems to be that however much we try to escape, we cannot.

MARCEAU: In that sense, of course, all life is pessimistic. We all have to die. The day man achieves immortality, we can be optimistic. Death is a great tragedy—we have to accept that. And we have to accept *The Cage,* too.

INTERVIEWER: In this respect, do you find yourself broadly in sympathy with what many contemporary dramatists are trying to say? Like Beckett or Ionesco, for example?

MARCEAU: Well, in one way, yes. I think *Waiting for Godot* is wonderful because it shows the fragility of time. It shows life without purpose—a terrible warning.

INTERVIEWER: Is it your purpose, then, to change people? This is said to be the function of all great art. You are a master of a form of theater which, because of the intensity of its impact, is capable of converting people. You are, therefore, in a powerful position. How will you use the medium of mime?

MARCEAU: In mime, a man can be put in extreme situations of tragedy or comedy. It depends on the inspiration of the mime. If it is not conveyed in a powerful form, it can be awful. But the great emotions, joy and sorrow, life and death, can be strikingly communicated in mime.

INTERVIEWER: Do you feel that words, as such, have become debased, or meaningless, that they fail to communicate? So that mime becomes the logical answer to playwrights like Ionesco and Pinter? (Beckett has, of course, already experimented with mime.) Do you feel that in some ways the success of your mime is due to people's disappointment or disillusionment with the power of words?

MARCEAU: No, I don't think so. I think that it is very difficult to find great authors, as it is difficult to find great mimes. You don't find a Shakespeare or a Molière every century, or a Shaw, a Brecht, or a Claudel every ten or twenty years. Word theater and mime theater are equally valuable. Certain extreme emotions, like those mentioned earlier, are better expressed in mime; ideas are better expressed in words. Music is the ideal medium for expressing feelings. Each art form has its own special territory.

INTERVIEWER: So you see mime as existing in the theater parallel to words, rather than taking their place?

MARCEAU: Oh, yes, it can't take the place of words. But when the theater has a great shortage of authors, the public will turn to mime, where they will find the imaginative content that they miss elsewhere. And—let's face it—people live in extreme predicaments these days; where are the words to describe them?

INTERVIEWER: Now that we have spoken of the content of your work, let us for a moment return to the form. Mime, as practiced by you, has fallen into three categories: the Style Exercises, in which you show man battling with the elements; the *Mimodrames,* in which you use a company of mimes, aided by décor and music, in order to narrate stories, mostly of literary derivation; and the comedies of Bip, the "comic hero forever on the brink of tragedy," as you once described him. We have already discussed the new developments in your Style Exercises; what, if any, will be the future of the *Mimodrames* and Bip?

MARCEAU: I think Bip will continue to be a popular type. There will be no big changes now.

INTERVIEWER: But he has changed a little, hasn't he?

MARCEAU: Yes, he's a little more cruel. And a little more sad, maybe, sometimes. But I think the great change will occur in the work with my company.

INTERVIEWER: In what way?
MARCEAU: In the themes I will choose, like *Faust*, for instance. Up till now we have had classical pantomimes, or romantic pantomimes. Now *Faust* will be an epic pantomime.

INTERVIEWER: The "epic" brings Brecht to mind. Has Brecht influenced you?
MARCEAU: Not directly; I think it's rather that I want to project men who are mythological—who are placed in history to give light to men in general. Faust, Don Quixote, Don Juan, the Greek heroes, Peer Gynt.

INTERVIEWER: And Bip? Will he disappear in due course, as Chaplin's tramp disappeared?
MARCEAU: I think that Bip will disappear, too, one day, when he is too old. He—his image, I mean—must always remain young. As we say in France: "The hero must die young." You cannot have an old Cid or an old Don Juan, and when you have an old Faust, he sells his soul to be young!

INTERVIEWER: You seem to be very interested in this question of growing old. One of your best mimes, *Reminiscences*, very movingly depicts an old man. Are you obsessed by the fact that you are getting older—you are only thirty-eight?
MARCEAU: I consider myself as a *very* young man. But I am aware that one day I will be old. I am not what you call an entertainer, content to do the same thing year after year; I want to give of my best at any given time of my life. Bip will be at his peak during the next ten years. After that—who knows? Chaplin knew when to stop playing the Tramp, he had the genius to know it, and to me the Chaplin of *Limelight* is as important as the Tramp. If he played the Tramp now, he would no longer be funny.

INTERVIEWER: Would you say that the mark of genius is to know what to leave unsaid?

MARCEAU: Yes, the mark of genius is to know exactly what to bring in your time, and to give of your best at different times. That's what Chaplin did. And musicians do it, too. Beethoven wrote differently when he was fifty than when he was twenty-five. Mozart is an exception, because he died at thirty-six—but even at thirty-six he wrote differently than at twenty-two. Chaplin could have stopped making films thirty years ago, and he would still have been considered great: the Tramp was created for all time. But if he had not created the Tramp, he could not have given us *Limelight*.

INTERVIEWER: Quite. Now, let us go from Chaplin to your own career. You are about to start the second phase of your career. The mature phase. You have been accepted internationally as a great mime; your technique is perfect. You are now intent on impressing on the public your views of life, your message, your attitudes to various contemporary problems. What, in quite concrete terms, are your plans for the future? What are you going to do in the next few years?

MARCEAU: I will not give up Bip for at least another ten years, because he is a popular character, involved in situations which will make people laugh. And there are always young people coming to the theater, who have not seen him before. Bip was created in 1947. At first he was purely funny. Then, in 1952, there was a new phase. It was the period of *The Butterfly, David and Goliath, The Lion Tamer.* . . .

INTERVIEWER: The lyrical phase?

MARCEAU: If you like. So Bip will continue, and in my *mimodrames* I will try to re-create men of great stature, like Faust and Don Juan.

INTERVIEWER: You've toured all over the world during the last few years—you've led a rather rootless kind of life. Are you going to continue like this, or are you going to settle in France for any length of time?

MARCEAU: I shall try to stay in France for at least two years, during which time I want to devise a lot of new shows with my company. I want to make films, which I should like to be shown all over the world. Time is short, and it is an awful waste of time to spend two or three years touring all over the world with the same material.

INTERVIEWER: It must be a great temptation for you to tour, because, due to the absence of language barriers, you can be readily understood everywhere.

MARCEAU: Yes, but there are so many millions of men, and I would prefer to project my art through films, which can be seen by everybody everywhere.

INTERVIEWER: So you see yourself as based in France, maybe with a company and a permanent theater of your own, making films which travel, instead of you?

MARCEAU: Every so often, every two years or so, I might go on a six month tour of the great capitals, say, London, New York, Berlin, Moscow. Of course, there will always be people who have never seen you; one could go on and on, presenting new material or old material. There will always be a potential public, once you are really established. But I am more interested in creating new material than in being seen by ever-increasing numbers of people. That's why I want to stay in one place. You see, there are lots of things I want to say. I want to use my creativity to the full. I want to strain my resources to the utmost. I also want to start a school of mime, so that our technique can be preserved, and our grammar taught. I want mime to be an accepted language of world theater. One day they will stop coming out of curiosity, in order to see a man who does something nobody else does. They will discuss mime, as they discuss a play. We will have kindled their imagination: they will be able to hear the music of silence.

Interviewed by FRANK MARCUS, 1962

ALAN SCHNEIDER

Alan Schneider is one of the most energetic and experienced directors in the American theater. He is no stranger to Broadway (The Remarkable Mr. Pennypacker, Anastasia, Miss Lonelyhearts, *among many others*), *and his work has included much of what is original and exciting Off-Broadway: Edward Albee's* The American Dream; *the first American productions of Samuel Beckett's plays* Waiting for Godot, Endgame, Krapp's Last Tape *and* Happy Days (*in its world premiere.*)

Mr. Schneider majored in political science at the University of Wisconsin, received his master's degree in drama from Columbia University, and has been a member of the Actors' Studio since its inception. In his time (Mr. Schneider was born in 1922), he has directed, all over the United States and in Europe, plays of Saroyan, Shakespeare, Ibsen, Sophocles, Molière, Synge, Wilder and Williams—to name only a few.

INTERVIEWER: Mr. Schneider, in 1948 in an interview to *The New York Times* you said: "The director defines. . . . His prime concern is an idea and an approach, a concept of what the play is about." Do you still feel this way?

SCHNEIDER: I didn't say the director defines, period. I said he defined relationships. To me a play is a series of relationships. A dramatic action, to me, means a change in relationship. I think I said that, and I'll stick by that.

INTERVIEWER: Has it ever happened with a play that you've directed that the playwright was so clear, and the actors so comprehending, that your functions weren't necessary?

SCHNEIDER: Certainly. It happens in every play to some extent. The trouble is that usually just having actors read the lines of the play leads to confusion and lack of definition. But sometimes, you know, an actress comes into a scene and has to sit down on a sofa and cross her legs—well sometimes you don't have to tell her how to do it, or it doesn't matter in that instance. Helen Hayes used to say to me: "Edit me, Alan. Don't direct me." I understood exactly what she meant. She wanted me to tell her when she was doing too much or too little. The director is a kind of editor. As a matter of fact I think there's a real analogy between an editor and a director, and I certainly don't figure an editor as important as the guy who wrote the original sentence. I'm not saying that in any modesty; I simply believe the director is a kind of necessary evil, rather than the fountainhead of the theater or anything like that. I'm delighted when I don't have to direct, when the actors have it all there, and when the playwright has got it very clearly established. Normally speaking an actor can't watch himself from the outside; he hasn't got a sense of perspective. And that's when the director is valuable.

INTERVIEWER: Do you have any preconceived idea of the whole play before you start work on it?

SCHNEIDER: I always like to think I know something of what a play's about. Sometimes what I know is very analytical, sometimes it's very general, sometimes it doesn't mean anything to anybody but me and I don't tell anybody. But, normally, when I sit down with a script to do preparatory work —which I don't always have time to do, unfortunately—I try to write down in my script what the play's about. It's this old business that the Group used to call the "spine." I try to avoid terminology; that is I don't care whether I express it in terms of a verb or one word or ten words or whatever. I just find it helps me to say something. And if I have a playwright who's around I ask him, "What are you trying to say?" Not in terms of propaganda, or even in terms of theme, but in terms of point of view and attitude. What is the statement of the play? What is the play about?

INTERVIEWER: You mentioned the Group. Is that the Group Theater?

SCHNEIDER: Yes.

INTERVIEWER: Were you a member of it?

SCHNEIDER: No, I wasn't old enough. I would have been delighted to be a member though, at the time. The Group was one of my earliest influences. When I was a kid in Baltimore they came by one Winter, and I saw *Awake and Sing* and *Men in White*. I felt they had the best ensemble acting I had ever seen. I felt they had a point of view, and I don't mean a political one. It was like a team that played better football than any other team, and even though I didn't like all their productions equally I always liked their work. If I had had more guts I might have run away and joined the Group Theater. But I was studying physics at the time—I wanted to be a scientist.

INTERVIEWER: Harold Pinter, talking about his play, *The Caretaker,* said the play was quite simply about the characters in it. Do you agree that a playwright's "idea," or point of view, is secondary to who his characters are?

SCHNEIDER: Certainly I think any play of serious import can be observed and experienced on the various levels. But Harold is probably bending over backward to counteract the current trend of giving some kind of symbolic or metaphysical significance to what an author very often sees on a simpler level. To me the best example of that is the business about Godot. I happened to be involved with an early production of *Godot,* and the big question at the time was what, or who, is Godot? Beckett's famous answer is: "If I'd known who Godot is, I would have said so." When *Godot* was done at San Quentin prison some years ago one of the convicts said he thought Godot was the warden. I think that was a wonderful way of putting it.

INTERVIEWER: Do you follow a set procedure, more or less, from your first reading of a script?

SCHNEIDER: Well, I'll tell you that the older I grow, the less set my procedure is. When I first started I knew very little about directing. I never studied directing, I had no ideas about procedure at all, so I found a kind of hit or miss method of moving the actors around on the stage to find interesting groupings that would have some meaning and rhythmical importance. In my first directing job, at Catholic University, I was concerned with what we now call "staging" a play. I staged it and then put in the production elements—music, scenery, lights, and so on—and that way the play went on. The next step in my learning process was when I came to New York and was more directly influenced by the things the Actors' Studio and other such groups were working with. The whole emphasis there was on the actor as the fundamental creative stimulus. The director's work was to make the actor do what was necessary. And I discovered America. I took a course with Lee Strasberg—which almost made me quit the theater because he was terribly critical of my work—and became terribly concerned with the actor, forgetting all the other mere technical elements of production that had previously preoccupied me. And that lasted for maybe five or six years. I remember I did an *Othello* in which I was so concerned with the problem of the soliloquy, which seemed to me an artificial form, that I hit upon the great device of giving Othello a deaf-mute confidant who followed him around like a dog, and to whom Othello would speak. I thought it was a great idea because it allowed the actor to speak realistically. After about five or six years of this the marriage of the Capulets and the Montagues took place. I came to a blend of the theatricalist and the psychological acting traditions.

In the last few years I have still been basically interested in working with the actor, but working with him in a theatrical way, as in my production of Brecht's *The Caucasian Chalk Circle* at the Arena Theater. Every play of course requires a different balance of the theatrical and the psychological approach. If I'm doing *School for Scandal* I don't try to make people pick their noses, obviously. I think one of the troubles today is that the younger directors are more fanatical than I have been able to be; all plays tend to resemble Chekhov, except Chekhov plays themselves, of course— that would be too conventional. I say that when you see a play you should almost be able to tell the style of the writer by the way in which the play is directed—just as when you see a painting by Mondrian or Braque or Renoir there is a difference not only in composition and subject matter, but in the whole texture or style. To me, the most important problem in directing a play is to find exactly what texture, what fabric, the author has created. When this problem is solved the production is successful.

INTERVIEWER: You are currently teaching classes in directing at the Circle in the Square. You feel, then, that directing is a craft which can be taught and developed formally?

SCHNEIDER: I believe that directing is a craft which can be passed along through the sharing of one's experience, just as a carpenter can have an apprentice. I don't believe in formal classes in directing. The kind of teaching that I'm doing has to do, in essence, with sharing my experience. It would be wonderful if young directors could get a chance not only to watch elder directors, but to work with them—as assistant stage managers or directorial assistants or whatever. Unfortunately there isn't enough opportunity to do this. One of the things I most regret is that I have rarely watched other directors. We're all so jealous of each other, or the thing is so private; it gets to be almost like a cult.

INTERVIEWER: As the director, can you, in plays that have some ambiguity, permit yourself the luxury of not being absolutely certain what each line means?

SCHNEIDER: Oh, sure. I don't believe for a minute that even in plays that aren't ambiguous, knowing what each line means is critical. Very often—I'm going to say a heretical thing—it's very dangerous for the actor to spend too much time figuring out what each line means. What I do know is basically what is the intention of the scene, or I decide what it is, and I try to make the actors work within that. Now lots of times, and this is a very important point, lots of times the actors themselves without knowing it, and without any opposition from me, change that basic conception. By their own personal aura and physicality they cause the scene to mean something a

little different than what I thought it meant, or what the
playwright thought it meant. I think that's inevitable, and far
be it from me to attempt to stop it. I count on that when I
cast a part. I think casting is the most important thing a director does.

INTERVIEWER: You mentioned *Godot*. Did you, after your
production of *Godot,* which was the first one in America, hold
symposia, and do you think they're important?

SCHNEIDER: I think anything that makes the audience think
about the play they've just seen is important. My main objection to theater today is that too often we go in at half-past
eight and leave at eleven, unchanged and unaffected, and go
have a sandwich or read tomorrow's newspaper, forgetting entirely what we've just seen. We've just wasted two and a half
hours instead of having—I won't even say necessarily a philosophical experience or a metaphysical experience or a sensory
experience—any experience at all. What we should have, I
think, is a sensuous experience. The theater is the richest of
the arts sensuously; that is, you can see and hear and be completely aware of the living life up there. The trouble is our
theater isn't that kind of experience. When I go abroad and
see the Berliner Ensemble or the Piccolo Teatro or some work
I've seen in London, I'm overwhelmed with the possibilities of
being affected in so many ways by what's going on on the
stage. This is exactly what I don't feel generally when I go to
Broadway or Off-Broadway theater. I think the reason the
musical has so strong a hold with us is because it's sensuous.
It does have music and color and life and theatricality, instead
of the same old business of the back porch or the back lot or
the two guys sitting on the sofa talking about did Myrtle go
to bed with John. I think we're fed up with that.

INTERVIEWER: I'm going to quote you back at you again. You
said that 100 years from now Samuel Beckett would still be
considered one of our major playwrights. It's often said that
Beckett's plays and characters are sterile or arid. And the im-
plication, I suppose, is that the playwright should try to go

beyond that. Do you agree that his plays are sterile and arid? And if so, do you think that matters?

SCHNEIDER: I have rarely been moved by a modern playwright to the extent that I've been moved when I read the plays of Beckett. The first time I read *Endgame,* and I hadn't been warned what to expect, I felt pretty much as if I had read *King Lear* or *Oedipus* for the first time. I felt I had had a tragic experience, and not tragic in the sense that *The Daily News* uses the word as an accidental catastrophe, but tragic in the sense that I was aware of what man was up against, against fate or his own nature, and yet somehow able to go on, to survive, to persist to the very end. Talk about sterility! Man's *striving* for life, man's *hope* for life, man's *zest* for life I don't think has ever been more strongly or more specifically stated than in his plays. I don't mind people disliking Sam Beckett's work but I'm baffled by people who say he's negative.

I find Samuel Taylor "sterile and arid," because, you know, he's giving me this business about girls going to a party, and while he's writing these plays the world is sitting around waiting for the atom bomb, and corruption and despair are permeating our pores. I think it's infinitely more positive to know a situation, and to go on in spite of it, than to pretend the situation doesn't exist, which is what our lesser writers are doing. This is far from a complete statement of my feelings about Sam. I just don't understand the word sterility applied to a conscious craftsman who is trying to see what are the boundaries of the theater, what are the possibilities of language, what are the limits of musical or symphonic or contrapuntal rhythm in the theater. Hundreds of years from now students of the theater will look upon the graveyard sequence in *Waiting for Godot* as a model of just language. I don't think Tennessee Williams will have any validity for the twenty-first-century man. He'll be a minor poet with a certain historical significance. I like Tennessee Williams, but Sam is saying something about man, not twentieth-century man or American man or Greek man, but Man.

INTERVIEWER: To talk about the form of Beckett's plays for a moment, rather than their content, do you think the material he chose for the theater is best suited to that medium? Isn't it, for instance, in *Happy Days,* more of an intellectual conceit than a dramatic device to bury a woman to her waist in the first act, and to her neck in the second?

SCHNEIDER: No, I think it's a metaphor. I think he's presenting something theatrically valid: a human being in a situation on the stage. He is trying, I know, deliberately to limit the tools of his dramatic form—he exercises the same sort of self limitation in his novels. He is trying to see how far you can go without plot, without characterization, without environment, and still have a novel. In the theater I think Sam is trying to do without interplay of character—and it isn't merely a question of going from four characters to two to one character, although that's indicative of what he's doing. He's removing the weapons from his armory, and seeing how much he can still forge with the weapons that are left. He uses one or a series of metaphors. The two bums on a darkling plain are looking for the answer that never comes: that's poetic image, and I think it's valid in the theater.

INTERVIEWER: Do you think it significant that what is perhaps the major inner force in the American theater is called the *Actors'* Studio? This is a contrast to the great directors' theaters of Europe.

SCHNEIDER: Well, I don't know that the Actors' Studio is the only major force here. It gets the most publicity. I think the Studio is representative of the search for reality which permeates our theatrical life. Certainly the major event that has influenced all of our playwriting, directing, acting, and audiences—the whole theater we have now—was the visit of the Moscow Art Theater in 1924, when suddenly we discovered Stanislavski. From that came the American Laboratory Theater and the work of Boleslavsky, and from that the Group, and from the Group the Actors' Studio and other manifestations— a very simplified version of history, but nevertheless fairly accurate. That original influence of the Moscow Art has resulted in our concern for "reality," and thus the publicity and importance of the Studio.

I have said that if the political situation had not been such that the Berliner Ensemble was prevented from coming over here, the whole situation would have been different. If the Berliner Ensemble were to come here tomorrow, or had come here then, our whole orientation would be toward theatricality rather than reality. Even though it hasn't come, its influence is beginning to be felt through the few Americans—including Lee Strasberg, who recently spent some time there—who have seen it. Its influence is beginning to be felt not only in terms of, "Let's do Brecht," but by a growing concern with such questions as, what is "big" theater, what is "historical theater," what is "historical realism"; is realistic acting sufficient to cope with all of this, and so on.

We are a nation always concerned with personality, with the emergence of a new personality, with the virile actor and the beautiful sexy gal—obviously this makes for the dominance of the actor at the Actors' Studio and everywhere else in the theater. There's no question but that with us, actors, who used to be pariahs, are now special sorts of Greek gods and goddesses. The Studio simply capitalizes, not intentionally, on this phenomenon. But we don't really have an actors' theater, nor do we have a directors' theater. I wish we had a playwrights' theater, but we don't. I don't think we have a theater. Fundamentally what we have is a series of accidents, or, if anything, a producers' theater. It depends on the whims and tastes of various producers what plays are going to be done or imported. We don't have any continuity, or any tradition. We have no sense of working regardless of success or failure, and thus we have no theater. Instead we have producing organizations. We're loaded with talent—acting talent, directing talent, not so much playwrighting talent, unfortunately, but scene-designing talent, whistling talent—every talent but the basic creative one of writing, and the talent that it takes to choose what plays should be done. I don't think we'll have a theater until we have definite organizations with definite points of view, organizations that limit themselves to a certain kind of work done in a certain manner. I used to think that that was the definition of theater, and indeed in all the history of the world it has been. How can I say it any other way? In New York we don't have the Royal Court.

INTERVIEWER: Do you think the theater-going public is different in London from what it is in New York?

SCHNEIDER: The thing I like about the public in London is that it's not as fashionable as ours—there's not so much of this theater party business or this Cadillac business. In London you can buy a ticket the day of the show, or the day before, and there's a whole aura there of informality and casualness. Perhaps I'm romanticizing the London situation a bit, but in New York it's hard and it's tough and you've got to get in there, and ultimately very few people enjoy the show. I've been consistently told, by people who know, that ninety per cent of the people who go to the theater in New York hate it, hate the theater. They go for reasons other than to enjoy a show. This is something I don't sense in London. A couple of the most exciting evenings I've ever spent in the theater were London openings, where people loved the theater and loved the idea of the play. Here openings are just a question of whether or not it will be a hit.

INTERVIEWER: What new plays in the London theater excite you? And do you feel there might be too much social consciousness about some of them?

SCHNEIDER: I saw *Look Back in Anger* at the Royal Court on opening night. There were a lot of things I didn't like about it, but I felt I was in on the beginning of some kind of revolution, just as if I'd seen *Waiting for Lefty* in the American theater. I admired Osborne tremendously, and still do. I've read *Luther* which I don't like as much because there's something phony or *ersatz* about it. I happen to like *Epitaph for George Dillon* best—perhaps because I directed it and know it better. I liked *The Entertainer*. I find it difficult to say that there's too much social consciousness about Osborne. I mean I'd like to kick Jimmy Porter in the rear end, because Jimmy Porter is asking for pity, but I think John Osborne has a right to write Jimmy Porter like that if he wants to. I was tremendously exhilarated to hear Osborne's language in the theater, especially at a time when most of the language I was hearing in the English theater was tepid.

Certainly Osborne is socio-political, but the more definitely social-consciousness kind of play is Arnold Wesker's. Arnold is a real tough working-class militant protester against things —he serves a function there—who writes with passion and a tremendous sense of dedication. I think the important thing about the five or six new English playwrights is that they're all interested in saying something of significance theatrically. The trouble with Christopher Fry, and the reason I think he never got anywhere, is that he has nothing to say. These new fellows have something to say, as well as having an interesting way of saying it. And they're writing plays. I was there opening night of *The Lady's Not for Burning* and I thought, "My God, the language is good but what's it all about?" On the other hand I was carried away by *Under Milk Wood* because there was something there about people. I think what Osborne did was strike a chord, say something a whole generation was afraid to say or wanted to say and couldn't say or didn't know how or didn't have a chance to say. And I wish he'd just go on writing more plays instead of making speeches.

INTERVIEWER: While we're on the subject of new plays, you've just directed a double bill of Edward Albee and John Mortimer —would you, economic considerations aside, put on a single one act play as a theater evening? What I'm questioning is: do you feel the actual amount of time spent watching a play is important?

SCHNEIDER: If a writer has to say something, and can say it best in one act—whether that act be twenty minutes long or as, say, *Endgame*, an hour and a half—I think he has a right to do so. Too often we arbitrarily decide on certain forms. When I grew up a play had to be three acts long. The playwright had to figure out, "How do I end my second act? " and "What do I do for a first act curtain? " I have no objection to that except that it stultifies a playwright's imagination, he has to repeat what someone else did. Then suddenly, about ten years ago, we broke away and began writing two act plays— you remember, Walter Kerr wrote a lot of articles on how maybe this was the best form of play, and we began having only one intermission. Well, I don't care whether a play has one act or sixteen scenes. The important thing is that you write the way you have to write, and not be conditioned by questions of whether it will get into a theater, or how expensive it will be to design the sets. Certainly I do think an audience that's used to spending two and a half hours in the theater will feel gypped at seeing only one act. But I've often hoped for a different kind of theater. We once had *Krapp's Last Tape* and couldn't find a companion piece that we liked, so we wanted to do it by itself twice a night at low cost. But we ran into trouble with union regulations and other economic problems, and had to wait. In direct answer to your question, though, I think it's obvious you can have a short play or a long play, as you can have a novel or a short story, but certainly most of us will recognize that the richness of a novel will, normally speaking, make it superior to a short story.

INTERVIEWER: Albee is sometimes referred to as "promising" because his plays so far have been one acters. Do you go along with this wait and see attitude, or do you take him on his own terms?

SCHNEIDER: I think again we're dealing with American diseases that have nothing basically to do with the theater. We want every play to be better than the previous play; we over-praise a guy on his first play because he's better than we thought he would be, and then we expect him to come through the next week to justify our own exaltation. *The Zoo Story* was shown to every producer in New York, and nobody would do it. It wasn't until it had been done in Germany that it was done here, and after the New York production Edward was hailed as the greatest playwright practically since Aeschylus. I don't think Edward himself thinks that he's doing anything other than beginning to learn his craft.

INTERVIEWER: You like Albee's plays?

SCHNEIDER: Yes, very much. Both Albee's and Beckett's. I say a director is like a midwife. He doesn't have to like all the babies he helps give birth to equally, but he has to like giving birth to babies, healthy babies.

INTERVIEWER: Do you see any relationship between current trends in other arts and current trends in the theater?

SCHNEIDER: Yes. We're about fifty years behind all the other arts. I think this has always been true, partially because theater has to have immediate acceptance. A painting can wait twenty years in an attic, but a play depends on certain social and institutional forms that aren't always there at the right moment —theater buildings, theater companies, the right actor for the right part, and so on. What interests me is that what is happening to new theater today—the critical controversy and the opposition to it I gather happened to the other arts fifty years ago. That doesn't mean that everyone writing like Beckett or Albee or Pinter today is automatically good, not any more than all the fellows who are painting abstract paintings are worth bothering about. But the fact that it is possible today to paint abstractly without being considered lunatic is indicative of what might happen to the theater twenty years from now, or ten—it happens faster in the theater, it's condensed—when people will write more non-realistic plays. I think realism as a form is dead. It's still moving about on the floor, but it's basically exhausted. It was wonderful once, but now with television and photography I don't think it's wonderful anymore. That doesn't mean I don't like Chekhov. But I don't think today you can sit down and write like Chekhov even if you're John Mortimer.

INTERVIEWER: Much of your work has been done at the Arena Stage in Washington. Do you prefer that kind of stage? Is it best suited to particular plays?

SCHNEIDER: I think plays of extreme theatricality or extreme mood work well in arena: Chekhov or Tennessee Williams, or anything that requires the nearness of the audience. I think any play can be done in arena. I think any play can be done in proscenium too, although I think some plays, like Shakespeare, suffer. I don't really prefer one kind of stage to another. What I do like is variety. I'm tired of the limitations of the conventional Broadway playhouse. And I think one of the reasons for the success of Off-Broadway—aside from its intimacy, its availability as far as location goes, and the lower prices—is that each of the smaller theaters provides a slightly different experience. The relation of the audience to the stage is different, the construction of the theater and the sets are different; you come there and the experience you have is not exactly the same experience you would have elsewhere. Broadway theaters all look the same, and the plays are pretty much the same. I like a theater experience that can't be duplicated elsewhere, where you have the pleasure of an individual set of associations. It's the same kind of thing as what makes one girl different from every other girl. I think that, somehow, coming down funny little stairs in a small theater, with the paint peeling a bit, the stagehand coming around behind, the actors walking around, I think all this makes a valid impact, creates a unique experience for the theater-goer.

INTERVIEWER: What would you suggest to a young man who wants to become a director, presuming he doesn't have an immediate opportunity to jump right in and direct?

SCHNEIDER: There is never an opportunity to direct. But I think the young man should do everything, everything possible to create an opportunity for himself. That's easier said than done, but still I say it. I think stage managing is fine, but it could be a dead end. If you're good you stay a stage manager. If you're bad nobody will give you a job as a director. Watching the work of as many directors as possible, from whatever vantage point, is very good. Acting allows you to do that. But creating your own opportunity is essential. I think the young director today has got to stop thinking in conventional terms of Broadway or Off-Broadway. If he really wants to create a theater the opportunity exists in any one of fifteen or twenty cities in the country, and ultimately that's where the opportunity lies. I think that's where the theater is going to be. Amen.

Interviewed by JEAN-CLAUDE VAN ITALLIE, 1962

JOHN SCHLESINGER

At the time of this interview John Schlesinger had been doing some strikingly imaginative documentaries on British television. Suddenly two of his films were presented in commercial cinemas. The first was Terminus, *a quietly witty and subtle short study of people in Waterloo Station. The second was* A Kind of Loving, *an adaptation of the novel by Stan Barstow. Some people might have mistaken this for just another in the current wave of north country working-class films. But it was, in fact, a perceptive interpretation of a rather ordinary story and it had considerably more depth, impact and authenticity than some of the flashier films in this genre.* A Kind of Loving *is, one feels, the beginning of a creative career that will prove to be one of the most important in British films.*

Schlesinger is a mild-mannered, rather avuncular man. He lives in a small house in Notting Hill and at the time of this interview he was in the last stages of filming A Kind of Loving. *The film was subsequently chosen to represent England in the Berlin Film Festival.*

INTERVIEWER: What was the first film you directed?
SCHLESINGER: Do you mean the first serious film or the first amateur effort I ever made?

INTERVIEWER: What about the first amateur effort?
SCHLESINGER: The first completely amateur effort that I made was a film about the school I was at when I was about eleven. It sounds precocious, but I had been given a nine point five camera when I was very young, because I showed a tremendous enthusiasm and interest in both photography and the

movies; I was fascinated by early cartoons. I decided to make
a film portraying the particular aspects of the school which
interested me, and in particular a visit to the seaside: a day's
outing from the prison-like atmosphere of the school. It was
banned by the headmaster, who considered it subversive.

INTERVIEWER: What did he consider subversive about it?
SCHLESINGER: Well, I was interested in candid camera technique. I still am now for that matter. Most of us spend our
lives hiding behind one façade or another. The headmaster,
for instance, had a façade of dignity which he didn't like to
see removed, and on that day's outing to the seaside the film
showed little incidents such as changing underneath towels,
and the moment when the headmaster emerged from the sea,
picking his way gingerly over cobbles on a stony beach. It
showed him perhaps in a comic light—certainly more human—
and I remember he said it appeared as if I were poking fun
at discipline, and he didn't want the school to see it.

INTERVIEWER: How did you eventually get into professional
films?
SCHLESINGER: I did it through the university. I made two films
there with Alan Cooke who is also a director now. We decided
in our first term at Oxford that it would be interesting to
make a film with members of the Oxford University Dramatic
Society. We tried to set it up within the bounds of the Film
Club at Oxford, but they didn't want anything to do with us.
So we set ourselves up as a separate company and, drawing
on just a few friends and my family, we made a very amateurish film called *Black Legend*. It was the story of a seven-
teenth-century hanging in Berkshire, where I lived. We made
it on a shoestring during a vacation, taking a fortnight to shoot
it in and editing it on the dining room table. Since we had
no money for a sound track, we used a lot of Vaughan Williams and William Walton records on twin turntables, and
gave public showings. One of these public showings was in
London, where Dilys Powell saw it and one of Michael
Balcon's publicity staff, who gave us splendid notices. The result was that we were summoned to Ealing by Michael Balcon.

He had seen the publicity that the film received, heard that it was made on a £200 budget, and I suppose thought that it must be something fantastic. He summoned all his heads of staff, directors, producers, to the theater at Ealing. It was an experience which I remember with cold shudders today because in fact, it was a very amateurish film; I think there are moments in it which still bear looking at, but on the whole it was a fiasco when viewed by professional eyes. Of course, the letter which I subsequently got thanked me for showing them "a good amateur film," which is all it ever set out to be. But we had hoped, of course, to get our first professional job out of it.

INTERVIEWER: Had you read books on filming and film techniques?
SCHLESINGER: No, very little.

INTERVIEWER: Then how did you go about editing?
SCHLESINGER: Just chopped it up. I have a horror of theory of all kinds. I admire people who can theorize about editing or acting, but I can't. I have read a few little technical books and handbooks—purely on exposure, but I have never read Karel Reisz's book on editing which I understand is very good. I believed very implicitly in trial and error.

INTERVIEWER: In other words, all your knowledge of films is self-taught?
SCHLESINGER: Yes, I would say largely self-taught. From working as an amateur and then willy-nilly in television which is really where I got my first opportunity.

INTERVIEWER: How did that come about?
SCHLESINGER: I made three sixteen-millimeter films which were given some sort of consideration. One was *Black Legend,* the second was a dreadful film called *The Starfish,* which was blown up to thirty-five millimeter and given a commercial distribution, quite disastrously. That was my first brush with Wardour Street. Then there was a period of years when I was an actor, playing in films and becoming increasingly in-

terested in the other side of the camera. While I had a tiny part in a production of Peter Hall's, I spent the rest of my day making a less ambitious film. It was a quarter of an hour's documentary about Hyde Park.

INTERVIEWER: How long did it take you to make this film?
SCHLESINGER: Oh, about a month or so. Working weekends.

INTERVIEWER: Was it a general study of Hyde Park in the afternoon?
SCHLESINGER: No, not really. It was a fairly candid look in a non-serious but lyrical way at people. How they behave, and their reactions to things and to each other on a Sunday afternoon in the park. The film suffered from a series of rather facetious jokes, and I am loath to be reminded of it now. I don't think it was very good, but it served its purpose. It was shown on the BBC.

INTERVIEWER: And was it this film which got you involved with *Monitor*?
SCHLESINGER: Yes, indirectly. It got me involved with a program called *Tonight*. Working on *Tonight* was like working on a newspaper.

INTERVIEWER: Strictly reporting?
SCHLESINGER: No, not entirely. The need for film in television devours material so rapidly that there is actually a chance for the individual film maker to say something quite quickly in a rather improvised fashion, which can be unique and spontaneous.

INTERVIEWER: What sort of things for example did you do for *Tonight*?
SCHLESINGER: I did a variety of things. The first thing was a straightforward impression of Petticoat Lane. Then I started experimenting with setting poems to film: such as *The Charge of the Light Brigade* set against the rush hour in the City. That was the first thing that I think caught people's eye as a sort of slick piece of counterpoint. But it worked! Then I

went on and did more experimental things. We took pop songs and interpreted them quite seriously, taking the lyrics down and literally translating them to mean something they were never intended to mean. In other words, we used things that were very current in our lives and transposed them into cinematic images. There is one song in particular which appealed to me.

INTERVIEWER: What is that?
SCHLESINGER: Something called *Song of the Valley* which is dreadfully sentimental—Tin Pan Alley at its worst.

INTERVIEWER: Do you remember the lyric?
SCHLESINGER: I don't remember exactly, but it went something like:

When I sing you the song of the valley . . .
Where the mountains seem to kiss the sky above . . .

That's all I remember.

INTERVIEWER: Now what did you do with this visually?
SCHLESINGER: I transposed it into being the thoughts of a man who is going to prison in the north, for armed robbery. He thinks over the various things he has left behind: his family, his children, left without a father, the streets which he knew, and so forth. I've constantly gone back to the north because there are things about it which attract me—not just the picturesqueness but a terrible sort of sadness—the streets, the isolation. I find these things enormously moving. This film seemed to evolve quite naturally. We went up to Halifax and filmed it in two days, and it's been revived ever since.

Then I was asked to do something for Armistice Day. It had always seemed to me that this had been previously treated in rather a hackneyed fashion. I don't think it is enough to see the impressive but cold ceremony at the Cenotaph. Our film was set in the Imperial War Museum, and seen through the eyes of a child, to whom war was just a series of exciting models, and we then contrasted the models with the real thing.

INTERVIEWER: And then when you began working for *Monitor,* didn't you do some films about children's paintings?

SCHLESINGER: Yes, that came about a year later. I had made a dozen films for *Monitor,* about one a month. *The Innocent Eye* was a film more or less conceived when I had been walking through Holland Park and saw something called an Adventure Playground—a place where children are given a series of everyday objects to play with: railway carriages, a ruined hulk of a car, logs of wood, ladders, anything. They are encouraged to use their imaginations to experiment with these objects. I wanted this to be the subject of the film, but the BBC wouldn't let me do it. Now I realize it was too tenuous a subject to treat in six weeks flat, which was the average time allowed to complete a film. But I did make a film about children's play, and particularly about children's paintings, and this was *The Innocent Eye.*

INTERVIEWER: The idea of seeing things through the eyes of a child had interested you before, hadn't it? Especially in your treatment of the Armistice Day theme. Do you find it offers you a certain kind of freedom?

SCHLESINGER: Yes, I think it does. And I find children very attractive to work with, and marvelous creatures to film. I get on very well with them, by somehow managing to get on to the same wavelength, putting myself on equal terms with them. I find that children give to a film a rather exhilarating sense of freedom and spontaneity. Perhaps I want really to express my own childhood, to hark back, to rediscover certain aspects of myself.

INTERVIEWER: Do you find working with children easier than working with adults?

SCHLESINGER: No, not really. Although I enjoy working with them, I do find it is sometimes necessary to cheat if one is really trying to get a sustained performance from a child. One has to play a sort of immense game. In *The Fallen Idol,* for instance, Carol Reed is known to have used various tricks to get the reactions from Bobby Henrey. After all, the greatest challenge to a director in working with children is to make the child appear spontaneous in front of the camera, and this is not always easy.

INTERVIEWER: Is *A Kind of Loving* your first full length feature film?

SCHLESINGER: Yes.

INTERVIEWER: Was it difficult making the transition from documentaries to a feature film?

SCHLESINGER: Yes, it was difficult. First of all, I had never really worked with actors in this way before. The techniques of filming are entirely different. In the documentary one works with seven or eight people, and that's all. With a feature film, automatically there are forty-five people involved. Naturally this alters your attitude toward the material you are shooting. There is much more pressure on you. You are less inclined to experiment when all the technicians are saying behind you, "Look, I don't think this is going to work."

INTERVIEWER: In other words, you are more restricted: you don't have the freedom you have when making a documentary.

SCHLESINGER: Exactly, your freedom is cut down considerably.

INTERVIEWER: But were you able to overcome these obstacles in this recent film?

SCHLESINGER: Yes, I think we managed to do this. In fact, after we had started working together with the unit we found that there was a definite common language. I'd always been frightened of the idea of making a feature film with an immense unit, because it seemed to me that British films, though technically perfect, are not spontaneous, and spontaneity in a realistic film is one of the most important things. In filming *A Kind of Loving,* I entered into the thing determined to make everybody tremendously enthusiastic about the subject. I began by giving both the technicians and the actors a feeling for the geography of the place, by taking them around all the locations we'd chosen before we actually started filming. I wanted to give them all a total picture of the setting. I mixed local people with real actors, and took them around to all sorts of places, so that they could get the feeling of the atmosphere of, say, a factory, a pub, a dance hall, or just a suburban street.

INTERVIEWER: Bringing them into the milieu?

SCHLESINGER: Not only the milieu of the setting, but also how it was going to be worked into the film. We all went for instance to a Saturday night hop. Everyone went, including the cameramen.

INTERVIEWER: In other words, you got the whole staff to live that particular kind of life before they began filming.

SCHLESINGER: Yes, I tried to, because I think it's ghastly to expect actors suddenly to arrive by air from London to Manchester and start filming the next day when they don't know each other or the places that they're filming in.

INTERVIEWER: This was the first time you worked with actors in a film. Did you have difficulty dealing with them?

SCHLESINGER: Actually, it was very interesting. The leading actor, Alan Bates, is a splendid stage actor who had worked at the Royal Court Theatre and had recently been playing in *The Caretaker* in New York. He flew back from America and almost immediately began working on this film, playing an entirely different character. The girl, June Ritchie, is from Manchester, and was straight out of the Royal Academy of Dramatic Arts. Ultimately, the two of them worked together marvelously but at first there was a certain breaking down of barriers that had to be done. Particularly on the part of Alan Bates, who is a much more conscious actor than June, who is more intuitive. She could ad lib a whole conversation much more easily than Bates could. He liked everything a little more carefully worked out.

INTERVIEWER: How did you manage to get them to work together spontaneously?

SCHLESINGER: I think this came about quite quickly, as soon as all of us got used to working together. It is, I think, a very difficult thing for an actor who has been closely involved in a part in a long run entirely to discard it in one week, and realistically play an entirely different sort of character, before the critical eye of the camera. I found that during the first weeks of shooting Alan needed more takes than June did, and whereas his performance improved by, say, take seven, she was always better in the earlier ones. I also avoided rehearsing anything too much. Obviously, you have to have technical rehearsals, but I preferred to rehearse the actors privately—in their dressing rooms or in a back street away from the unit— so that there was no feeling of pressure. I also wanted to avoid a too perfectly drilled kind of scene, which I find in so many commercial films. It does not matter to me so much if the actor turns too far away from the camera, or is not perfectly framed, if the performance comes through spontaneously. I even encourage any sort of departure from the script, or from accepted technique, if it will add something to the spontaneity of the scene.

INTERVIEWER: Do you feel that your approach is similar to a whole new trend in British cinema?

SCHLESINGER: Yes, I do. I think perhaps it began with *Room at the Top,* which I thought was a terrific departure from the conventional type of British film because it was direct, honest, and personal. It was extremely fresh and well-observed. I preferred *Saturday Night and Sunday Morning,* which for me had a tremendous impact. Part of this was due to the fact that it had unknown actors—new faces not seen on the screen before. I carried this through in *A Kind of Loving,* for hardly any of the cast had done a film before. The present day trend —if you can call it a trend—started, I think, as a result of *Saturday Night and Sunday Morning.* It was a great commercial success, and therefore encouraged other companies to jump on the bandwagon. Suddenly it was possible to make realistic subjects, more directly, done largely on location with unknown actors, and the public were prepared to accept them.

INTERVIEWER: Then you feel that all this is the beginning of a new upsurge in British films?

SCHLESINGER: Yes, I do, but there is a limit to making just "real" films. We have not yet started in any way to explore the techniques used by Antonioni, Resnais, Godard, or Truffaut in their last films. It is certainly true that British films have had a style of their own. There was a style about the Ealing

Comedies, but they were not stylistic in the techniques employed. It is very difficult to experiment technically in the commercial cinema, although Tony Richardson started to do so with *A Taste of Honey*. The distributors have had a stranglehold on the British film industry for many years. It is they who have dictated the public taste, although finally they are finding some of their ideas disproved. I believe that they have underestimated the level of intelligence of the average British audience. It is going to be possible in the next few years, I hope, to experiment with many more types of subjects, although the cost of production is still too prohibitive to risk making a really uncommercial film.

Victim, for instance, was a commercial success, but the public went to see it because it was sold as a thriller with homosexual overtones. It never really got to the root of this particular problem. I think that now the time is ripe for us to try and expand the range of subjects with which the cinema deals. It will be difficult, but there are producers who give a far more liberal hand to the director in the making of films now than there ever used to be. It is a very healthy sign.

We have made *A Kind of Loving* entirely as we wanted to. The distributors, Anglo-Amalgamated, had hitherto only made sure-fire commercial successes (such as the *Carry On* series) and a few thrillers. But they never came near us during the production of *Loving*. If the film fails, we can only blame ourselves.

Interviewed by ROBERT RUBENS, 1962

TONY RICHARDSON
and LINDSAY ANDERSON

*The first time I met Lindsay Anderson was in the alley be-
hind London's Royal Court Theatre near the stage door.
Amidst the usual bustling activity—actors throwing a football
around, people rushing in and out of the theater—a medium
height man with short-cropped graying hair came up to me.
He had the look of a serious harlequin with an occasionally
mischievous smile. We went for coffee somewhere just off
Sloane Square, and he told me immediately that in the interview he wanted to discuss mainly the more pressing problems
of the theater. In other words, let the other directors talk about
the artistic nuances of directing, he wanted to talk of the
theater in terms of the need for more national support and the
problems that have arisen because of the lack of subsidy.*

*But our first conversation wasn't as heavy as all that. We
soon started joking about old favorite actresses, about the days
of Cecily Courtnedge and the Theater Guild in America of the
thirties and forties. He was curious about Katherine Cornell
and the other American actresses of her day who seemed so
terribly English. We arranged to meet the following week to
have the interview at the Cambridge Theatre where he was
restaging* Billy Liar *after some major changes in the cast.*

*We didn't actually have the interview until several weeks
later, when we went up to an empty dressing room in the Royal
Court. He spoke rapidly and without hesitation, and, if anything, the tape recorder seemed to stimulate him into discussing
all sorts of things we hadn't touched on in our previous talks.
Except for a few minor changes, mainly punctuation, the interview here is an exact transcription of our conversation.*

My meeting with Tony Richardson was a far more business-

like matter. I had to be fitted into a busy schedule at the London office of Woodfall Films in Curzon Street, from which Richardson directed the highly thought of films, Look Back in Anger *and* A Taste of Honey. *Extremely tall, lean, and highly articulate, words seemed to flow almost before I had asked the questions. He was most anxious to talk about New York, where he had spent a considerable amount of time.*

At the time of this interview both Richardson and Anderson were deeply involved in the new movement in the English theater, of which the Royal Court was the center. Richardson, who directed Osborne's Look Back in Anger *(and his* Luther*) was one of the original founders of the Royal Court. Anderson, whose first production there was Willis Hall's* The Long and the Short and the Tall, *was one of the most respected directors on the staff.*

TONY RICHARDSON

INTERVIEWER: Could you tell me how you began in the theater and how you came to be involved in the founding of the Royal Court?

RICHARDSON: I've always been interested in the theater ever since I was a child, and I did a lot of amateur theater both while I was in school and during my holidays. When I was at Oxford I joined all the dramatic societies there and directed a lot of shows. I was at the same time running an amateur theater in Bradford, which is my home. Immediately after Oxford I went into television, doing various odd productions on the side, but I was always thinking of the cinema.

During that time I met George Devine. We both had an idea of the sort of theater we wanted to see in London, the kind of theater we felt there was a complete lack of. A theater that would present new interesting work and a large number of foreign plays which otherwise couldn't be seen in England. Our scheme for starting the Royal Court Theatre (1954) fell through because we had no one to put up the money. Two years later, however, the English Stage Company, which was a curious collection of individuals brought together for no particular reason, was formed and invited George Devine to be its director. We revived the scheme we had had two years earlier. Actually it was very lucky that it was delayed two years because I don't think we would have been able to do it as successfully then. I don't think there was the amount of material around in 1954 that there was in 1956.

INTERVIEWER: Besides the difficulty in finding financial backing, what were some of the other problems in the early days of the Royal Court?

RICHARDSON: There is always the problem of economic necessities in running a theater like that. The fact that it's a small theater, that it costs a lot to put on the sort of plays we were doing, the fact that we were entirely dependent on the critics —if we get good notices we sell out, if we don't get good notices no one comes at all. This is one of the constant problems: one cannot build up any sort of permanent audience in London.

But the great problem was simply the material itself; where to find the young writers and where to find the talent. In the beginning we went out and contacted novelists and every sort of writer to try to persuade them to write plays; for instance, Nigel Dennis, who had never thought of writing for the theater. He did an adaptation of his novel *Cards of Identity*.

Our great stroke of luck, the thing that saved us, we would have had to close in a couple of months, was the discovery of John Osborne. As soon as his talent was recognized he created a breakthrough in the theater, and all sorts of young people started to think of writing plays in a way they wouldn't have before. They suddenly saw that it was possible to write a play that said something real and could be successful. Playwriting suddenly became expressive of a whole generation.

INTERVIEWER: How did you actually discover Osborne? Did he just send in a manuscript?

RICHARDSON: Yes. As soon as the scheme for the Royal Court was announced, about a year before the first play was produced, one of the very first manuscripts which came in the post was *Look Back in Anger*. This was a stroke of absolute luck; one of those pieces of historical luck without which the thing could not have functioned. That's what I meant by saying that if we had tried to do it two years earlier we probably wouldn't have succeeded. It was a question of the opportunity and the man coming along at the right time.

INTERVIEWER: Who actually first read the play? Was it you or Devine?

RICHARDSON: Both of us read it at the same time. We were living in the same house, and we were immediately struck by the power of the writing. It was quite obvious from the start that this was exactly what we were looking for. What we didn't, of course, realize was that it would be a success. We thought it might be a total failure.

INTERVIEWER: But this wasn't his first play, was it? Hadn't he written *Epitaph for George Dillon* before this?

RICHARDSON: He'd written several plays, some of which had been produced in rep., a lot of verse plays, but this was the first play he had written entirely by himself apart from the very early ones. *Dillon* was a collaboration.

INTERVIEWER: What was the immediate reaction to *Look Back in Anger?*

RICHARDSON: It wasn't a success at first. It had very bad notices in the daily and evening papers, and we thought we were going to have to take it off, but the Sunday notices saved the play. Once it had been established as a success, suddenly all sorts of new people began writing plays. This was the first time that a play had been written in England which had presented life in England as it then was, with the feelings and aspirations and humor of people under thirty. It was the first time for generations that this had been done on the stage. The English theater had been a completely class-bound entertainment reflecting the ideas of society before the war and it hadn't begun even vaguely to relate to the vast social and economic changes that had been taking place inside English society.

INTERVIEWER: Then the production of *Look Back in Anger*

caused a flood of other plays in the same vein? Who were some
of the people writing them?

RICHARDSON: I don't say that all the new writers wrote because
of John Osborne, but he created a climate in which it was possible for people to present their plays. I mean people like John
Arden, Arnold Wesker, Shelagh Delaney, Harold Pinter, N. F.
Simpson, Willis Hall, Keith Waterhouse and Brendan Behan.

INTERVIEWER: You've spent some time in America. How did
you find the New York theater in comparison to the London
theater?

RICHARDSON: First of all, on a more immediate and superficial
level, it's a thrilling and exciting theater to work in, because
you get the sense that New York is a town geared to theater,
in the most extraordinary way. It seems to be a society built
around the theater, everyone goes to the new plays, everyone
talks about them, all the people in the theater go to see each
other's work. You meet all the people in the theater. It is absolutely extraordinary—the whole life of the city seems centered
around the theater and it's immensely exhilarating and exciting
because of that. This isn't so in England at all.

INTERVIEWER: Yes, but what about the actual productions?

RICHARDSON: Well, when you come to *what* is presented in the
American theater and *how* it is presented it's a totally different
matter. To me the American theater is as bad now—at any
rate, the Broadway theater—as the British theater was fifteen
years ago. With very few exceptions I don't believe that there
has been any creative work done in the last decade on Broadway. I think it's become more and more a theater oriented
toward the expense account customers who want a certain sort
of musical which is totally predictable. Although I am a great
admirer of American musicals as such, I feel that even those
have fallen into a pattern that is pretty stale. The economics of
Broadway have grown and grown to such a crazy height that
there is now no possibility for the serious American theater
except outside of Broadway.

I think the exciting thing that is happening there is the grow-

ing power of the Off-Broadway theater where interesting new
work is being done by writers such as Edward Albee who are
suddenly making some sort of beginning of a new movement
in the American theater. This isn't reflected on Broadway at all.
To me the whole of Broadway is at the moment just a cultural
desert.

INTERVIEWER: If, as you explain, the London stage has been
class-bound, simply a reflection of a society that existed years
ago mirrored in countless drawing room entertainments, would
you say that theater is class-bound in the same way on Broadway?

RICHARDSON: Yes, I think it is. The New York theater is purely
interested in materialistic goods. It is an entirely materialistic
theater which goes for certain sorts of what are called production values: a lot of jazzy music, a lot of sets, an over-emphasis
on certain pictorial effects—spectacle in a production that has
nothing to do with the content or the actual thing which is
being said. In the same way that the thirties theater reflected
certain upper middle-class tastes and ideas of what life was like
in England, I think the Broadway theater at the moment reflects entirely the tastes of a certain economic class in America.

INTERVIEWER: Do you think this is true even of some of the
serious productions, such as plays by writers like Arthur Miller,
Tennessee Williams, or even someone like William Inge?

RICHARDSON: I think there are exceptions. I've admired Tennessee Williams greatly and also Arthur Miller. I don't admire
William Inge very much. But I think they are the exceptions.
They are the last kick of the Old Guard of the forties, because,
after all, that was when their most significant work was done.

Otherwise I think the Broadway theater exists to a large
extent on imports which again is a sort of snobbish taste. That
sort of moneyed audience wants to feel that it is seeing the best
of Paris in New York, because this is part of the American
image of themselves. They feel they are the Babylon of the
world to which all the riches are brought and that they can get
it very easily and see all the masterpieces of the world in one
place.

INTERVIEWER: What about Off-Broadway?

RICHARDSON: I don't think it is as exciting as it will be in five or ten years' time. I think something has begun Off-Broadway. I remember when I first went to America in 1956, Off-Broadway was almost exclusively concerned with revivals. Now, obviously revivals play an important part in the theater. Every cosmopolitan city should provide an adequate place for revivals to sustain its theatrical tradition, making the great drama of the past available. But I don't think that revivals can be done Off-Broadway authoritatively with good enough actors or directors, and the right size theater or scenery.

Now, however, Off-Broadway is thinking about new plays, which is exactly what I think they ought to be doing, and whether you admire them or not there are people like Albee, Arthur Kopit, Jack Richardson, who offer some signs that there are people in the American theater who are going to do something new.

INTERVIEWER: What about the films? This is a great interest of yours and you've done considerable work in it. Can you explain why the English cinema has been so static in the last twenty years?

RICHARDSON: I think it's been a great mistake that the English cinema has felt forced to compete with the American. It has been too consciously set up for the American market. The problem is that we think all the time in terms of speaking the same language, instead of trying to make films which are specifically English; our own. But because everything is geared that way (we're not really good at making films on the American model) everyone plays too safe and is too cautious.

INTERVIEWER: Do you mean that until recently England never found its own particular cinematic style?

RICHARDSON: It never really developed its own style. There were some good films produced. The Ealing tradition had a certain value and freshness when it first started, then it petered out. Korda before the war made certain sorts of films (not the kind that I particularly like) but they had some sort of vitality even on just an entertainment level. But since then there has been nothing. It's been a desert—the English film industry.

INTERVIEWER: What about the future of English films?

RICHARDSON: I think there are one or two tiny oases springing up, and we're trying hard.

INTERVIEWER: And do you think these oases will come from the same spring that seems to be producing so much new talent in the theater?

RICHARDSON: Yes, they're all basically part of the same movement. The same writers want to make films. Perhaps there will be others who will spring up entirely independent of the theater but the way it is going at the moment there is quite a lot of cross-fertilization.

LINDSAY ANDERSON

INTERVIEWER: What are you directing at the moment?

ANDERSON: At the moment I am really in a state of suspension; I am waiting to begin a film, the first feature film that I have had a chance to make. In the meantime, I have a production running in the West End. It has been running over a year and we've had to put new actors into it, so I have been rehearsing that. The play is *Billy Liar* by Willis Hall, whose *The Long and the Short and the Tall* was the first play I did in the regular theater of the Royal Court (as opposed to Sunday Night productions). It was written by him in collaboration with Keith Waterhouse who wrote the novel.

INTERVIEWER: Why is *Billy Liar* being done in the West End rather than at the Royal Court?

ANDERSON: Because it is a commercial play.

INTERVIEWER: And why have you decided to do this particular commercial play?

ANDERSON: Because it is a good one. I think that to make a rigid distinction between commercial plays and good plays, or commercial plays and art plays is a mistake. *Billy Liar* is an interesting case, by the way, for I don't think the Royal Court was ever given the opportunity to do it. That is, it was offered to a management that felt the play would have a better chance of success if it wasn't done in the rather rarified atmosphere of an art theater. At the same time I think it is possible that the Court wouldn't have wanted to do it, in which case I think they would have been wrong; we do suffer a bit from a kind of intellectual snobbery about plays that can be called popular. And *Billy Liar* is a play that attempts to have it both ways, and to a large degree succeeds. It has great popular appeal, while at the same time having a nub of content, a certain poetic vein and a definite social significance that makes it worthwhile doing.

INTERVIEWER: Do you find that there are many plays that have genuine artistic merit and yet have practically no popular appeal?

ANDERSON: Yes, I think this happens frequently; one can't expect that innovating works should be popular. This is true of all the arts. When artists make new departures or go into new experiments with style, their work is generally apt to be inaccessible to the large public, and often apt to be inaccessible to the critics as well. This is really the history of art, isn't it?

INTERVIEWER: Could you explain what particular sort of commercial play has been dominating the English theater for the past twenty or thirty years? And how would you say it reflects certain aspects of English life?

ANDERSON: Well, I suppose that the English commercial theater of the past twenty or thirty years has reflected what has been a rather static and constipated social scene. That is to say they have been plays rigidly segregated according to class. We have had plays which were designed for the lowest level of popular response, represented now by the Whitehall farces, which have an enormous popular appeal, largely to provincial audiences. On the other hand you have the theater designed for the upper- and middle-class audience, which reflects a more or less fantasy idea of upper-class life—gracious living and gracious dressing—which the lower middle-class play-goer will go to see because it is what he aspires to and which the upper-class play-goer will go to because it reminds him of home, or what he thinks home should be like. And both these types of theater reflect a tradition common to all classes in this country; that is, a fairly secure philistinism. They have been plays which don't touch, or move, or disturb, but are designed in the most facile way to entertain.

INTERVIEWER: When they do touch on serious themes, how do they go wrong?

ANDERSON: Well, I think that Terence Rattigan is a good case in point. Rattigan is someone who has several times broached interesting or serious themes, and knows very well where to stop, where to draw back, so that finally his plays do not disturb or come out of the category of mere entertainment.

His plays tend to titillate more than anything else. Something like *The Deep Blue Sea* has the apparatus of a psychological study, but doesn't really go beyond a fairly intelligent magazine story, with all the consoling qualities of a magazine story. And a play like *The Winslow Boy* is another case in point, where you have a very interesting theme, much the sort of theme that Ibsen attacked in *An Enemy of the People*, but this theme is only pursued, with a great deal of cleverness and astuteness, for two acts, and the third act is really devoted to running away from the theme and turning toward rosy comedy and ending with tears and smiles all around.

INTERVIEWER: How has this kind of play affected acting in England? Has it turned acting into a sort of formula based on this kind of elegant facility of the West End plays?

ANDERSON: Yes, I think this is absolutely true. The kind of acting we call the Shaftesbury Avenue style goes with the Shaftesbury Avenue kind of play, and the Shaftesbury Avenue kind of direction and decor. They are very homogeneous. And this has meant a particular sort of stylized acting; it is acting that corresponds aesthetically to a photograph in *Vogue*. That is to say it is peculiarly unreal with a kind of commercialized elegance. A great, often an admirable, technique—photographs in *Vogue* are, after all, often the work of extremely good technicians; they are very slick indeed. So you have a tradition of English acting which is technically of a high standard, but emotionally and intellectually very poor.

INTERVIEWER: What happens when this Shaftesbury Avenue kind of actor has to take another sort of part?

ANDERSON: I think the answer is that they don't. It is fairly noticeable for instance that a theater like the Royal Court which has existed for about five and a half years and which has been the center of what we may now call the theatrical revolution in Britain, has relied far more on the younger and newer actors than it has on the established ones; and of the established stars only Sir Laurence Olivier and Dame Peggy Ashcroft have consistently, generously and courageously come here to act, while the others have consistently refused to appear in plays by Brecht, Beckett, Miller, or Osborne. It is significant that after *Look Back in Anger,* Olivier wanted to appear in a play by Osborne; one has to remember that when *The Entertainer* was done, Osborne was by no means an established playwright. It was a courageous and imaginative gesture on Olivier's part. But he is one of the few exceptions.

INTERVIEWER: Recently Sir John Gielgud was interviewed by Harold Hobson in *The Sunday Times.* Did you read that? And what did you think of it?

ANDERSON: Yes, I did read it and I did find it extremely interesting; in two ways. First of all, I was disappointed by a kind of fear that is evident in the interview, fear of things that are new, a noticeably timid attitude toward work by people like Genêt, Ionesco or Beckett—but an unnecessarily timid attitude. In an interview like that, one senses the extraordinary gulf that exists between generations, and the lack of understanding. Gielgud is not in any way an ungenerous person, and I wouldn't want to seem to be attacking him, because I get the feeling from the article that he would like to be able to understand, to come to terms, but circumstances make this impossible. In fact our theater is so divided that he hasn't quite the self-assurance that he can come in and take part in these newer movements and contribute to them. This I think is a great pity.

Now the second thing I would like to say is that it is very interesting when someone like Gielgud talks of the emphasis on style and technique, which is something the younger generation of actors in this country have reacted against, but which is something I would agree with Gielgud that they desperately need to cultivate. Having reacted against a false style, it is necessary to develop a true style. One can't do everything with a kind of rough and truthful naturalism; but of course, they can only do it through truth and naturalism and then returning to style, not by copying an old style that is now out of date.

INTERVIEWER: Then you feel that most of the young English actors have not yet found this feeling for presentation and style?
ANDERSON: The basic problem here is that to find it you have to be able to practice. This is where we really come up against the present organization of theaters, which makes it difficult for a young actor to get the kind of training which enables him to develop a variety of styles. The big subsidies still go to the more or less established theaters of the Old Vic and Stratford-on-Avon which preserve a conservative attitude toward acting and toward the theater generally, and I don't think they are the best places for young actors who need to develop.

INTERVIEWER: Although many of the younger actors have reacted against the Shaftesbury Avenue style, isn't it true that very few of them have taken up the deeply introspective Method acting? And why is this?
ANDERSON: Well, Method acting, to use a rough term, has had a certain vogue here and of course actors like Brando and James Dean did make a great impact on young British actors. On the other hand, I think that apart from a few groups on the fringe the rather obsessive psychoanalytical school of acting is something to which the English do not really respond; it isn't a part of them.

The most talented younger British actors have a sensitive and serious psychological approach, but they are fortunately not tempted to get bogged down in too much self examination. I am not a great admirer of the masturbatory school of acting which I think the American tradition of Method acting can very easily become. I think the best chance for the development of a good tradition of acting in this country is in this psychological awareness which is balanced by a feeling for presentation and style.

INTERVIEWER: Is it true that more of the younger actors of today come from a greater variety of backgrounds than those of twenty or thirty years ago? And were most of those Shaftesbury Avenue actors actually from the class that they generally portrayed on the stage?

ANDERSON: Very much so. Someone like Gielgud is genuinely unable to understand the problems of the younger actors today partly because they are such a very different and more varied group than his contemporaries were. If you take the most prominent actors of today, who were all promising actors twenty or thirty years ago, you will find that they are all middle-class: Olivier, Gielgud, Guinness, Richardson, Edith Evans, Peggy Ashcroft, and Redgrave. None of them are working-class by origin. And in fact twenty years ago or even ten years ago when a young actor who came from a working-class background went to a drama school the first thing that was emphasized to him was that he had to cut off from his background. He had to learn how to speak *posh*. This was not put to him then as it would be now, that he had to learn another, i.e., an upper-class dialect, but continue to keep his own speech. Then he was made to feel that this was something disgraceful, something shameful that he had to get rid of if he was going to be a success. This had a disastrous effect on a lot of talented actors because when in fact you cut yourself off from your background and your way of speech you cut yourself off from something very basic in yourself. The result was that there were many actors who lost their true personalities. Alternatively if they did keep their proletarian accents and personalities they found themselves playing small parts as comic relief.

This is not the case today. We have experienced in a characteristically English way something of a social revolution. Today we are getting young actors who are proud of their origins, in fact who capitalize on them. For them the problem of conserving what comes out of their background and yet to be able to play Restoration comedy or *Hamlet* is obviously a difficult thing. I don't think it's in any way an impossible thing, but at the moment we don't have the kind of theater where this interesting experiment could be carried out.

INTERVIEWER: You spoke of the division in the English theater between Shaftesbury Avenue and the Royal Court. Could you explain how this division has come about?

ANDERSON: With the Royal Court we have to include the very potent influence of Joan Littlewood and the Theatre Workshop. I think the Royal Court is the key to this development in the English theater. It happened in a typically English way with a group of people getting together (one of them was a writer, Ronald Duncan). They wanted to found a theater, if possible with a company, where a non-commercial kind of play could be performed. They got finance from a number of angels who provided about £30,000. Since they were not themselves directors they chose George Devine, who had worked in the theater with people like Gielgud and in the Old Vic after the war.

But the kind of theater that these sponsors were interested in was not in fact the kind of theater that George Devine was interested in. The English Stage Company was originally founded to promote a tradition of poetic or at least of literary drama of the Eliot and Fry schools. But Devine's and his assistant Tony Richardson's interests lay in something more contemporary and of more actual social significance. And this is why the first season of plays included both the first play by John Osborne, *Look Back in Anger,* and two plays by Ronald Duncan, and there is no doubt that these hit on the contemporary nerve, and this is the line which has been followed ever since by the Royal Court. It has had a considerable effect on the theater generally.

INTERVIEWER: What are some of the problems that are still facing the Royal Court?

ANDERSON: The chief problem is money, lack of subsidy. In spite of the fact that in the last ten years the theater has attracted a great deal of publicity and respect, it still isn't considered reputable. In Britain it still isn't accepted that a civilized country supports its theater in the same way that it supports its art galleries or orchestras, ballet or opera, and as a result the subsidies available here have been quite ludicrous. It is really because of lack of finance that the Royal Court has not been able to do the full job that it set out to do. It also wanted to have a company of actors under regular salary, but it was realized after one season of doing experimental plays that we could not get the kind of audiences or support that would enable us to maintain a company of actors. Therefore the Royal Court has never been able to build up a tradition of presentation and style and direction which should have gone together with the production of the new plays.

INTERVIEWER: How much does the problem of money affect the choice of the plays?

ANDERSON: In a way, I think it is remarkable that the Court has done most of the plays it wanted to do. The activities of the theater could probably have been more varied and they might have done more way-out experiments than they have, but it's more a question of not being able to run the productions, or to put the plays into the repertoire so that the public and the critics might get used to them, and so build up support. For in fact if you put on a new play and can only run it for three weeks before it comes off forever, and if that play really is original, it is very unlikely that it is going to be able to capture an audience.

INTERVIEWER: How about the future?

ANDERSON: My mood is one of cautious optimism. I think the theater is very alive in spite of all the obstacles—of course, when one works in the theater one is apt to be more conscious of the obstacles—and is potentially tremendously promising. I feel the logic of events is going to move toward the creation of companies. Probably reluctantly, subsidies will be pushed up, and if this happens one can look forward to a real renaissance of the theater in this country, and the last five years will seem only to have been a beginning.

Interviewed by ROBERT RUBENS, 1962

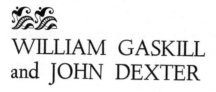

WILLIAM GASKILL
and JOHN DEXTER

At the time of these interviews, William Gaskill and John Dexter were on the staff of London's Royal Court Theatre where they directed numerous plays by the new group of playwrights who brought about such a striking change in English theater. With the Royal Court as its center, providing an outlet for such talents as John Osborne, Arnold Wesker and Harold Pinter, British theater moved away from the stratified, drawing-room naturalism of Noel Coward and Terence Rattigan. It was an important break, echoing many basic changes that took place in English life at the time.

William Gaskill, highly articulate, university-educated, with a direct, forceful manner, was considered by many to be one of the more intellectual of the younger directors. At the time of the interview, he had directed John Osborne's Epitaph for George Dillon *and N. F. Simpson's* A Resounding Tinkle.

John Dexter was animated, candid and surprisingly self-effacing. When I watched a rehearsal of Arnold Wesker's The Kitchen, *I was struck by the seemingly effortless way in which Dexter was able to work a huge cast, by constant jokes and teasing, into just the frenzy of emotional tension he was after.*

WILLIAM GASKILL

INTERVIEWER: Mr. Gaskill, how did you begin in the theater?
GASKILL: I began like almost every British director—in the universities. I directed amateur productions during my three years at Oxford, and then I went to Paris to study for a year. (I went through an intensely Francophile period.) After that I came back and went into provincial rep. I stage managed, acted, and

directed in about five repertory companies. Later I went into commercial television (when it first started) directing such things as *Zoo* programs for children. It was about this time that I did a Sunday Night production at the Royal Court. It was N. F. Simpson's *A Resounding Tinkle.* They liked that very much and I was asked to go on the staff of the Court. I stayed there as a permanent member of the staff for about two years, directing such plays as *Epitaph for George Dillon,* Osborne's first play, and others by Simpson and John Arden.

INTERVIEWER: Have you found many changes in the English theater in the last ten years?

GASKILL: Well, in the last five years, not in the last ten. All of my working life in the theater has been since the war; and in this time there seem to have been quite definite "periods." The first period, about the time I was an undergraduate, was the time of actors returning from the war, of the big classical revivals at the Old Vic, of Gielgud's season in the Haymarket, and of the dominance of H. M. Tennent Ltd. That period was marked, in creative writing, by the works of the poetic school: Fry, Eliot, and, to some extent, Whiting.

Then came 1956, the founding of the Royal Court, and the historic date of *Look Back in Anger.* Of course, Joan Littlewood had been working in the provinces for a much longer period before this, but her work came to London and reached fruition at about this time. So we had these two parallel movements emerging at more or less the same time—that is, about ten years after the war.

The changes are probably more marked for us in England than they would be for people coming in from outside, because, in a way, we were far behind many other movements that had taken place on the continent. I would say that the last foreign dramatists to make any serious impression on the English theater were . . . Chekhov and Ibsen. Pirandello, who is the mainspring of nearly all modern French dramatic writing, has never been revived successfully in England and has never had any major influence here. Similarly, the kind of social writing of Odets and the Group Theater didn't really penetrate England. Though, indeed, there is a long tradition of working-class and

middle-class theater which dates back to the repertory movement of about 1910, the period of *Hobson's Choice* and *Hindle
Wakes,* the classics of what are now called the Manchester
School. Incidentally, these plays have had an interesting revival recently on television, and they bear a strong resemblance
to the early plays of Osborne.

INTERVIEWER: You don't feel, then, that the social works of
Odets, Rice, and the Group Theater in New York have had
much influence here?
GASKILL: No, not really. Almost everyone read *The Fervent
Years* by Harold Clurman at one time or another; but though
one could argue that Wesker as a writer has affinities with
Odets, I don't think one could call it a definite influence (he's
really much more like Chekhov) anymore than one could state
that Ionesco was the dominant influence on N. F. Simpson, or
Beckett on Pinter. I remember talking to Simpson when I first
directed *A Resounding Tinkle* and he assured me he had
never read or seen any Ionesco. Anyone with half an eye can
see that his work is much more influenced by Lewis Carroll.
I think the changes in dramatic writing have been created more
by the social mood of the times than by any direct literary influence from abroad—unlike France where a writer like Pirandello has had a definite and marked influence on a literary
group.

INTERVIEWER: Then you feel that neither the experimental
plays of Ionesco, Genêt, etc., nor the American social realism
have had any tangible influence here, and that the new drama
in England is more or less a natural evolvement?
GASKILL: Yes, I think it has been almost entirely a product of
social and cultural change. I think England tends to reject literary influences rather strongly.

INTERVIEWER: Why is this?
GASKILL: Because it is an island, and England has an insular
tradition—and it is still very suspicious of foreigners. I know
it's a music hall joke that the English don't like foreigners,
but there is a basic truth in it. They tend to create for them-

selves. I think much of the new movement has been a discovery of England by the English, and I think this is what is so puzzling to people outside; they say, "Well, it's not all that new." It may not be to them but it is to us. You have to remember that up to 1956 working-class parts were *always* comic, that actors never used a regional accent in a straight part, and that plays did only depict one section of society. The exploration of new areas of society in drama has been one of the main creative forces in the movement. Naturally this means that many of the plays have a regional or insular quality which makes them puzzling to foreigners and I wouldn't say that many of the plays are international masterpieces. We may enter a phase where the writing here reaches an international standard, and I think perhaps we have already entered that phase.

INTERVIEWER: Having been so closely associated with this new movement, what would you say the new playwrights are actually trying to achieve?

GASKILL: Well, what any writer tries to achieve at the time he writes—is to show "the very age and body of the time his form and pressure." With Arnold Wesker, for instance, there is a quite definite political motivation; he wishes to make social change through his work, but I think he's exceptional. I don't think this is true of Osborne, Simpson, or Pinter, or Arden. They are all socially aware and could, if you like, be described as socialists, but I don't think they are writing with a social function to the degree that Odets was writing.

INTERVIEWER: You once said that these people are striving for a new architecture in drama. Could you explain what you meant by that?

GASKILL: I think there has been a lot of misunderstanding about the new writing, because much of it has been dismissed as being imperfectly constructed, as not composing a "well-made play."

A well-made play is the invention of those people who admired the work of Ibsen; or who have come to admire the work of Ibsen seventy years after it was written. As Simpson said to me when he was watching *Rosmersholm,* "It's all very well, but the admiration that people are now lavishing on this play comes seventy years too late. If they had been onto it at the time, it might have been worth something." In fact, what people mean is that the new plays are not written in the form of Ibsen. They have not stopped to consider that every play in its own time finds its own form. If you take the structure of a Greek tragedy, you will find it is not that of a well-made play. I think certainly that writers like Pinter and Simpson are striving to find a new form which is expressive of what they feel about the time. I don't know how well they are succeeding. I think perhaps they are still groping toward it . . . but it is certainly not the structure of the three act tragedy, whatever it may be.

JOHN DEXTER

INTERVIEWER: Could you tell us something about your beginnings in the theater?

DEXTER: My beginnings in the theater were amateur and provincial, and I became aware of the theater later than most. I left an English elementary school at the age of fourteen, less than half-educated, and almost unaware that drama could impinge on my life at all. You must remember that in 1939 there was little or no cultural activity in the provinces; it took the blitz to force the theater out of London. Repertory did exist in some towns, but not in mine . . . and certainly none of my teachers at school ever suggested one should visit a theater rather than a cinema. Then suddenly in the space of a few months I went to the Old Vic, Sadler's Wells, and saw *The Doctor's Dilemma.* This was a tremendous *physical* thrill. But it was not until I was eighteen and going into the Army that I felt I could be a part of this activity. It seemed to be the exclusive domain of people who "spoke nicely" (I didn't), and of people who were educated (I wasn't). After the war I worked unpaid and once or twice I was even paid. Small parts followed, then some larger ones; but I'll let you imagine the effect of Derbyshire vowels on the works of Coward and Maugham.

Even at this time my work and thought were confined to a re-creation of West End manners and conditions—in the chaos of weekly repertory there was time for nothing more. It was in one of the many periods of resting (I wasn't a very good actor) that I began to read and explore theater south of the Trent and the Thames.

INTERVIEWER: Then could you explain the ways in which your experience as an actor prepared you for directing?

DEXTER: Well, I was conscious that, as an actor, I was all right, but nothing more. I was also conscious that the directors—the people who were telling me what to do—weren't really being much help. I suppose I am always most aware of the actor's deep need to relax. Only from confidence and relaxation can the imagination flow. I aim to create time and atmosphere in which this can happen, and in which I can be aware of the actor's needs before he is aware of them himself.

INTERVIEWER: When I watched your rehearsal of *The Kitchen* the other day, I noticed that you certainly do achieve a relaxed atmosphere. You seem to do this partly through a constant sense of humor; joking and laughing with the actors as you direct them. Is this part of your particular formula for directing?

DEXTER: I don't think there can be a formula, except that which emerges during rehearsal and changes with each play. Kazan said that rehearsals are a love affair between the director and the cast. I think it's more of a calculated courtship with love at the end if you're successful. I must know an actor or actress very well before I can work with them. I must understand what they laugh at, if they don't laugh at all, where they come from, how they think politically. I don't think actors are really difficult people. I think, oddly enough, that in most cases they are rather shy. They are not quite the sort of extroverts they are popularly imagined to be. Even the most experienced actor needs coaxing and easing into a performance. So, really the most important, and in some ways the most harrowing, aspect of directing a play is in the casting. Technical ability is easy to discover, but imagination, flow of feeling, rhythmic patterns, personal tensions—these take a great deal of time and expenditure of nervous energy in order to comprehend. Finally, if all the qualities I seek are evident, but I have no personal response to the artist, I must begin all over again.

INTERVIEWER: Your approach to directing, in other words, is more intuitive than cerebral.

DEXTER: I think it must be, because intuition is all I've got; so that's what I must work with. It's no use my trying to make myself a cerebral director—whatever that is—because I am simply not that sort of person. Having had the advantage of not having had a university education, I think I should use it. Although this may give me an uncluttered approach to certain directorial problems, it also makes me a rather risky proposition for commercial managements who cannot risk thousands of pounds on the chance that my intuition may be right. That is why I am happiest at the Royal Court. The atmosphere is relaxed, there is time to experiment and to grow slowly with a company. One has freedom and responsibility in a way I have found nowhere else.

INTERVIEWER: How do you feel about the Stanislavski Method acting?

DEXTER: I have never worked with a Stanislavski Method actor, and I don't know anyone who has. The books contain more practical common sense than is generally supposed by those who incessantly quote from him. I have worked with one or two actors who imagined themselves to be method actors, and I didn't think much of them. They tend to work in a much too self indulgent fashion for my taste; everything is related to their own personal experience and the imaginative factor is almost totally ignored. I believe imagination is far more important for an actor than experience.

INTERVIEWER: You have been called a social-realist director. Do you think this is an accurate description?

DEXTER: Oh, dear, how I hate this definition game. What do they mean by social realism? If Felsenstein is regarded as the apotheosis of the social-realist director, then I accept the title. But I try to react to each play on its own terms. I feel, for instance, that I responded to Wesker's *The Kitchen,* which on the surface looks like very social-realist writing, by trying to create something quite unreal. I was aiming at a kind of formalism, through the use of a bare stage, exposed lighting, and the most deeply theatrical of all techniques—mime. I wanted the audience to be constantly aware of a theatrical re-creation of a kitchen; not of a flat photograph which can be seen through any hotel basement window. Anyone seeing the play should realize that it is hardly realism, in spite of the definite social awareness of the author. The fact is that I am not necessarily a social-realist director at all. I don't really know what sort of director I am and I hope I never will.

INTERVIEWER: You directed Lillian Hellman's *Toys in the Attic,* which was highly praised in New York. Could you explain why it failed in London?

DEXTER: Yes, I suppose I could. We can always explain our failures, and I certainly learned more from *Toys in the Attic* than from any other play I have directed. It was a total failure for which I was more than three-quarters responsible. I suppose an English director is always faced with this problem in American plays; especially anything as particularly American and as complete as *Toys in the Attic.* I know now that I shouldn't have tackled it, not having absorbed a good deal more of that particular background. In any play, I always have to come back to intuition and imagination. In this particular case, my intuition was right; my imagination wasn't rich enough to interpret things completely alien to my experience. It is a question of how far you can step out of the realm of your personal experience. I have never been a Norfolk farmer, but I was able to interpret something there which was in Wesker's play. But I couldn't reach out and catch this atmosphere that Lillian had put down on paper. My imagination failed; it wasn't enough. Then, of course, there was the problem of the cast. I was unable to contact the actors on the right level, partly because I was never certain myself of the style of acting the play needed, never at ease in the specialized milieu of southern American decadence. Also, I think I was a little bit intimidated by the combined experience of the group of actors and actresses I had working with me. If I had chosen them myself and knew them better, there might have been more harmony. It was a splendid cast who worked very hard, but all in all, with one exception, I never made them completely confident in me. They did everything I asked them to do, and in many cases did it a great deal better than I could have asked; but what I asked wasn't enough, and the stimulus I gave them wasn't enough. It isn't until after the disaster that you know what you should have done. It wasn't until the last week of rehearsal that I suddenly began to realize, after talking to Lillian, watching the play, and reading it again and again, that there had been this failing somewhere. Now I see that it was a failure of compassion, a failure of feeling. It isn't enough to admire and even love a play if you have no real compassion for the characters. One has to be with them all the time and I wasn't. I was outside them, intrigued, watching in a sort of cool, interested way, and no more than that.

Interviewed by ROBERT RUBENS, 1961

GORE VIDAL

I first saw Gore Vidal on Umnak Island, in the Aleutians, during the war, in the midst of a roaring blizzard. He caught my attention at once by his self-possession. He had just landed on the island, which is remote, desolate, sad. What I remember most is that he was very young, and that he kept looking about, taking everything in, while the other soldiers, mostly older, were grumbling and cursing and pulling their fur parkas about their faces. I watched him as he stamped his boots in the snow and turned his head this way and that. (An observer observed!) Later, in New York in 1946 when Williwaw *was published, I bought the novel at once on the peculiarly Aleutian recommendation of the name (that of a howling wind that comes from the Bering Sea and crosses the islands) and recognized the photograph of the author. I was impressed by the tightly-written, unpretentious quality of the book, and followed the work of Vidal from then on.*

In a Yellow Wood *came in 1947,* The City and the Pillar *in 1948,* The Season of Comfort *in 1949, and two books in 1950:* A Search for the King *(an historical novel on the Richard-Blondel theme) and* Dark Green, Bright Red. *Then came a breathing spell before* The Judgment of Paris *in 1952, and a longer pause before* Messiah *in 1954. (Since then there has been a collection of short stories, a book of television plays, and the comedy,* Visit to a Small Planet.) *The last two novels had small success, to my complete mystification, for they are of high excellence, balanced, intuitive, witty, and with a distinctive and unforgettable acid flavor all their own.* The Judgment of Paris *is an account of a young American's wanderjahr in Europe, crowded with amusing characters*

*and incidents. Messiah is black satire: an image of America
dominated by a television god; it has a Jacobean consciousness of mortality, a dry style—moreover, the reader is not
invited to identify himself with any of the characters. All is
lucid, understated, bitter. When I read it, I thought, if this had
been translated from the French, how the reviewers would fall
out in a dead faint, and how the readers would argue over it.
But it was home-grown and somehow got lost in the shuffle,
while several big slovenly novels from semi-literate writers made
the news. When I heard Vidal was coming to Italy, I couldn't
wait to see him. We had been acquainted briefly in New
York in 1946, but now, years and books later, I was full of
questions to ask. We met in Rome, and he agreed to an interview.*

I

A small salon in the Grand Hôtel, Rome.

INTERVIEWER: Shall we do the statistics and so forth? Your
frame of reference?
VIDAL: I was born October 3, 1925, at West Point, New York.
Within a year my family moved to Washington, D.C. I was
raised there and in nearby Virginia.

INTERVIEWER: And your name: were you named after your
grandfather, the Senator?
VIDAL: He was Thomas Pryor Gore of Oklahoma; my name is
Eugene Luther Gore Vidal. I wasn't named for him, although
he had a great influence in my life. He was blind from the age
of ten; I read to him on and off for seventeen years.

INTERVIEWER: He was a very interesting figure, wasn't he?
What did you read to him?
VIDAL: Oh, yes, he brought Oklahoma into the Union in 1907,
and he was the first Senator. What did we read? Well, I read
him Constitutional history and British common law mostly; for
pleasure we had Brann's *The Iconoclast* and the Victorian

poets. In his attic in Rock Creek Park, D.C. (I describe that house in a short story, *A Moment of Green Laurel*) there were 7–8000 books. The first that I could read by myself was called *The Duck and the Kangaroo*. My favorites were Lane's *Arabian Nights* and a nineteenth century *Stories from Livy*.

INTERVIEWER: Your education . . . ?

VIDAL: Lots of schools. From eleven until fourteen I was in St. Alban's, in Washington. I was a year at Los Alamos, then three years at Exeter which were among the happiest of my life. You know, getting away from the family and its problems. My first novel was written at Exeter when I was fifteen. At least, part of a first novel, because I had a terrible problem for years: I could finish nothing. But I did about 100 pages of that one, all about Mussolini, his mistress, spies, very florid—the result of a trip to Rome in 1939. I wrote quite a few short stories, too.

INTERVIEWER: And verse?

VIDAL: Some rather didactic verse. As a poet I was a profound moralist with a resolute meter—terrible, thumping stuff.

INTERVIEWER: Then you always knew you were cut out to be a writer?

VIDAL: Oh, no! There was an awful crisis in my mind—the choice between politics and literature. I was brought up with the idea of going into politics; all the family were in politics. Even my father, an aviation man, was in Roosevelt's Little Cabinet as Director of Air Commerce. And the Gores are forever running for office all around the south. The family was originally from Mississippi.

INTERVIEWER: Did you write a great deal then? When did you first publish?

VIDAL: In the *Exeter Review*, of which I was an editor. I published three stories before I graduated in June, 1943; went into the Army in July, 1943, was sent to Army Training Group at the Virginia Military Institute for one term, where I wrote part of another novel. The writer I had read and studied and chosen for my model was—this may surprise you, but then I

was an unworldly seventeen!—Somerset Maugham. I had also
met, in the bridge-playing world of my mother, Michael Arlen
who knew Maugham, so the novel I was trying to write was
really *Cakes and Ale* all over again, with Maugham instead
of Hardy, Arlen instead of Hugh Walpole, and myself as
Maugham writing it. It was a beautifully weary book, in what
is now the grand tradition of adolescent novel writing.

INTERVIEWER: You must have started *Williwaw* about
then. . . .

VIDAL: Well, let's see: when I left hospital I was dumped into
the infantry, and then got into the Air Force, then into crash
boats, then passed an examination as a first mate, knowing
nothing of navigation save what I learned from memorizing a
book on the subject. Finally, I was sent to the Aleutian Islands
as first mate of the F.S.35. Fortunately, it was so foggy that no
one ever discovered I couldn't set a course. We relied on point
to point navigation: a symbol? Anyway, up there making a
regular run between Chernowski Bay and Dutch Harbor, in
December, 1944, I wrote half of *Williwaw* in pencil in a gray
ledger marked "Accounts"; then, for the fourth time I gave up,
convinced I couldn't finish anything. Meanwhile, I had slyly
contracted arthritis, was hospitalized in Los Angeles. After, I
was sent to Florida to train eighteen year olds. One night alone
in headquarters—I was officer of the day—there was a hurricane
warning up, and everything was shuttered against the coming
storm—I had just seen Boris Karloff in *Isle of the Dead*—that
night I finished *Williwaw*.

INTERVIEWER: How did *Williwaw* come to be published?
VIDAL: I first took the novel and a bunch of poems to Roger
Linscott at Random House who liked the poems but wouldn't
read the novel because it was in longhand. He seemed to lack
dedication. But I had the book typed. There was a woman
doing a life of Amelia Earhart, and when she came to interview
my father, who had known the flyer, I showed her the manuscript. She suggested I take it to Nicholas Wreden of Dutton's.
I did and we got on well; he said he'd publish it, and offered me
a job when I got out of the Army. I worked at Dutton six

months, until *Williwaw* came out in April, 1946, and I quit on the strength of the notices. Couldn't stand going to an office. I have never gone to an office since. So, having attained some recognition, I fled to Guatemala where I lived off and on for three years and wrote *In a Yellow Wood* and *The City and the Pillar*. Those three books were written between the ages of nineteen and twenty-one. And it is depressing to think that I am still known primarily for such green work. My later books are a good deal more right, and very different. But literary reputations change slowly.

II

Amalfi. We had driven down—a party of four—in an ancient Mercedes touring car suitable for a retired or deported gangster. We spent the night wandering about the deserted streets, hearing only the stream that tumbles down the mountain and rushes through the city to the sea. Vidal used the town for an episode in The Judgment of Paris, *but he had not visited it for some years. The next morning we breakfasted on a terrace overlooking the sea and continued our conversations.*

INTERVIEWER: If you please, I should like a bit of history on *The City and the Pillar*. One has heard so many contradictory statements concerning it, why you wrote it, whether or not it's autobiographical, all that.

VIDAL: Well, first of all, it is not "about" homosexuality. The actual theme is not unlike Alain-Fournier's: if one continues always to look back, to relate everything to a first affair, one is emotionally, even humanly destroyed. The pillar of salt. Oh, I realize that the ending of *The City and the Pillar* smacks of *Tosca,* but it was inevitable. I think now that if I had not written the novel so realistically, I could have made that ending work. But I deliberately chose a flat gray style which I thought would give immediacy to certain human facts which up till then had not been frankly handled in America. I wanted an undecorated, a graphic effect. And I did very much want to shock. As for autobiography, the book, like all of my work, is invented, down to the last detail. There were absolutely no originals of the characters.

INTERVIEWER: You rely on imagination more than observation then?

VIDAL: What Thackeray called the "fancy." I am incapable of reporting anything. For me, the fact that something *happened* is quite enough, and needs no further comment. The act of writing is creating something that was *not,* and to make it *real.* A novelist, as I see it, must invent the truth.

INTERVIEWER: What effect did the publication of the book have on your life, literary and personal?

VIDAL (*pauses, then smiles slowly*): Let me take a deep breath and tell you. First, I was at that time the author of two books embarrassingly admired—embarrassingly because I was under twenty-one and newspaper praise is a false thing at best, though, I suspect now, preferable to blame. I was the Huck Finn of the younger novelists, photographed against ships for *Life* magazine, boyishly scowling. I seemed as safe as . . . who? Herman Wouk? I was in the running. Then came the bomb: *The City and the Pillar.* I remember I read it through once before it was sent to the printer, and I thought that if I ever read it again I'd never publish it. . . . So I sent back a hardly-corrected proof. Then the reviews, what few there were, began and I discovered what happens in America if you tamper with the fragile—people avert their eyes, and go on talking. Half of my former admirers did not review it at all. *The New York Times* refused to advertise it—and when the publishers took the matter directly to Mr. Sulzberger, he decided to uphold his censor. Of the reviews received, a few were thoughtful and lengthy, most quite bad. Two words popped up to haunt that book, and all my writing ever since: "clinical" and "sterile." "Clinical" is used whenever one writes of relationships which are not familiar—I dare say that if the story had dealt with a boy and a girl instead of two boys the book would have been characterized as "lyrical." "Sterile" is an even deadlier curse upon the house, and comes from a dark syllogism in the American *zeitgeist*: the homosexual act does not produce children,

therefore it is sterile; Mr. X's book is concerned with the homosexual act, therefore the book is sterile. (This syllogism was first
proposed by the Russians when they turned on André Gide
and it used to be a standard Stalinist line.) But despite the
absence of reviews and no advertisements in *The New York
Times,* the book was a bestseller. Aesthetically, the book was
very youthful, very naïve, hasty but "felt," and I suppose in
a way that the rudeness of its execution was part of its strength
and the reason why it goes on year after year being read. I still
think publishing it was a virtuous act and I would do it again,
hard fate though it has been in some ways. One quite lost the
newspaper reviewers, which was sad because their gentle
twittering was always a great comfort; after all, I belong to no
literary clique; I am outside the Academy; I have no friends
who slyly review me. . . . The business of literary politics has
never figured in my life. Do I make myself seem a dark literary
prince? More sinned against, etc.? I certainly mean to! And
one does get what one wants, despite the querulous tone, the
occasional misgivings. Forcing the world to adjust to oneself
has always seemed to me an honorable life work . . . that one
fails in the end is irrelevant.

INTERVIEWER: Did you receive many letters from readers?
VIDAL: Just before the book was published the Kinsey Report
came out, and I received a charming letter from Dr. Kinsey
complimenting me on "my work in the field"! But I also received about 2,000 letters, mostly of a confessional nature, from
every corner of the world (the book was translated into French,
Italian, Dutch, Norwegian, German, etc.).

INTERVIEWER: Do you still have echoes of it?
VIDAL: Oh, yes. Letters still come. Critically . . . well, for
instance, there was a young critic who began a distinguished
critical career by particularly admiring and celebrating the
heterosexual love scenes of *In a Yellow Wood* but then later,
after the appearance of *The City and the Pillar,* declared that
I was unable to write convincingly of the man-woman relationship: a *volte-face* which I forgive him but which I find con-
tinuously burdensome as I proceed upon my "clinical" and

"sterile" way. One could write *Anna Karenina* now and get the same reaction.

INTERVIEWER: Let's see, you finished that book in Guatemala; where did you go next?

VIDAL: I finished *The Season of Comfort* down there, too. I lived in the ruins of a sixteenth century Carmelite convent in Antigua. Well, after *The City and the Pillar* was published, I came to Europe in March, 1948. I went straight to Rome where I had a friend, Frederic Prokosch. Then I met Tennessee Williams and we drove all around Italy in a jeep. All this time I was writing *A Search for the King*. Then back to Paris, to the U.S., a last trip to Guatemala (to write *Dark Green, Bright Red*), then Paris again, and back to the U.S.

INTERVIEWER: I'm dizzy. What year are we now?

VIDAL (*chuckling*): 1950 was a crucial year—when I published two novels: *A Search for a King* which had good reviews and no sales, and *Dark Green, Bright Red* which had bad notices and no sales—and optimistically bought the house at Tarrytown on the Hudson River where I still live; went broke; wrote in an absolute explosion of delight *The Judgment of Paris*, a picaresque book which is my best. It was quite well received; sold pretty well enough. To support myself, I took to lecturing —colleges, ladies' clubs—a chilling experience. Then at my wit's end, I wrote three mystery stories under a pseudonym. And, as is usual with works of the left hand, they were all successful. Meanwhile, I was working on *Messiah*, which was published in 1954, to sink serenely beneath the waves, although it was well regarded in Europe. Survival was now a desperate matter. So I hit upon a kind of five-year plan: an all-out raid upon television, which could make me enough money to live the rest of my life. It's been a fascinating, wearying experience. The plan was finished two years ago, and barring the unexpected I am, in a modest way, financially set for life. If one has the stamina, there's a lot to be said for piracy.

INTERVIEWER: Will you write more novels?

VIDAL: Oh, yes. I have one in my head now but curiously

enough, whereas I could never think of ideas for plays a few
years ago, now I think of nothing but ideas for plays: the old
novel instinct has gone temporarily into the theater. One tends
to invent in one form or the other. The unexpected thing about
my five-year plan is that I came to enjoy playwriting and as one
enjoys it one respects it, which I didn't at first.

INTERVIEWER: Which gives you greater satisfaction, your novels
or your plays?
VIDAL: The novel. If only because I don't get the play deep
enough or the characters rich enough for my purposes. I think
this failure has to do with language. I'm not happy with
naturalistic dialogue: I don't much use it, as you'll see, in those
books I've written since twenty-one, and yet I haven't found an
alternative to the terrible naturalistic gabble in our theater,
the racket of "Do come in," "Drink?" "Yes," "Where'd you
leave it?" "Upstairs," "Well, go look," etc. I don't do it much
better than the others, but what I have done, and what interests me, is to clown, to be funny, bizarre—I enjoy comedic
invention, both high and low; there is almost nothing quite so
satisfying as making an audience laugh while removing their
insides.

INTERVIEWER: Tell me about your television adaptations, about
dealing with Faulkner, James, etc.?
VIDAL: I did them for money of course—but I always tried to
pick a writer I respected—or at least that I thought I could do
something respectable with. I was most successful with Faulkner and James. I have a considerable affection for James, but
not much for Faulkner. I failed entirely with Hemingway,
and so has nearly everyone else, which makes one wonder about
the original . . . or at least about its viability in *our* time.

INTERVIEWER: You were saying you invented everything, but
weren't there some characters in *In a Yellow Wood* who were
recognizably well-known New York literary and social figures?
VIDAL: Well, let's say sometimes I drew small caricatures in the
margin . . . peripheral doodling. The thing accomplished is
"made," not recorded. Odd how people—even knowing ones—
think it's always one's own life. I suppose they are so accus-

tomed to the self obsessed Thomas Wolfe sort of thing that the whole idea of invention is both discredited and disbelieved.

INTERVIEWER: Interesting, too, how *The City and the Pillar* was considered scandalous in America, and considered a moral work in Europe.

VIDAL: I am, and don't entirely understand why, a moralistic writer in a very American way. I seem always to be writing about a moral choice and . . . well, that's for the critics to worry about.

III

On the terrace of the Trattoria Paris, in the Trastevere section of Rome. The motorbikes roared and blasted past us, a thin hedge away, as we dined and talked.

INTERVIEWER: Do you feel that your early interest in history and politics has done a great deal in shaping you as a novelist?

VIDAL: Yes. You know Bernard Shaw used to say that religion and politics . . . in the large sense . . . are the only things that should concern a man; they certainly fascinate me though they are currently unfashionable preoccupations. The contemporary novel has split: on the one hand there is the private universe novel, unrelated to the society around it, unrelated to the fact of death. I suppose Nathalie Sarraute has taken it quite as far as anyone in our period . . . the anti-novel (old-fashioned actually . . . the Goncourts used to write them, and very glum they were). Then there are the busy popular novels. All that concern over who divorces whom and why this marriage failed and who's to get custody of those children and finally, who cares? Even Maisie has got to know a very great deal to save that sort of novel. And love! Dear God, the horror Love has become in our culture! Mr. X. don't write so good, but he does feel Love is the only thing which matters, and Compassion, too . . . and everyone gets a warm glow from Mr. X's stylized compassion. It is the stunning cliché of our literature, and the largest lie about man's estate. Whitehead once wrote that the way to assess a society is not by what it says of itself but those things it does not say, the never-mentioned, the taken-for-granted. Well, it seems to me that the underlying assumption of our society is that Love (something vague, anodyne, splendid) is every man's due and of course not only is it not every man's due, it is not always desirable. Flaubert was fascinated by that theme! Bovarism . . . only his Emma was a woman of meager intelligence while some of our very best writers are neatly impaled on this same folly. A satire on the Romantic assumption is in order now. How wonderful to be the first contemporary novelist *not* to tack the ensign of Love to his mast. Paul Bowles of course attempted the reverse in *Let It Come Down*; at the end, his protagonist achieves perfect alienation. . . . I suppose it's the same thing turned inside out but it was amiable to read.

INTERVIEWER: Then you would deal with the grand problems?
VIDAL: Yes! The great emotions, the great crises . . . anything to keep from surrendering to the idea that we are all victimized by the hugeness of society. Even if this is true, one should still attack the giant head-on; the alternative is paralysis or, worse, deliberate smallness. *We all know so much more than we write.* And why don't we write it? Because we are afraid of being thought stupid or wicked or . . . unlovable.

IV

Bricktop's Club, under the Via Veneto, Rome. After Bricktop sang her definitive version of Miss Otis Regrets, *we settled down in a corner for some quiet drinking, and to finish our interview.*

INTERVIEWER: Could you tell me a little of your working methods?
VIDAL: Novels in longhand, plays on the typewriter, the morning hours. I begin with a vague idea of the knot to be tied or untied. I always think of every writer having in his head a repertory theater with a resident company of players. Some play themselves over and over again, some are more protean. When I decide the knot, I "cast" the novel, using the actors I need. Sometimes I miscast. Sometimes I curse the shortcomings

of my company but I can't fire them: they are aspects of one's own personality. . . . They have term contracts.

INTERVIEWER: Do you rewrite much?
VIDAL: I write first drafts with great speed but the older I get (a familiar observation, I know) I rewrite more and more. When I first started, it was like working in egg-tempera—flat, quick drying, on a wall, one got it right or one didn't. In shorter works like *Williwaw* I got it right. In others I got it wrong. I'm more an oil painter now. More deliberate. A good deal less certain.

INTERVIEWER: Do you make notes or outlines: keep a notebook?
VIDAL: No, I always lose them, because I hate to reread them. I jot things down occasionally, then never look at them again. Never have more than one page of random notes for an entire novel.

INTERVIEWER: What would you consider the perfect novel: the novel you'd most wish to read?
VIDAL: The terrible thing is, I don't want to read *a* novel—I never have. When I read fiction with any delight it has always been when I've the time to read the whole of a man's work, rather than one book.

INTERVIEWER: Who gives you greatest pleasure?
VIDAL: Well, different works at different times and in different moods. I suppose my greatest pleasure still comes from Apuleius and Petronius, "the bright pagan world." Then I've read all of Flaubert, Proust, Henry James, Meredith, and Peacock, who for a certain kind of thing I often try to do, is the most relevant model. The novel of ideas: a most imprecise designation. Everybody, of course, would like to have written *Le Grand Meaulnes*.

INTERVIEWER: Any others who have been signposts for you?
VIDAL: I don't know. One's tendency is to fake influences later, to rearrange history. I suppose Gibbon has had as profound an effect on me as any writer. I don't mean stylistically so much as the effect of his attitude. Then one goes through phases:

Lawrence's *Women in Love,* and Mann's *The Magic Mountain* and *Tonio Kröger.* When I was very young the greatest influence—don't know if I dare say it—was Shakespeare. I read all Shakespeare when I was fourteen at Los Alamos. *The Yale Shakespeare,* a play to a volume, I read the lot.

INTERVIEWER: And contemporaries?
VIDAL: I am much drawn to the moral fabulists William Golding (*Lord of the Flies*) and John Bowen (*After the Rain, The Truth Shall Not Help Us*), to Paul Bowles in his short stories. Or to mention someone doing what I try to do: Lawrence Durrell in his Alexandria novels—*Justine, Balthazar,* etc.—it is dazzling work.

INTERVIEWER: Now a question of style: what led from the documentary style of your first books to the extravagance of *The Judgment of Paris?*
VIDAL: I found that naturalism wasn't natural for me. When I began at nineteen to write in a hard flat style it was because that seemed to me the only way to write; it was the national manner. Not till I finished my third book did I realize the style was inadequate for my purposes, and that I must find my own voice and tone. *The Season of Comfort* was the midway work, an experiment and a debacle.

INTERVIEWER: That historical romance, *A Search for the King,* how did that pop up in the list of your books?
VIDAL: A *jeu d'esprit.* I like the fabulous, the invented, and I dislike repeating myself. I am not captive to one region nor to one unflinching attitude toward life. I am always conscious that we live, in Sir Thomas Browne's phrase—"in divided and distinguished worlds," and I should never be so presumptuous as to say finally, "That is it!"

INTERVIEWER: Have you consciously designed the different pitch, or tone, of each of the books?
VIDAL (*thoughtfully*): It comes out of the subject and out of oneself at the time. I am a dry clown who has often miscast himself in the drama; when I've gone wrong in novels it has

usually been that my view was not, simply, the useful one of
the subject. . . . It seems to me, when I am playwriting seriously, that I'm not writing. Yet the emotional concentration is
the same. Final relief is more gratifying, yet it's like doing
charades. Cousin germane to prose yet not prose.

INTERVIEWER: A couple of last points . . . didn't you stir up a
hornet's nest in America a year or so ago? . . . some opinions
on the novel . . . ?

VIDAL: Yes. I wrote in *The New York Times,* and again in
The Reporter, articles stating very tentatively the proposition
that the novel as a popular art form was ended. Now its
decline, from the point of view of general interest, is a fact,
and I took the line that the fault (this is the reverse of the busy
reviewers) is the public's, not the writer's. We have never
had more interesting writers than we do today. But the public
has sneaked off, and I suggested that the novel, which after all
is only 300 years old in our language, was perhaps an inter-
regnum form, and that the public, from the Greek mysteries
to television, had always preferred the dramatic event.

INTERVIEWER: Your contemporaries mounted high horse over
this?

VIDAL: Yes. Yet no one bothered to argue the central premise:
the brief life of the novel in our language—of which we can
observe the origins, flowering, and decline. But then they don't
read too carefully, which rather proves the point. Anyway,
from what I have seen of the young today, the bright ones are
interested in sociology, philosophy at second hand, and of
course, criticism.

INTERVIEWER: Ah-ha, and now we come to the inevitable question. What about criticism in America?

VIDAL: It's either a monkish avocation conducted in the
Academy or it is simply garrulous newspaper writing, and that
perfect justice of which we all dream (even if it is summary
execution!) is denied us.

INTERVIEWER: Have you noted any critical ideas of any importance in America?

VIDAL: I wouldn't know! I read a good deal of criticism, but only as a vice, not so good as reading science fiction, rather better than reading mystery stories. But I do admire the confidence of our nobler critics. They've got it made, and they know it!

INTERVIEWER: Do you think writing for movies, television and so forth is corroding to a writer's more serious work?
VIDAL: Unfortunately, one has to earn a living. For me it was less compromising to write for films than to teach, or review other people's books. Or journalism. Yet there is a destructive element in writing for hire and it is, simply, indifference: a man's defense when he believes or is made to believe that he is misusing his talent (and the world which was indifferent to the talent itself is usually eager to point out its misuse). The sullen response—and especially if he is successful in a worldly way—is indifference. And it must be fought against in the dark hours, for indifference is death to the artist. Somewhere in that is a peculiarly American tragedy.

> *Note*: A decade has passed since this interview. Vidal lives in Rome now, and flies off to Hollywood, London, New York, Washington at the slightest provocation. He writes in *Life*, debates on television, has produced *Julian* and *Myra Breckinridge* (so titillating to the masses that its ultimate lofty ironies have scarce been perceived). Vidal is successful, rich, yet the dry humor persists and the busy industriousness remains as was. One is tempted to believe he eats Mexican jumping-beans for breakfast, washed down by a split of *brut*.

Interviewed by EUGENE WALTER, 1960